W9-CGW-514

The Secondary Colors

THREE ESSAYS

Alexander Theroux

AN OWL BOOK
Henry Holt and Company   New York

Henry Holt and Company, Inc.
Publishers since 1866
115 West 18th Street
New York, New York 10011

Henry Holt® is a registered
trademark of Henry Holt and Company, Inc.

Copyright © 1996 by Alexander Theroux
All rights reserved.

Published in Canada by Fitzhenry & Whiteside Ltd.,
195 Allstate Parkway, Markham, Ontario L3R 4T8

Library of Congress Cataloging-in-Publication Data
Theroux, Alexander.
The secondary colors: three essays/Alexander Theroux.—1st ed.
p.   cm.
1. Colors.   2. Colors in literature.   I. Title.
QC495.T48   1996   95-40041
814'.54—dc20   CIP

ISBN 0-8050-4458-2
ISBN 0-8050-5326-3 (An Owl Book: pbk.)

Henry Holt books are available for special promotions
and premiums. For details contact: Director, Special Markets.

First published in hardcover in 1996 by
Henry Holt and Company, Inc.

First Owl Book Edition—1997

Designed by Paula R. Szafranski

Printed in the United States of America
All first editions are printed on acid-free paper. ∞

10 9 8 7 6 5 4 3 2 1
10 9 8 7 6 5 4 3 2 1   (pbk.)

for my dear sisters,
Ann Marie and Mary

Colors are the deeds
and sufferings of light.
—Goethe

Aren't orange, purple, and green like
costumes made of felt, *Munchkin* colors?
—Laura Markley

Orange

ORANGE IS A BOLD, forritsome color. It sells, it smiles, it sings, it simpers, combining the aura of Hollywood musicals, the leisure of sunshiny Florida—*Moon Over Miami* in Technicolor—and South American festivals. Orange is "hot," gives back light, and sits at the center of one's *ch'i* (cosmic or vital energy). It is an active, warm, advancing earthy color, indicative of and supposedly preferred by social types with an agreeable, good-natured, and gregarious personality, glad-handing and salesman-hearty, yammering and bumptious and irrepressible, although it carries the added connotations, predominantly in its mode of near-phosphorescence, of fickleness, vacillation, lack of steadiness, and, many even insist, a lack of warmth. But, surely, it is nothing if not unshy and bottomlessly flippant and even pagan, a color that takes place, in the parlance of twenties journalism, in full view of the spectators.

It is a color that, as Vachel Lindsay said of Hollywood, has "crowd splendor" and a deep saturation that, with spectacle and a kind of high-spirited presence, along with an almost unanalyzable loveableness often denied other colors, energizes mass. While at times it may seem thick and impenetrably opaque, it can just as often be lucid, as clear and ringing as a wineglass. "Orange clients are convivial," notes Eric P. Danger in *How to Use Color to Sell.* It is a color that rides over opposition through its sheer pluck and inventive ability and radiates with plenitude and exhilarating expenditure a brash and noncollaborating dynamic, a shouting hue that, dominating, exuberant, everywhere superabundant, speaks out all at once. Its patron saint is St. Medard, Bishop (c. 470–558), who was portrayed in the Middle Ages—*"le ris de St. Medard"*—laughing with his mouth open.

Loudness is orange, with an inviting rotundity as round as the ovals and circles of the fruit that bears its name, not unlike the spherically comical name Ogleby, which sounds, as W. C. Fields exclaimed in the movie *The Bank Dick,* "like a bubble in a bathtub." It is the color of Falstaff and Boule de Suif and Happy Hooligan with his triple nephews all wearing tin cans for hats. It is flame, fire, foolishness, and fun, the color of poodles, sambamaniacs, and people with zipperoo. For centuries, orange—pronounced "ornch" in Philadelphia, I believe—was not the name of a color, in fact. Chaucer describes Chaunticleer: "His colour was betwixe yelow and reed." (Chaunticleer's colors, according to Chaucer scholars, correspond to the arms of Henry St. John Bolingbroke.) And in "The Canon Yeoman's Tale," Chaucer uses the term *citrinacioun,* turning to citron. ("When the materials of the philosopher's stone were in a state favorable to the success of the experiment," notes scholar F. N. Robinson, "they were supposed to assume the color of citron.") Chaucer knew the color; he simply did not have a word for it. Once named, however, orange jumped in with both feet, gumball-bright and saucy and kicking with life, proving itself worthy of its new baptism. It gives, like a good many people I know, an exaggerated sense of event. At times orange and purple seem almost more like flavors than colors, and the colors, despite oranges and grapes, more artificial than natural. Orange is sharper than shy and flashier than frail, with nothing of diffidence or doubt in what is announced of its high saturation, and somehow always reminds me of what Ty Cobb once said of the game of baseball: "It's no pink tea, and mollycoddles had better stay out."

Orange is the wife of blue and belongs to that category of colors that are also *things,* rose, chestnut, olive, grape, walnut, and so forth. The two matchable colors have what in Hollywood jargon is called "he-she chemistry," like Alan Ladd and Veronica Lake. A van Gogh color—very, very rare in Picasso—orange is in its complexion and cast a committed color, always ardent and emotional, appearing, often with its complement, on football jerseys, sweaters, socks, and guidons, and "generally belongs," as Guy Davenport once perspicaciously mentioned to me, "to the strenuous limb." ("There is no blue without yellow and without orange," said van Gogh in 1888.) In 1881, the National League's first year, all second basemen were identified by uniformly orange-and-blue shirts, belts, and caps. (Pants were white.) The color orange has always combined for me, in a subjective portmanteau, the French words *orage* (storm) and *orant,* a praying female figure in art, yoking in passive and active acts two disparate qualities.

Is Robert Burton correct in *The Anatomy of Melancholy* when he points out that humors affect the colors of objects? Or is it the reverse? We know that red, yellow, and orange stimulate the appetite, that blue, green, and mauve suppress it. Orange seems for its flush almost too gamesome or facetious to appear seriously on national flags, and that rectangular third of it on Ireland's flag has always looked, at least to me, slightly fatuous for it—and the Houston Astros used to look like rubes, the hysterical fire orange stripes of their uniforms recalling for me the incicurable blazes of teenage fender painting on hot rods or the lapping flames I once saw daubed on the outer walls of the sex cabaret El Infierno in Tijuana's Zona Norte! A secondary color, however, never takes a backseat to a primary color, for, in its Platonic remove from yellow and red, orange, in the way a child recapitulates his or her parents, restates both. I remember reading on Willa Cather's gravestone in Jaffrey, New Hampshire, "That is happiness, to be dissolved into something complete and great."

It is an adult's seventh color preference, a child's fifth, a pratfallish color, a fat clown's, with little subtlety, less grace, and in its mouth a hearty "Hail-Fellow-Well-Met." In China, orange stands for power and happiness, where it is also the auspicious hue of celestial fruit and the color of pride, hospitality, marriage, ambition, benevolence, what Ann Landers with her characteristic preschool rhetoric calls, I believe, a "day brightener." It has strut and swank and "side." It stands for cleanliness and purity and chastity, but for daring as well, of the artist-and-model ballgoer of the Parisian 1890s, of the Vienna *Gigerl,* of the gay blade, of young farm couples laughing on their way to the state fair, of hot guitarist Albert Collins playing "Snowcone" or Buster Brown singing "Fannie Mae" and Ray Sharpe "Linda Lu" and Mariah Carey "Emotions." In Yucatán— Mexico is still a solid orange on our atlases—orange leaves are used in baths for a new mother. Oranges were often used as pomander balls in hot, crowded places before the institution of bathing and air-conditioning. (Oil of orange is still employed in hospitals to ward off bad odors.) It is the color of splendor and mercy in the Kabbala, for adult library cards (yellow for children) when I was growing up, and even of pop singer Madonna's house, overlooking Lake Hollywood, in Hollywood, California—it was once Bugsy Siegel's residence—which from afar, with its red and yellow stripes, gives the effect of orange. "Orange for outrage," as William Gass writes in *The Tunnel.* An orange car, a GTO called "The Judge," was made by Pontiac in 1968. And in the 1950s the Underwood Company even came out with a small orange portable typewriter. H. L. Mencken noted the existence of a person named Memory D. Orange. Orange Seeley was one of the pioneer settlers of Utah. A Mr. and Mrs. Orange also pops up, funnily enough, in Dickens's *Holiday Romance.* Many towns and places here and abroad are named for the color. One of my favorite song titles is "When It's Apple-Pickin' Time in Orange, New Jersey, We'll Make a Peach of a Pair." Curiously, there is no rhyme in English for the word *orange.* As Ogden Nash once, not wittily, observed,

> *English is a language than which none is sublimer,*
> *But it presents certain difficulties for the rhymer.*
> *There are no rhymes for orange or silver,*
> *Unless liberties you pilfer.*

There are orange-striped cattle, sunsets, chiles, tobacco leaves, caviar and roe, and giant (eight-inch) centipedes, as well as orange perfumes, channel bass, and popping plugs. It is the color of the Magdalene's hair, as well as Donald Duck's. Tide, the first artificial detergent (1949), comes in a strident orange box. Tarnish on silver is orange, as are baseball paths, pedicurists' orange sticks, old-time Russian lampshades (according to John Gunther in *Inside Russia),* Rhodesian Ridgeback dogs, citronella, vitamin-D pills, crabs, paragoric, ambeer— tobacco juice!—the tint of fresh coffee (stale coffee is grayish), ribbed Catholic confessional partitions, the lifeguards' trunks and floats of TV's *Baywatch,* the hair of jackals, and Monet's border of nasturtiums *(capucine)*—they are edible!—now profusely overrunning the sunlit paths of Giverny.

A secondary color, orange—artificial, like cats and tinsel and concocted drinks (or any mixture)—is made up of the combination of yellow and red, the "classical colors," according to German cultural historian Oswald

Spengler in *The Decline of the West,* "the colors of the material, the near, the full-blooded." The color orange is loud, showy, unrestrained, clamorous, even bullying, and in many of its fluorescent flushes or tones—or should we say "keys"?—hideous. The title credits of Technicolor films are usually in orange, as are those in Cinemascope *(A Farewell to Arms, The River of No Return, Guys and Dolls,* and so forth). The Georgia license plate (peaches, oddly, are apparently thought of as orange in that state), as well as peach stones, is orange. A perfect "peach orange," to my mind, is the color in the Walt Disney film *Pinocchio* of that autokinetic puppet's cap (orange with a blue stripe, the exact reverse of Jiminy Cricket's hat, blue with an orange stripe). The glad cinematic imagery of orange here is very strong, including Geppetto's apron and shoes, hearth and fireside, toys and clocks and pendula, Cleo the goldfish, Gideon's coat, Jiminy Cricket's spats, doorways, clothes, and entire settings. "He dreamt of peach stones, and a lady with a lace parasol, whose face he could not see," wrote Ronald Firbank of a uniquely extravagant and entirely imaginative soul in his lush story *Lady Appledore's Mésalliance.* The *Financial Times* newspaper, incidentally, is printed on orange paper, using that simple, generous color, I've heard it said, because it creates less contrast with the print and is more inviting—what, giving it a fireside's warmth?—to read. (Also, the ink doesn't smudge.) In Paintball, the currently popular war game—an adult version of water guns, a wilderness hide-and-seek played in a real woods—the balls are often orange. In 1973, Charles Finley, owner of the Oakland A's, introduced orange baseballs, as Larry MacPhail in 1938 once tried yellow ones, but they failed to catch on. Golf balls are popularly orange, however. So versatile is orange that it can be listed variously in libraries, via the Dewey Decimal System, under 630 (fruit trees); 152 or 153 (psychology); 616, 618 (emotional); 709 (art history); 750 (painting); and so forth.

As to literature, I still believe, subjectively, that the definitive orange sentence—evoking love, languor, and New England autumn—is Grace Metalious's opening line in *Peyton Place:* "Indian Summer is like a woman."

I have visions of orange, set pieces or box sets of the color, suggested by dreams and completed by nothing more than my own projections and quirky biases: a corpulent Indian sweating cardamom through his enormous pores. Goofy, Disney's orangish cartoon dog, eating a wedge of pumpkin pie. A round harvest moon, shining above spooning lovers in some 1940s Technicolor musical starring Gordon Macrae and Doris Day. A marketplace, with rustic bowls of nuts, pecans, almonds, red-skinned Spanish peanuts, in maybe northern Thailand. Sundried apricots in a bowl in a window in Oxnard, California. Al Jolson singing "Latin from Manhattan," and ending the song with the joyous shout, "Velveeta!" Or, along the same vein, Lupe Velez, the Mexican Spitfire, doing her rhumba number in *The Cuban Love Song* (1931) or singing "Say What I Wanna Hear You Say" in the film *Hot-Cha* (1932). Cole Porter, sitting in an orangerie in Haiti at sunset, composing. It is the *marceline* of a beautiful sunrise, the orange that melts into saffron and the saffron that goes into mauve and the mauve that rises to the sky to embrace its azure limpidity in perfect fusion.

Tithonia, or the Mexican sunflower, a bloom that attracts hummingbirds and butterflies, shows, in my opinion, more than anything else in all of nature the *deepest* orange. It is a fire-drake so tropically dense, so sulphurously ripe, so madly glorious, that in the daring and almost insolent boldness of its pure orange fulgor, it could actually be burning.

A citrus fruit, of course, the orange—the fruit and the color, while inextricable, are not absolutely linked— is native to China. (The bitter orange *{bigarade}* is a native of India.) "The first known reference to oranges," observes John McPhee in his book *Oranges* (1967), "occurs in the second book of the *Five Classics,* which appeared in China around 500 B.C. and is generally regarded as having been edited by Confucius." The Greeks and Romans did not know the sweet orange, but they probably did know the bitter orange, the citron. The Provençal word *auranja* (after *aura,* gold; French *or)* goes back to the Spanish *naranja,* to Arabic *nāranj,* from Persian *nārang,* and that word from the Tamil *naru,* fragrant. The Sanskrit word for this twenty-million-year-old fruit was *Nâgrunga,* meaning "fruit flavored by elephants," from which the Italian words *Naranzi* and *d'Aranzi,* the Latin terms (of the Middle Ages) *Arantium, Arangium,* and later *Aurentium*—which produced the French word *orange*—were all derived. (A bitter white glucoside called *naringin,* found in the blossoms and fruit of the grapefruit, is cognate to orange.) It was the crusaders who brought bitter oranges from Palestine into Italy, and the Arabs, whose apt word for orange is, wonderfully, *burtuqal,* where the best oranges were presumably grown in Moorish times, when the fruit was introduced into Spain and the south of France, as well as probably into East Africa. The peripatetics of the orange, then, go from China to the Malay Archipelago to the east coast of Africa, beyond the desert to the Mediterranean, and then across to the Americas. "There were no oranges in the Western Hemisphere before Columbus himself introduced them," explains McPhee, who also points out that it was Pizarro who took them to Peru, Hernando de Soto in his travels who brought the fruit to the area of St. Augustine, Florida, in 1539, and Spanish missionaries in the Far West who brought them to California. Seedless oranges, incidentally, were not grown in the United States until 1871. The first ones came from Brazil and were planted in California.

Is an orange the unidentified "fruit" of the Edenic tree in the garden (Gen. 3:3)? Possibly for John Chapman, a.k.a. "Johnny Appleseed" (1774–1845), America's romantic sower of seeds, who once said, "Be sure the Lord wouldn't keep anyone from eating an apple. How many times is the apple mentioned in a favorable way in the Good Book? Eleven times, that's how many!" In the Holy Koran, the banana plant is the Tree of Knowledge, the equivalent of the Christian Tree of Knowledge, and the fruit that God forbade Adam and Eve to sample was the banana. The "apple" that is mentioned in the Song of Solomon (2:3,5; 7:8; 8:5) and in Joel (1:12) may be the apricot or the orange (the "apples of gold," Prov. 25:11) that flourished in Asia Minor. (Curiously, "Applesins," slyly like *Apfelsine,* the German word for orange, is the slang word for orange in Anthony Burgess's novel *A Clockwork Orange.*) There is not a single mention of oranges in the Bible. (André Gide in *La Symphonie Pastorale* mistakenly asserts—had he not read Mark 15:17?—that there is not a single mention of color in any of the Gospels.) In spite of the paintings of Fra Filippo Lippi, Duccio, Raphael, Bellini, and so forth, no orange trees existed in the Holy Land during the time of Christ, who in all probability would never have seen an orange. On the other hand, would Christ have seen a fox? No, and yet that was his derisive name for Herod Antipas, Tetrarch of Galilee. Therefore, we might be entirely mistaken about what he did and did not see. The true truth, unfortunately—the *"verita verissima"* of the Neapolitans—can never be known.

In Hebrew, the fruit is called *tapus,* evidently a variant of *tapuach,* apple. So it is intriguing to speculate, as many do, that the forbidden fruit of Eden in Genesis 3:6 might have been the orange. It is, after all, as Joyce's Leopold Bloom conjectures in *Ulysses,* the fertile and citrus-yielding land of Agendath Netaim: "planter's company. . . . Excellent for shade, fuel and construction. Orangegroves and immense melonfields north of Jaffa. You pay eight marks and they plant a dunam of land for you with olives, oranges, almonds or citrons." It suffuses, does the color orange, the entire "Calypso" episode of Joyce's novel, establishing the theme of the *Drang nach osten* while evoking the perfumed aura of sun-warmed orange groves. As a color, it commodiously runs the gamut between warmth and light. Andrew Marvell in "Bermudas" gave as an elemental image:

> *Orange bright*
> *Like golden lamps in a green night*

How did people refer to the color orange before the discovery of the fruit? There are several possibilities. Yellow over the past centuries has had a broader range than now. "Gold" and "amber" and "yalwe" appear as colors before the late-sixteenth-century arrival of the word *orange.* Thus, for instance, from the *Secretis secretorum* of the early fifteenth century: "Whos colour ys gold, lyke that ys meen bytwen reed and yalwe." According to Jonny Morris, "The most common term was probably tawny. Holland's Pliny of 1601 has 'without forth of a light tawny or yellowish-red.'" One should probably refer to heraldic terms, before any other source, as one may find greater accuracy of definition in that ancient field than anywhere else. So Gerard Leigh's *The Accidence of Armorie* of 1568: "Now to the sixth coloure, whiche we calle Tawney, and is blazed by thys woorde. Tenne . . . is made of two bright colours which is redde and yellowe."

In 1597, Francis Bacon does say, "Userers should have orange-tawny bonnets, because they do Judaise" *(Essay* XLI), for it was not only the ancient color almost always appropriated to clerks and persons of inferior condition, but it was also the color worn by the Jews. And remember when Bottom the weaver asks Quince what color beard he was to wear for the character of Pyramus in *A Midsummer Night's Dream* (I.ii), he replies, "I will discharge it in either your straw-colour beard, your orange-tawny beard, your purple-in-grain beard, or your French-crown-colour beard, your perfect yellow." Curiously, Shakespeare never uses the word *orange* as a color by itself, only the safer compound orange-tawny, and that only twice in the same play, alternately describing a beard and a bird bill.

Although orange is thus a relatively modern name for the color, it is not as if in the ancient world a specific name for the color failed to surface for lack of opportunity. To take only one example, the word *smurna* (σμύρνα), from which we get the name Smyrna, is a word of semitic origin, the scriptural word for myrrh— one of the three gifts of the Magi (Matt. 2:11)—which is specifically reddish yellow, a color, however, never once described in any of the many references made to it (Psalms 45:8; Prov. 7:17; Song of Sol. 1:13; 5:5; Exod. 30:23; Esther 2:12; and John 19:39).

It should be noted that the original name for the fruit, seen no doubt as a variation of yellow, was "a norange," and through verbal elision, with the swallowing of the letter *n* by confusion with the indefinite article, became "an orange." (Umpire was, in middle English, originally "noumper," an extra man haled in to settle arguments, just as napron, from French *naperon,* was the original spelling for the protective garment we know as an apron. Some other words changed by elision are a nadder [adder], a nauger [auger], and an ewt [newt].) It was dyes and varied usage in the dyeing in-

dustry that easily allowed for so many shades and varia-
tions of "ochre" to be known. The darker extreme is
known as "burnt ochre," the brighter as "yellow ochre."
It was the brighter shade of burnt ochre that became
informally the name of the fruit when the citrus became
a regular household object. Technically speaking, orange
is the only word for itself. "I'm always trying to think of
some other word for it, both fruit and color, and there
isn't one," John Updike once told me. Tangerine, for
instance, is a color but a modern name for one—you
have to know that fruit to know that color.

Tawny—born of the word *tenné,* a heraldic tincture
indicating orange or bright brown—incorporates with
an almost maddening latitude the full range and degree
of hues of any given group tanned by the sun (brown as
a berry, bronze god, red as crabs, golden tan, I'm turn-
ing black), recalling for me lines from Wallace Stevens's
"The Green Plant,"

> *The effete vocabulary of summer*
> *No longer says anything.*
> *The brown at the bottom of red.*
> *The orange far down in yellow.*

Catullus in his poem "Atys" speaks of a lion's tawny
mane. Dio Cassius, the Greek historian, noted of British
warrior Boadicea, "a great mass of the tawniest hair fell
to her hips." But the hues of tawniness are multiple and
can be inexact. Martians, notes Swedenborg in *Earths of
the Universe,* creatures who live on fruit and dress in
fibers made from tree bark, have faces that are "half

Menagerie one sunny autumn day when I was seventeen and finding something of symbolic delight, even trans-figuration, in its vivid original fruit-orange hardcover binding. To me it is a wistfully *violet* play, however. And were you aware that one working title for *A Streetcar Named Desire* was *The Primary Colors*?

But whether over books or bottles or boats, aren't our dreams only our desires after all? Of all God's gifts to the sight of man, John Ruskin thought color was the holiest. Constable collected colors on the picturesque heath of Fittleworth Common, tints and specimens.

And what of Rubens and his rainbows?

Color is fictive space.

Isn't that why Baudelaire said children talk to toys?

What about curry orange? Coral? Russet? Or the dis-tinctive school bus orange of food dye no. A001M, which can be found, say, in Cheez Whiz, that processed "cheese food," created in fifties America, that contains not only mozzarella, Muenster, and Gouda, along with mustard, salt, and Worcestershire sauce, but that inde-scribably delicious preservative sorbic acid? There is an orange-flavored prophylaxis in dentistry, used in polish-ing, that in color is of a deep burnt orange. A flavid orange can be found in marmalade, a comestible that painter Claude Monet, for one, particularly loved. I re-member S. S. Pierce's (pronounced "Perse" by cultured Bostonians) five-pound stone jars of orange marmalade, or "mama" in diner slang. But in England, Cooper's Oxford Marmalade (orange, extra chunky) is apparently matchless, and British spy Kim Philby, who loved it, had it sent several times a year to his secret address in

Moscow, where even his telephone was ex-directory. The old, self-pitying, crumpled, and unshaven drunk Marmeladov, incidentally, in Dostoyevsky's *Crime and Punishment*—"whose very name indicates his lack of willpower," observes Dostoyevsky biographer Joseph Frank—with his "yellow, even greenish complexion," is actually and suitably named for that confiture.

There is cuprous orange. Mark Twain in *Life on the Mississippi* insisted Irishmen were lined with copper! "Give an Irishman lager for a month, and he's a dead man. An Irishman is lined with copper, and the beer corrodes it," he wrote. "But whiskey polishes the copper and is the saving of him, sir." Could that be why "stills" are famously made of copper, their kettles and coils? In the "Circe" (or fifteenth) chapter of James Joyce's *Ulysses,* the phrase "lumps of coal and copper snow" describe cones of ice sweetened with fruit juice, what we today refer to as snow cones (or "slushes" in the Boston area), clearly allusions to grape and orange ices.

Terra-cotta is orangeish, an ancient, perhaps prehistoric hue: "originally colored," as Aldous Huxley has a character, one of Vulca's artists, describe it in his short story "After the Fireworks," in *Brief Candles* (1930). ("By Vulca," wrote Huxley, "the only Etruscan sculptor [anyone] knows the name of. . . .") A good painterly example of terra-cotta is Picasso's oil *Two Nudes* (1906), with its red browns and rawness of facture. Isn't rawness in fact orange? And flare? And tang? Many oils are orange. So is grease, paint remover, naval jelly. As is ancient henna, with so much red simmering provocatively within it. I love some of the names of the Bruning paints in the orange category: Sedona Clay, Coronette Orange, Orange Torch, Tigerstripe, October Bronze, and Glowing Ember. Are not the very insides of trees orange—when cut, the inmost circle or core of trunks is almost always a ripe sunburst or autumn orange—along with much of nature, from resins to reef coral to the pebbled orangewood stick, or emery board, used in the care of fingernails. Aurora is orange, skies burning with the fires of dawn, the rising light of the morning, the ghostly flashes of the supernal borealis. "Like an orange in a fried fish shop" is Gulley Jimson's cheekily original and bold description of the sun in a morning mist in Joyce Cary's *The Horse's Mouth.* The red light of traffic signals has some orange in it (and the green, blue) in order to make it even more easily distinguished by the color-blind (who of course depend on the traditional layout—vertical lights, red on top, etc.—as well). Did you know, by the way, that ten times as many men as women are color-blind?

I look at the color orange and figuratively find conspicuous exuberance, the kind of power that excites the imagination, in such diverse works as Hogarth's *The Shrimp Girl,* a joyous youngster free from all frills, unashamed in her rags, regarding the world with bright eyes and the beauty of health, or the lines from the Song of Solomon (4:17–21):

> . . . *come, O south wind!*
> *Blow upon my garden,*

let its fragrance be wafted abroad.
Let me beloved come to his garden,
and eat its choicest fruits

or Johann Sebastian Bach's magnificent chorale *"Schmücke dich o liebe Seele"* ("Make Yourself Beautiful, Beloved Soul")—which so affected Mendelssohn that he supposedly told Schumann, "If life were to deprive me of hope and faith, this one chorale would bring them back"—or even Bach's joyous cantata for the Easter of 1715, *Der Himmel lacht.* Trumpeter Ruby Braff once saw orange in hearing Louis Armstrong. I wonder what color would have filled his mind when he first heard Johnny Hodges alto "Squatty-Roo" or "Isfahan" or "Jeep's Blues" or listened to Rex Stewart hit E above C above high C on his trumpet, as he was said to do. Duke Ellington's surprisingly open-ended definition of jazz, you may recall, was "freedom of expression," which incorporates a thousand majesties—*and* sillinesses, no doubt. Like Paul Whiteman's three-foot baton. Heisenberg's Uncertainty Principle, which lies at the heart of quantum theory. Sister Flute, "raked" with spiritual heat, wildly shouting, clapping, and moaning in the aisles in a black Baptist church. I find something paradigmatically orange in them all.

I mention high C. It is to my mind a definitively orange note, as bright as the homonymous American bug juice of the same color, Hi-C, and as neon-intense and vitaminized, like the hundreds of high Cs "with the F on top" that Louis Armstrong loved to hit on stage and in ballroom appearances (rarely on record, where he was tamer) in songs like "Ding Dong Daddy," "Sendin' the Vipers," and "Potato Head Blues," for example, and that last poignant note that comes out of Mimi's lovely throat as she exits with Rodolfo in the first act of *La Bohème.* It is the essential of a soprano's equipment. (In Jules Massenet's *Esclarmonde,* however, the beautiful American soprano Sybil Sanderson, with whom, incidentally, Massenet was in love, sang a famous top G, which, at least according to Diaghilev, "is supposed to be the highest note the human voice can reach.") Lillian Nordica, for one, with her great passion, thrilled audiences when she hit high C in the "Inflammatus" of Rossini's *Stabat Mater.* She sang with Jean de Reszke, who, Tristan to her famous Isolde, also loved that high note, as did bold Francesco Tamagno, a true *tenore di forza,* who capriciously added five successive orangeaceous high Cs to the stretta in the last act of *William Tell.* "It is a vocal sound fat, round, euphonious, and well-focused right up to a full-voiced and resonant top," writes Henry Pleasants in *The Great Singers,* like Enrico Caruso's tenor, as well as the baritone of Titta Ruffo, who, ringing in high notes extending to a high B-flat, was supposedly deficient only in *lower* notes! The one recording the two men made together, in 1914, when both men were in their prime, the *"si, pel ciel"* from *Otello,* was ample, sumptuous, emphatic with floridity, and, according to Pleasants, "stands alone as an example of sheer vocal wealth unmatched and unapproached among the great documents of vocal recording." I heard it once at Harvard, sitting alone in Paine Hall one rainy day in 1975, with tears in my eyes.

Orange is the color of Halloween. The Irish brought Halloween with them to America, where the day was not widely celebrated until about 1900. November first was the Celtic New Year. October thirty-first was celebrated by the Druids with many human sacrifices and a festival honoring Samhain, the lord of the dead. The Druids believed that sinful souls who died during the year would be in a place of torment unless Samhain was placated with sacrifices. As the Druids believed that the sinful lost souls were released upon the earth by Samhain for one night on October 31 while they awaited judgment, people feared these spirits and so carved demonic faces into pumpkins or large turnips, placing a candle in them to keep the evil spirits away from their houses. Pope Gregory the Great decided to incorporate the Druids' holiday into the church. He decreed that November 1 was to be a universal church observance. It is the season for fat orange moons ("All Hallows moon, witches moon"). Candy corn, with its festive two-tone kernels of orange and white, was introduced on this holiday obviously to make more money for the candy industry, always on the lookout for new reasons to compel customers to buy their products.

Orange in the field of astrology is the color of the second level of the building devoted to the planet Jupiter in the Temple of Nebuchadnezzar. It is the color of the doctoral hood for engineering (apricot for nursing, maize for agriculture), in meteorology the color of weatherfront markings on maps for the intertropical convergence zones, and all of the screen grids and second transistor bases in electrical chassis wiring are of this exact and irrepressible color. Jacinth, a gem almost pure orange in color, indicates modesty and cures heart ailments. I am not certain if fire opals have salutary qualities, but I once saw a Mexican fire opal in a jewelry store window that in its bright deliquescent orange scintillants sparkled like godsong. Topazes are said to symbolize divine goodness, faithfulness, sagacity—"an exuberant name for such a gem of a knight," wrote Skeat of Chaucer's pilgrim, Sir Thopas—love, and the sun; it conjoins mineral orange to copper red, or chalcedony. I have already mentioned jazz trumpeter Ruby Braff. As a boy growing up in Roxbury, in an epiphanic and life-altering moment, he first heard Louis Armstrong playing his trumpet over the radio on "The 920 Club," and he would later say of the experience, "It was unearthly. An orange tone suddenly filled the room. It was like nothing else I ever heard in my life."

What took place?

Had color found music? Is color just the refraction of white light? Is color elusive and the mind orange that found what consumed its dream? Was philosopher John Locke right in distinguishing primary physical qualities, inherent in material objects, from secondary qualities, that exist only in the mind of the observer—"subtle deceits," as Herman Melville suggests in *Moby-Dick* (Chapter 42), "not actually inherent in substances, but only laid on from without"?

So many things are orange. Gourds, horn, clown hair, Aspergum—I was once happily addicted to chewing this stuff, something like medicated orange Chiclets, and at one rather extreme point in my life began going through whole boxes of it daily—DPW trucks, pennies, dried lather soap, highway repair cones, Princeton, dental plaque, old radio dials (lighted), goldfish, the century-old violins of Cremona (Amati, Stradivari, and Guarneri), battery mold, tree fungi *(Pholiota aurivella)* protruding from the rotten trunks of trees, plywood, Mexican terra-cotta, sap, harvest moons, tigers, Archie Andrews's socks, chamois cloth, leather work gloves (cotton, with blue wristlets), chorizo, fishing boots, gasoline, achiote, good wooden umbrella handles, shellac, autumn leaves, rock lichen, French dressing, amber cigarette holders and filters with their tangerine tips, the fingers of smokers ("his cigarette fingers are the color of whiskey," writes Frederick Seidel in "A Negro Judge"), the crusts of bread loaves, amber, price stickers, toucans' bills, the glow and smell of punk, mushrooms on logs (which are cultivated in Japan), the five ball in pool, ceramic pots, 1950s leather luggage, Mexican bull rings, the bracts of royal palm trees, dashboard knobs, tamarind, domestic caviar, bourbon, Orange Crush bottles, star anise—a large tree of the magnolia family found only in North Vietnam—waning sunlight on windows, the handles on Fiskars scissors *(the* sewing scissors—an orange handle has made them a machine), resin chairs, earwax, butterscotch, foxes, old celluloid film, and the most popular embroidery thread on Mexican girls' blouses. Nor should we forget those ugly, enveloping biomorphic orange modular couches of the eighties, Pears soap ("tar-black when dry, topaz-like when held to the light," as Vladimir Nabokov notes in *Speak, Memory),* or Grand Canyon sandstone, especially in late afternoon in the coppery sun. We read in Thomas Pynchon's *Gravity's Rainbow* of a man's fair skin being "stained by afternoon a luminous synthetic orange [someone had] never before associated with skin." Suns, even moons, can be richly and dramatically orange.

So is nicotine, smoked salmon, the painted skin on murals of hieroglyphed Egyptians, duck bills and feet, the eggs of sea urchins, cod's roe, the robes of Buddhist monks, women's scented face powders, liquid foundations, and old Boston tramcars. It is the color of foot soles, petrified wood, the sunset, rust, pigeons' eyes, and the fluid orange ridge of flame moving unevenly down a piece of burning paper, as well as bulb filaments, autumn brambles, many honeys, oaten biscuits, Rexall signs, auto-polishing cloths ("And thick, color/orange and black, with a nap," notes poet Charles Olson in "Letter 22"), melba toast, king bolete mushrooms and chanterelles, sanding wheels, sawdust, goonch—licorice seeds from India—and Neutrogena soap. There is always something of comfort and nurturing assurance in orange, from the glow of gaslights to Fresnel lights to the revolving holophotal lights of old lighthouses to the magic immemorial tints of a suffusing, soft-hued day in autumn. But also pain. I often sorrowfully recall that unforgettable photograph taken on June 11, 1963, of the suicidal but selflessly propitiatory Vietnamese Buddhist monk, Thich Quang Duc, protesting American involvement—he was gazing into a decade of horror—sitting full lotus in a swirl of flames on a hot summer street in Saigon, back erect, shaved head held high, while orange flames, blazing up, consumed him in his orange robes as he stared transfixed into the middle distance with blackened hands raised like a statue in dying benediction. Orange in its high saturation is a color not easy to forget.

Wax is mostly orange, isn't it? Car waxes, floor waxes, canned waxes, various polishes, and emulsions. Are you aware that candles are never mentioned in Scripture? Nor is wax, amazingly enough. Wax, as in "He waxed wroth," is in fact used only and always as a verb. Everywhere in the Bible the word *lamp* should be substituted for *candle,* and any reference to wax in modern translations is bogus.

Most redheads have orange or rust-colored hair. No better example can be found than Judy Garland's over-hennaed pageboy in the musical *Meet Me in St. Louis,* a movie filled with radiant "chocolate box" colors that made the world look bright as song. (Judy never looked thinner, and I remember once reading somewhere that stale Coca-Cola was used to shade her cheeks.) What about the clownish epigones of Aschenbach in Thomas Mann's *Death in Venice?* Ian Fleming's cruel Auric Goldfinger (Gert Frobe) wore a bright carrot red crewcut. And Fagin, the crafty old Jew in Dickens's *Oliver Twist* had matted red hair. (The word *ruffian* in English and Italian *ruffino* come from the same root as "rufous," meaning red-headed.) Alexander Hamilton's hair was a gold-corn reddish color. So was that of Willie Nelson, actress Samantha Eggar, Ezra Pound—Ford Madox Ford jokingly said of its crinkly gold-red that it looked as if it had been "soaked in vinegar"—and everyone from various Klimt women to giant Ruebezahl, the Carrot

Counter of German fairy tale fame. In 1914, Billie Burke, who had orange hair, married the impresario Florenz Ziegfeld, a man who expressly disliked both dyed *and* bobbed hair, which he said made women "all alike as two peas in a pod. It [bobbing] has destroyed that elusive and priceless quality which women of charm must have—personality." I would like to have seen orange-haired composer Ignace Paderewski gaily riding in nineteenth-century eccentric Isabella Stewart Gardner's carriage, going round and round the Fenway, with his long locks—mocked in staid Boston—blowing in the wind. Lucille Ball's fluffy Hollywood hair, never red, was of an orange brighter than naphthacene or arsenic disulphide, although she did make an appearance in 1935 as a platinum blond in the Stooges' film *Three Little Pigskins.* Vincent van Gogh, whom children followed and cruelly taunted with, *"Fou roux! Fou roux! Fou roux!"* had orange hair. So did Mortimer Snerd. And the same goes for Bonnie Raitt, Sen. Strom Thurmond, architect Stanford White, Clarabelle the Clown, and attempted murderer and thug Robert ("Sideshow Bob") Terwilliger on TV's *The Simpsons* ("Whaddya mean 'attempted'? Do they give a Nobel Prize for 'attempted' chemist?"), Cindy Lauper, Sioux City Sue, Wilma Flintstone, puffball-headed singer Reba McEntire, Squeaky Fromme, and Howdy Doody with his copper-penny freckles honoring the number of American states (at the time). Betty Boop had orange hair in Max Fleischer's *Poor Cinderella* (1934), the only color film ever done of that cartoon character. Gore Vidal described Edith Sitwell as having "thin, tea-colored hair." Punk rocker

Tony James of Generation X, to achieve the perfect hedgehog hair, used a concoction of lemon juice, spit, and orange juice. ("I used to walk around smelling like a carton of Kia-Ora," he said.) And Sid Vicious of the Sex Pistols used orange food coloring to dye his hair. Orange hair, in a sense, implies comic puffery and chaos, almost certainly wildness, and almost always needs something of severity in dress to tone it down. As critic James Wolcott wrote of Arianna Stassinopoulos Huffington, "She wears beautifully tailored dresses, which offset her fiery orange helmet of power hair."

Regarding what we might call "contained" reddish or orange hair, one thinks perhaps of Broadway musicals' Gwen Verdon or fifties model Suzy Parker, with her perky russet hair and cool sartorial demeanor, or even Duke Ellington, whom joshing fellow musicians and certain intimates good-humoredly called "Piano Red" and "Sandhead." Bette Davis playing Elizabeth I in the movie *The Virgin Queen* sports a high, shiny, plastic orange wiglet that is a far brighter orange than, though it oddly resembles, a Brillo pad. After David Bowie's television special *The 1980 Floor Show,* starring the Diamond Dog himself wearing tight, flaring pants and an orange hairdo (or "hair don't," as film director John Waters would say)—along with Amanda Lear, Marianne Faithfull, and the Troggs—American teenagers the next day maniacally descended on local drugstores to scarf up boxes of copper henna. "Manic Panic," an orange hair dye, is popular among slackers and punks nowadays. And baseball player red-headed Daniel J. ("Rusty") Staub, who played for the Montreal Expos in 1964, was commonly referred to in that town as *"Le Grand Orange."*

No one even makes the pretense that Li'l Orphan Annie's hair is anything but sunset orange. The murderous doll Chuckie in *Child's Play,* along with having mad staring blue eyes, has thatch orange hair. So does Alfred E. Newman of *Mad* magazine. And Red Buttons, that frazzled goofball with freckles, had nothing red about him and properly should have been called "Orange"—playing agent Arthur Landau in the movie *Harlow,* at one point he actually wears an orange suit that perfectly matches his oddly shaped head. And Sylvia Plath's could have been denoted orange, who wrote in her poem "Lady Lazarus," "Out of the ash/I rise with my red hair/And I eat men like air." Haven't we agreed orange has a kind of fatness? Roundness? Walter Hudson, the fattest man in the world—*Forbes* magazine listed his gross weight at a full fourteen hundred pounds (seven-tenths of a ton)—and a man who spent nearly all of his life in bed, wore his hair in twin braids wound with orange ribbons. He died at the age of forty-six, at 1,125 pounds, of the flu. Doesn't the "roundness" of orange in the robes of Hare Krishna pursuivants somehow match their shaven heads in welcoming simplicity? Speaking of orange and roundness, Sarah "Fergie" Ferguson, the Duchess of York, was judged in the compilation *Who's Had Who,* by Simon Bell, Richard Curtis, and Helen Fielding, as being a fully and "genuinely orange" person because of her "bright orange hair, bright orange freckles, and generally orange shape and demeanor." And it was Anne Sexton who, putting on weight, while ingeniously—and uniquely, I believe—using the word *orange* as a verb, wrote the following lines from "Moon Song, Woman Song,"

> *I have been oranging and fat,*
> *carrot colored, gaped at. . . .*

No, it is always orange I think of in flaming hair, not red, as for example in Daniel S. Libman's story "I Am the Light": "I went to Mr. Donuts once and saw a girl whose entire face was covered with burns; but her hair was beautiful. It was a brilliant fiery red. It seemed likely that her hair was what had set fire to her face."

And in Carson McCullers's lovely story *A Tree. A Rock. A Cloud,* the nameless man with "faded orange hair" in the streetcar café who discloses to the paper boy the secret of love also crucially needs to have been burned, as it were, in order to discover his truth.

There is in the world of maquillage much orange, I believe. Doesn't orange simulate, even exaggerate, healthful skin? Robustness. The song of the outdoors. Lancôme lipsticks of an orange hue are called Orange Boheme, Rouge Symbole, Orange Brulée, and Oranjeque, and Elizabeth Arden orange lipsticks have names like Papaya, Neoclassic Peach, and Coral. Pancake makeup is orange. "He's alive. He's wearing a suit. And he's orange," a critic in the *New York Times* observed in 1994 of actor William Shatner, dressed as *Star Trek*'s Captain Kirk, sitting in Orso, ready for lunch. And an immensely tall black man I know—he looks like a Somali or a thin, spear-long Watusi—has orange gums.

And according to Evangeline Bruce in her *Napoleon and Josephine: An Improbable Marriage,* the empress Josephine, Napoleon's wife, is described on her passport, believe it or not, as having "orange eyes."

Singer Cindy Lauper, I believe, wore various shades of orange lipstick on a lot of her album covers. Many street prostitutes in the slum courts and side streets of Mexican cities, having an odd sense of what will attract men, often wear orange lipstick and orange fingernail polish. And wistfully sexy Rita Hayworth, who as a young girl danced in the Foreign Club on Tijuana's Avenida de Revolucion, always seemed to be wearing luscious orange lipstick, which, with her raised and du-bious eyebrow, a beautiful superciliousness, seemed al-most a part of her irony—she was haunted all her life and tried to keep people away. Is not orange lipstick, something like Maybelline's roll-on kissing gloss in lus-cious honey orange, generally popular with all tall, big-lipped women like Jayne Meadows and Toni Tennille and Rhonda Fleming? Dr. Clayton Forester (Gene Barry) wears orange-rimmed eyeglasses in the film *War of the Worlds.* And remember in that overtinted drive-in shocker *When Worlds Collide* that the fat planet Bellus, as it comes hurling forward, is pure orange. It is a *very* orange movie: all of the people's dresses and jackets, ties, all of the earthmoving equipment, the fire extinguisher, the long struts of the spaceship going to Planet Xyra, the ominous sign board that is slowly counting down D day (explosion day). And, forgive me, but aren't those orange *Christmas* trees on idyllic Xyra in the final apoca-lyptic scene?

An orange phenomenon took place in the Ziegfeld Follies of 1922. As lovely Mary Lewis began singing "Weaving My Dreams" in the "Lace-land" number, the dancers' costumes, along with hers, all looked properly lace-colored until the lights went suddenly dim and were then cut, when, lo and behold, all of the girls glowed orange against the black curtain, a zippy radium effect that was produced by a special paint purchased in Paris and that cost something like two hundred dollars a pound.

Orange clothes, as much a force as a fashion, have always been popular in dress, from beachwear to B movies to Miss Sarah Bernhardt. When Bernhardt played the role of Camille in Vienna in an orange-and-black-lace bodice, that poor victim's cynosure of a dress as she passed away stimulated a greater response in print by way of descriptive prose than did the dying throbs themselves. It has always been a popular color with the shiny set—shallow power charity queens and clothes hamsters and fashion victims of *W* and *Women's Wear* and *Vogue*—from Donna Karan's jersey sarongs to tangerine-colored Balenciagas to Bill Blass dresses with sable trim. And frankly, between you and me, there is not a long step from such couture, and such people, to the world of science fiction.

Elvis, by the way, loved orange silk pajamas. And Frank Sinatra, when dressed in his single-breasted tux to sing, often wears an orange pocket handkerchief. As a color, it is *so* retro now. "I live for meetings with suits [male executives]," pop singer Madonna told *Vanity Fair* in 1991. "I love them because I know they had a really boring week and I walk in there with my orange velvet leggings and drop popcorn in my cleavage and then fish it out and eat it. I like that. I know I'm entertaining them, and I know that they know."

Weena's (Yvette Mimieux's) dress in the thumpingly bad but delightfully campy film *The Time Machine* is optimistic orange. And in Electra Woman films, "Lori"—what *is* this thing about awful space movies and the color orange?—wears a very kitschy orange leotard (with a yellow "EW" on her chest) as well as cartoonish orange boots with yellow thunderbolts down the front. In the crapulous film *Prince Valiant,* the young hero's (Robert Wagner's) tunic is orange leather. Giving her "the appearance of a heroine of a county fair," on the other hand, Paul Gauguin makes mention in *Noa Noa* of the wife of the chief of Punaauia wearing a "bizarre dress of orange velvet." Joan Fontaine in *Frenchman's Creek,* a film based on the du Maurier novel, wears an orange Karinska ball gown that matches her hair. Don't Alice Faye and Carmen Miranda, with her fruity hats, rubber smile, and outlandish gestures—La Miranda, along with Betty Hutton, was philosopher Ludwig Wittgenstein's favorite movie star!—often wear orange in *Springtime in the Rockies* and *The Gang's All Here?* Doesn't splashpool diva Esther Williams almost always wear orange bathing suits in that rash of her escapist MGM films she made? Robert De Niro's orange hunting jacket in *The Deer Hunter* is the only vivid color in the toneless landscape of those bleak winter hills, just as Astronaut Dave's (Keir Dullea's) orange space suit in Stanley Kubrick's *2001: A Space Odyssey* is a vital and energizing comfort among all of that steel and vastness of space and cold technology and cosmic nothingness. Orange suits somehow become textual defenses of vitality and hope in the reaches of that soulless, gadget-filled cosmos where Hal the 9000 series computer—who alone knows the true nature of the mission—disdainfully sees humans as the source of imperfection and error and tries to kill them.

A scant orange bikini bathing suit darkly becomes to the protagonist in Larry Woiwode's novel *What I'm Going to Do, I Think* (1969), the symbol of his wife's secret infidelities in New York prior to their marriage, and sets him on a long course of danger, suspicion, and violence. Big, slovenly Dinah Brand in Dashiell Hammett's *Red Harvest* ("Her big ripe mouth was rouged evenly this evening") at one point wears an orange silk dress, covered with spots and stains. Marianna in Nabokov's *The Eye* wears "apricot-colored" stockings. And William T. Vollmann in his story "Scintillant Orange," from *The Rainbow Stories,* gives us a hip apocalyptic retelling of the tale of Shadrach, Meshach, and Abednego descending into the "scintillant orange magma" of the Fiery Furnace, where, horribly, "liquid fire dripped from the ceiling as if a million plastic party glasses had been set aflame and oozed their jelled orange light down through the cracks of the world" and where "the walls were like orange prisms of heat and light, and Shadrach's hair became orange, and his face became orange as Meshach looked upon him, and his beard burned fiercely, and it seemed to Meshach that the three of them wore the rare orange garments of kings."

There was a strong domination in early color film of fiery red-orange. The color imagery in *Gate of Hell,* for example, the first Japanese film to use color, especially in the opening scenes of chaos in the Imperial Palace, is a good example. To study the technology of color, many Japanese technicians and directors came to Hollywood. Herbert Kalmus, who launched his Technicolor research in 1918, was by 1923, according to Arthur Knight in *The Liveliest Art,* "marketing a two-color process in which the red-orange-yellow portion of the spectrum was photographed on one negative, the green-blue-purple portion on another. When laminated together, they produced a pleasing though still far from accurate color scale."

There are so many films spiced up by the color orange from the world, as Johnny Mercer put it, of that "screwy bally hooey Hollywood." Fred Astaire sings "Funny Face" to Audrey Hepburn in an orange-red darkroom—and so everything seems wonderfully that color. And Astaire and Lucille Bremer, waving silver fans, do a snappy number in *Ziegfeld Follies* (1946), wearing Chinese orange pantaloons, slippers, and hats. Regarding Hepburn, she is equally pretty as Liza Doolittle singing "Show Me" in *My Fair Lady* wearing a chic peach-colored suit and elegant hat with flowers designed by Mr. Cecil Beaton. Gloria Grahame in *The Greatest Show on Earth* looks sparkling and available in an orange sweater-and-skirt ensemble. Natalie Wood as Maria with skin like pecan wood in *West Side Story* effectively wears this festive color in several scenes, most notably as she sings "I Feel Pretty" in an orange jumper. And Mitzi Gaynor in *South Pacific* sings "I'm in Love with a Wonderful Guy" while wearing a joyful orange top. Doris Day wears a sequined orange dress in *Do Not Disturb* while dancing, when, suddenly spying her rival, she angrily asks for a divorce and creates a huge kerfuffle as she dumps a bowl of potato chips over Rod Taylor's head. Alexander Korda's campy *The Thief of Baghdad,* starring Sabu—isn't he, in his primitive young tawniness, half orange himself?—is a passacaglia of orange turbans, robes, vests, and pilasters, the full orange sails of evil Japha's galleon, and oranges piled high in market stalls. There are many orange dresses, much orange imagery—shirts, lanterns, and so forth—in the Havana sequences of *Guys and Dolls.* In the film version of the musical *Carousel,* Gordon Macrae as Billy Bigelow wears a long-sleeved orange jersey as he sings "If I Loved You" to Julie (Shirley Jones), who looks so beautiful in her innocently open-necked orange frock when later she tells him she is going to have his baby. And when, as Curly, Macrae sings, "Oh, What a Beautiful Morning" in *Oklahoma!,* wearing a sunrise orange shirt, I am once again reminded of the orange rotundity of W. C. Fields's Ogleby, for as Philip Furia in *The Poets of Tin Pan Alley* perspicaciously notes, "the long vowels of that show's opening phrases are recapitulated in the final phrase 'Oklahoma—O-K' and reverberate through such varied lines as 'I cain't *say no,*' 'Don't throw bouquets at me," and

> *Everything's up to date in Kansas City,*
> *They've gone about as fur as they can go!*

And Olivia Hussey as Juliet in the Franco Zeffirelli film *Romeo and Juliet* is wearing with sweet innocence and purity, when we first see her, a sun-bright orange bodice and mantua. What a stark contrast to the mental hospital–looking orange tunic Hedy (Jennifer Jason Leigh) wears in that dark scene in the film *Single White Female* when she makes a violent and obscene phone call. In Tony Gatlif's film *Latchmo Drom* ("Bonne Route," "Safe Journey"), the long, flowing, flimsy, floating shirt and tunic of the dancing gypsy girl spinning in circles in the desert are orange. And Kay Hanna in the film *The Chairman*, a very orange film—everywhere can be seen red and orange jackets, flowers, and so forth—is wearing an orange jumpsuit in her passionate confession of love to Gregory Peck before he leaves for China on his dangerous spy mission, where there is more red and orange imagery visible than on the loud breastworks of Graumann's Chinese Theatre.

Auntie Mame (Rosalind Russell), on the occasion of her nephew Patrick's first visit in that film, wears a great flaming orange banyan over a sequined suit and touchingly covers him with it as she tucks him in bed that night. While Cary Grant in *An Affair to Remember* finds Deborah Kerr's stylish orange coat as splendid as the orange-and-beige dress she wears to match her perfectly coiffed auburn-orange hair. And it might as well have been a movie when in 1967 Jackie Onassis visited Cambodia in a striking tangelo dress, splendidly wearing what Catherine Bowman in her poem "Jackie in Cambodia" called her "heavenly wardrobe/from iceberg to tangelo."

The ultimate orange movie is, at least to me, the ironically named *Blue Skies* (1946). It is almost all orange flowers, dancers' skirts and dresses, lighting for scenes, neon signs of Johnny Adams's (Bing Crosby's) nightclubs, like "The Hole in the Wall," "The Cracker Barrel," "The Top Hat," and so forth, all of the babes and bunting in the "heat wave" scene, everything up to and including Joan Caulfield's lipsticks and Bing's visibly orange toupee. The film's a feast of the secondary colors in general, with purple and green hues everywhere. A good runner-up would be the movie *Tootsie*. So much of the comedy of that film depends on the caricatured and exclamatory outspokenness of his/her—Dorothy's (Dustin Hoffman's), farcically playing now a man, now a woman—orange blouses, orange skirts, orange lipsticks, orange nail polish, and so forth. Even characters with minor roles wear that color. And all of the imagery is orange, from fur coats to the jackets of strangers to street signs.

Orange is a strongly unromantic color, perhaps for the inherent humor, even goofiness, in its extravagant voice. Consider, for example, comic Jim Carrey's all-orange combination tuxedo, top hat, shoes, and cane in the cloacal comedy *Dumb and Dumber.* It is a color virtually nonexistent in song titles, whether blues or rock-and-roll or pop tunes, with the exception of Charlie Mingus's "Song with Orange" and "Orange Was the Color of Her Dress, Then Silk Blue," both recorded in the early sixties, as well as "Orange Crescent" by Steve Turre (performed by Woody Shaw's quintet in 1982) along with a few rare songs with orange blossoms in the title. Nat King Cole's "Orange Colored Sky," with Stan Kenton and his Orchestra—the first hit song, by the way, ever introduced on television (September 30, 1950)—stands pretty much alone. With so many other colors so prominent in music, isn't this odd?

On the vapid TV show *The Brady Bunch,* which ran from 1969 to 1974, the actors of which were described by someone as "lively young nowsters who dressed in flowery jumpers, billowy mod shirts, and burnt orange bell-bottoms," we no doubt found that color at its nadir. It was a period, the early seventies, of earth tones, with orange represented by colors such as sienna fustian, mustard, and Albuquerque loam! (Didn't that simpering father on *The Brady Bunch* always wear the Ban-Lon saffron shirts of a yahoo and orange "floods"? Or is it the revolting fact that everybody did?) Orange (or lemon-white or puppy-shit yellow) full bodysuits or leisure suits with gold stitching, which Jack Hyde of *Men's Wear* said made everyone who wore them look like a bus driver, were very popular during that dull decade of disco and dumbness, sappiness and sideburns. Rank stupidity, a kind of invincible ignorance, adhibits to the color. Bill Cosby, an opportunistic, face-pulling buffoon, in my opinion, not a comedian, maybe because of the shameless and incessant spate of commercials he does on TV, looks to me not black, but orange. So does NBC's weatherman, fat, pop-eyed olio Willard Scott— beachball orange! Also drama junkie/diet cheerleader Richard Simmons, whose behavior is beyond the ramparts of even German Expressionism. And right-wing radio newsdork and bunco-artist Paul Harvey, who, like the shill he is, works commercials without a break right into the news. All have the garish look of those comic postcards from the 1930s, with their fierce, spurious colors, mostly orange. I think that, along with people and types, even certain goofy and nitwitish surnames, like Sinkler and Titcomb and Barnicle and Henchy, have an orange cast to them, worse by far than anything like Dagwood Bumstead or Egbert Sousé, at least in my opinion. On the other hand, Jesus himself had relatives named Zadok and Zerubabbel and Jehoshaphat! Gilligan's rugby shirt in the fatuous television series *Gilligan's Island* was of a moronic orange. Mr. Toby Crackit, one of Fagin's touch confederates in *Oliver Twist,* always wears an orange neckerchief. Temperamental Nora Bayes often sang her songs, undulating, screened by an enormous fan or orange feathers. (My question is, feathers from exactly what *bird?*) She reportedly refused to perform in costumes that were not ferociously expensive.

Orange jackets are formal wear on the Singapore stock exchange. Flyer Jackie Cochrane's jumpsuit—it is on display at the San Diego Aerospace Museum—is orange. And holy men in India, who own nothing and spend a lifetime piously following their dharma, wear poor orange cloth tunics, just as the tambourine-shaking pursuivants of Hare Krishna all wear pale, thin saffron robes, delicate as thread.

"During the summer of 1964, Monty got involved with decorating the brownstone," writes Patricia Bosworth in her biography *Montgomery Clift,* pointing out that "record producer Ben Bagley hung bright orange awnings on the outside of the house. Nancy Pinkerton, a young actress Monty had met in Ogunquit . . . asked, 'Monty, where did you get those psychedelic awnings? They're terrible.' And he said, 'But look!' He was sitting on the stairs, as he often did. 'Look at that light!' he said, and, sure enough, the light filtering through the orange awnings and into the room was the most beautiful light I'd ever seen. It was like being under an amber gel. Everybody who sat in that room would look like a million dollars. Monty said he didn't care how his house looked from the outside, he was creating his ambience for himself inside, and it was pleasing to him aesthetically; everybody would have a scrim."

Orange has always had a celebratory aspect. Carousel horses. Fun fairs. Surfing equipment. Take jukeboxes: Ever since they were first introduced in 1889, when Louis Glass installed a coin-operated cylinder phonograph in San Francisco's lush Palais Royale Saloon, they have been predominantly vibrant orange—the better to *glow.* The grilles were almost always all orange, along with the pilaster caps, the back-colored illuminated curved plastics, and the translucent fluted panels of plastic, not forgetting of course the "bubble tubes." Among some of the classics from the "golden years" of the juke, with their illuminated plastics, were Wurlitzer model 1015 ("The Bubbler")—modeled in 1940s ads by pert Betty Grable, wearing orange lipstick and bright orange high heels—Rock-Ola's 1939 luxury light up; and the showiest of all Wurlitzers, model 850 from 1941, featuring two colorful orange peacocks in the center. Many early radios, thick and shiny, were made in many colors, not from plastic, but of mineral-bright, almost wet-looking catalin—orange was a favorite—a name obviously taken from catalinite, the agate beach pebble from Santa Catalina Island in California.

I believe, if, as Cecil Beaton once warmly said of Sarah Bernhardt, she had a "brown velvet voice," that there are orange voices—optimistic, risible, responsive, often sensually warm and fibrillating—and among them I would include Edgar Bergen and Charlie McCarthy, Donald Duck, Audrey Hepburn (as in *The Nun's Story* she could make even repellent words like *garlic* and *blackwater fever* sound positively alluring), Bart Simpson, the actress Glynis Johns, radio's Henry Aldrich, the Great Gildersleeve (Willard Waterman), Grace Kelly, who had lovely sexual tremulousness, Jack Benny, cabaret singer Karen Akers, who also has a wonderful scylla blue one, Walter Denton (young Richard Crenna) in *Our Miss Brooks,* Red Skelton, Doris Day, Robert Preston, the Scarecrow in *The Wizard of Oz,* and Sylvester the cat. (Greta Garbo's voice was dark blue; Walter Winchell, whose reedy vocal pitch was an octave higher than usual when he was on air, had a smudged yellow voice; and in my opinion Dylan Thomas's voice was a bright green. I would say Henry Kissinger's and the Reverend Jerry Falwell's, for two, are devil black.)

A subjective list of things that seem orange to me are: the human knee, owls, fan lights, the word *Dixie,* Winnie the Pooh, laughter, old classrooms, the poems of Eugene Field, face-to-face coitus, the whole concept of bread, prep schools, patently futile stupidity—like the dumb giants of storybook fame—cashmere, Bix Beiderbecke's cornet wailing on "Riverboat Shuffle,"

"I'm Comin' Virginia," and "Singin' the Blues," Holly-
wood, the boogie-woogie, circuses, the smell of popcorn,
Italian shoes, duck quacks, certain woefully dopey fifties
celebrities, like Robert Cummings, Bill Cullen, and Art
Linkletter, the state of Florida, ostentation, bad writers
(Rod McKuen, Maya Angelou, Ayn Rand, etc.), Audie
Murphy's face, the Mysterium Tremendum involving
clouds and light in which Jesus Christ will come again,
and real southern cooking ("Put some South in your
mouth"), especially that of the Cajun variety with its
orange roux ("Cajun napalm") and file powders and rich
étouffée sauces.

There is with this bright color a great laughing con-
nection to food. Fried chicken. Baked ziti. Spaghetti and
spaghetti sauce. Ravioli. Crepes. (Isak Dinesen in Rung-
sted served Truman Capote orange-flavored crepes.)
Squash. Fungi. Yams. Sweet potatoes. Welsh rabbit and,
Jackie Onassis's favorite lunch, toasted cheese sand-
wiches. Curiously, a lot of "mommy food" is orange. It
clearly predominates in the packaging of crackers, corn
snacks, and most air foods and finger foods. (And
hugely—why?—in laundry detergent boxes and plastic
bottles. "The [Tide] box," writes Thomas Hine in *The
Total Package,* "seems at once to be promising power,
with its aggressive orange and yellow, and restraint, in
the blue in which the name of the product is written.")
And of course carrots. Are you aware of the fact that
carrots were not orange until fairly recently, like some-
time around the last century? They were in fact origi-
nally purple and became white, yellow, and finally
orange only as the direct result of selective breeding, and

you can look it up, as Casey Stengel used to say. Edith Sitwell, nevertheless, to my mind the essential poet of the color orange, wonderfully compares carrots to flames of fire in her poem "Aubade." "The Yiddish word for carrots is *meren,* which sounds like the Yiddish word for more," writes Rabbi Richard Israel in *The Kosher Pig,* who goes on to assert, discussing tsimmes, a slow-cooked stew based on carrots—where, cut into discs like golden coins at Rosh Hashanah, the hope is for a prosperous New Year—that such a dish probably didn't exist prior to the late fourteenth century "because carrots were then considered a novelty," but I believe he is mistaken. Carrots at one time were taken as part of the cure with the waters of Vichy, but generally considered scraplow, they were more often disdainfully dismissed—literally, they were held as common fare for the beasts—as elephant food. (Carotene is now being used in medicine to reduce the growth of oral cancers.) But even when eaten by humans, carrots had small repute as a value. "What'll you give him for a birthday-present?" Bruno inquires in Lewis Carroll's *Sylvie and Bruno Concluded.* "A small saucer of chopped carrots," replies the professor. "In giving birthday-presents, *my* motto is cheapness!"

Was this scrimp view of carrots, or "humbler esculents," as Thoreau called them, theological? "It was a pet theory of Thoreau's friend and neighbor, Bronson Alcott," wrote Clara Endicott Sears in 1915, "that man's diet should not be confined to vegetables merely, but to those species of plants that showed their higher nature by growing up toward the sun and not down into the earth. Thus one should eat corn, but not carrots, which were considered 'humble.' "

Simone Signoret speaks in her autobiography *Nostalgia Isn't What It Used to Be* of seeing American soldiers during the war eating—as she wasn't—from small packages. "What's that orange pâté you're eating?" They would answer, "K-rations. You want some?" I recently asked a veteran what he thought the food in question was. He laughed and said he could not imagine. "Maybe meat."

But no meat is orange, is it? Orange food I tend to think of as mushy, marrowful, and meatless. It would surely color the decor of Murder Free Menus, the restaurant a friend of mine on Cape Cod and I once wanted to open where nothing is served that has or had a face. (John Reed in *The Ten Days that Shook the World* sympathetically mentions eating at a restaurant in the Soviet Union called I Eat No One!)

I also think of vinegar as pinkish orange. It is educational to know that the Roman army's main drink was vinegar and water. Again, you can look it up. When the centurion offered Jesus Christ on the cross a sponge soaked in vinegar as an anodyne, he was performing a charitable act, not, as the nuns often told us, a mocking one—for it was the soldiers' own standard drink. The use of vinegar has always had its place in the story of human diet. In biblical times, there was Ruth's husband and his solicitation: "And Boaz said unto her, 'At mealtime come thou thither and eat of the bread, and dip thy morsel in the vinegar' " (Ruth 2:14), and later, in Greek and Roman antiquity, the words *oxybaphon* and *acetabulum* were names for certain bowls, filled with vinegar, that were placed on the dining table for guests to dip their bread in. And if we can have a vinegar drink, why not pumpkin beer?

In good old colony times a pumpkin beer *was* made. ("And pumpkins sweat a bitter oil," as Roethke writes in "The Coming of the Cold.") Pumpkins, one of America's few indigenous foods, are actually squashes. In Roman times, the pumpkin, or their version of ours *(pepo,* Latin), was symbolic of stupidity, and somewhere in Robert Graves's novel *I, Claudius,* the stuttering narrator, whom Suetonius in *The Twelve Caesars* slandered as a twitching fool, is denounced as a "pumpkin." I think it is because the color orange, even if harmlessly, is common and foolish looking. Seneca's satire *Apocolocyntosis,* or *Pumpkinification*—printed anonymously, as he wanted to keep his head on his shoulders—mockingly dealt with Emperor Nero's ejection from Mt. Olympus. Calling someone a *calabaza* in Mexico is derisive. Mo, the junkyard dog of the Three Stooges, often walloped Larry and Curley, snarling "You pumpkinhead!" (But I think of *all* the Stooges' sound effects as being orange, the poke in the eyes *{"goinggg!"},* the punch in the gut *{"kaboom!"},* the ear twist *{"roixxx!"},* the golf on the head *{"thunkkk!"}* and so forth.) Wasn't comedian Jimmy Durante's signature goodnight line, "Goodnight, Mrs. Calabash, wherever you are" ultimately a pumpkin joke? Agatha Christie's five-feet-four-inch egg-shaped-head detective, Hercule Poirot, once retired to raise pumpkins. Pumpkin was nineteenth-century slang *(kin* meaning little) for the vagina. There is more to do with pumpkins than make pies. Pumpkins can be roasted, fried, baked, gratinéed, and made into soup. Candied pumpkin, or *dulce de calabaza,* is eaten in Mexico on the Day of the Dead. José Donoso mentions "pumpkin doughnuts with plenty of brown sugar sauce" in *The Obscene Bird of Night,* a novel in which a great pumpkin scene not only takes place but the gubbins of a split one is best described: "the rich orange velvet of its viscera spilling out seeds joined by slobbery ligaments to the meat that lodged them in the hollow" (tr. Hardie St. Martin and Leonard Mades). "The [heavens] act on a man during his life," writes Kepler, "in the manner of the loops which a peasant ties at random around the pumpkins in his field. They do not cause the pumpkin to grow, but they determine its shape." And remember in Herman Melville's *Mardi* (1849), whoever arrives at Nora-Bamma in search of its celebrated golden pumpkins will fall into a profound sleep even before plucking the first one and will be able to wake up only when the darkness of night has fallen. (Local currency there in that primitive land, by the way—shades of Poe's grisly *Berenice*—is human teeth!)

Remember the "pumpkin papers"? In August 1948, Whittaker Chambers, a senior editor of *Time* magazine, told the House Un-American Activities Committee that he had once been a Communist and an underground courier, naming as he did so ten other men as his former associates, the best known being Alger Hiss, formerly a high official at the State Department. Chambers accused Hiss of handing him secret government material, which

Chambers supposedly preserved by placing it in a pumpkin at his farm in Maryland. In 1975, after Hiss was indicted, tried twice, and sent to jail for almost four years, the secret "pumpkin papers" were ultimately found to contain nothing secret, nothing whatsoever confidential.

As to cucurbitic insults, by the way, the word *pumpkin* is also offensive in Japan when used abusively, in an accusatory or condemnatory way. "Ichiume was hardly a compelling beauty," we read in Liz Dalby's *Geisha.* "She was always ready to fend off teasing remarks by deprecating herself first. The other geisha knew that if they called her *kabocha,* pumpkin, they could make her furious and make her cry."

It may be mentioned here that the traditional color combinations for Geisha robes and sashes, for the most part named after flowering plants, are specific for each month of the year and are gracefully composed of combinations of colors, often with lovely names like peach, cicada wing, and artemesia, which meet at the sleeve openings and the breast, where the garments overlap. January's colors, for example, are pale green layered over deep purple, a combination called pine. But for our purposes, May's combination is called mandarin orange flower, the actual blossom of which is white, which consists of purple and a color elegantly known as deadleaf yellow.

Orange is an appetizing color. It is the color of bowls of Indian pudding, of braided egg-glazed challah, Wheaties boxes, beer, the pulp of papaya, fish sticks, sea clam valves, saffron, French Company spice boxes and tins (food colors, vanilla extract, cinnamon, and so forth), Clark bars, Reese's candy wrappers—it's a huge candy-packaging color—Manischewitz boxes, salsa, orange pekoe tea, bad hot dogs, Nehi soda, apricots, many lentils, innards in general, sweet orange marmalade (Paddington, the honey bear from South America, although he *was* found at the London station he's named after, has a passion for marmalade sandwiches), knishes, hush puppies, toasted English muffins (also called "garbos"), chorizo, corn dogs, cottage fried potatoes, nachos, Fritos corn chips, Yorkshire pudding, squash, chicken paprika, fried fish, Texas rice, cheese popcorn, and orange roughy, harvested mainly around New Zealand, which we see imported as frozen fish, but as it swims it is orange. Madeleines are orange, and so are prickly pears on California cacti, mangoes, and Nesselrode pudding. Nor should we forget about French, Russian, and Catalina salad dressings, in all their bottled orangeaceousness.

A shipboard comestible called "duff" (from dough), flour boiled in water and eaten with molasses—as tasty, no doubt, as Duff, Homer Simpson's favorite beer—was orangeish and looked upon as a luxury. ("Many a rascally captain has made up with his crew for hard usage," writes Richard Henry Dana in *Two Years Before the Mast,* "by allowing them duff twice a week on the passage home.") One of the hottest of the hot, the virtually merciless, scalding habañero pepper, which grows primarily in the Caribbean and Yucatán—it's thirty to fifty times hotter (200,000 to 300,000 Scoville units) than the legendary jalapeño—is visibly a harmless orange. I think of Indian food, with its cumin, ground cinnamon, ginger, chili powder, paprika, curry powder, and garam masala, as almost exclusively orange. Murghi kebabs. Mashed eggplant. Dal curry. Onion bhajis. Chapatis and chutneys. All of it, orange as andalusite. A lost delicacy, by the way, called orangebutter, the recipe for which can be found in *The Closet of Rarities* (1706), was made in the eighteenth century by beating two gallons of cream to a thickness and adding a half pint each of orange-flower water and red wine.

And what about cheeses? Cheddar, Double Gloucester, and Leicester are good orange English cheeses. There's Pecorino, made from sheep's milk. French Pouligny–Saint Pierre. And from Norway Port-Salut, mature Gouda—which in their glossy wheels look like Ezekiel's wheels—Tilsit, Norvegia, orange Ridderost, and Jarlsberg, with its large holes. Nor should we forget to mention Cheez-Doodles, Cheez-Its, and Cheetos, which incidentally reminds me of a joke. A man bursts into a doctor's office and complains with alarm, "Doc, my penis is turning orange!" "That's strange," says the doctor, "how do you explain it?" "I don't know." "Is it from work?" "I don't think so," says the fellow, "I don't work." So the doctor asks, "Well, do you have hobbies?" The man shrugs. "Not really," he replies. He pauses a moment. "Well," he says, "I do rent porno movies and eat Cheetos."

There is much orange in Asian cuisine. Red curry of prawns. Thai shallow-fried fish cakes *(tod mun pla)*. "Orange wedding rice" is a brilliantly colored rice sold on the streets of Vietnam and often prepared at home there for holidays, banquets, and weddings. An intense, almost henna-red orange powder, called *xoi gac* or "carrot powder," it is taken from a dried fruit not found in the United States, although the powder can be found in certain Asian stores. It has little flavor, but its color is what is especially prized. Speaking of Asia, a brilliant orange brandy sauce *(nuoc sot cam)* that accompanies roast chicken or duck perfectly goes as follows:

> 2 *three-inch pieces lemon zest, cut into strips*
> 5 *three-inch pieces orange zest, cut into strips*
> 1 *T. butter*
> 1 *minced carrot*
> 1 *minced clove garlic*
> 1 *T. brandy*
> 1 *T. soy sauce*
> 2 *tsp. honey*
> *1/2 cup fresh orange juice*

Combine zests and cook for thirty seconds in small saucepan and water. In another small saucepan, over medium heat, melt butter; add zests, carrots, and garlic and cook one minute. Add brandy, soy sauce, honey, and orange juice. Increase heat and cook, adding some pan juices, until slightly syrupy, about two minutes. Pour over the meat.

The papery orange-yellow blossoms of the zucchini plant are a Mediterranean delicacy. "The whole blossom is edible, although according to Italian-food expert Marcella Hazan," notes *Gourmet* in August 1995, "only the male blossoms (those on a thin stem that never grow into zucchini) have a crisp texture when cooked and are good to eat. (The familiar zucchini is the fruit of the female blossom.)"

As to fruits, there are mangoes, melons, persimmons, tangelos (a hybrid fruit—portmanteau of tangerine and pomelo—obtained by crossing a grapefruit with a tangerine or a mandarin orange), and the sweet orange pepper called "Corona." Quinces have orange flesh. So do cantaloupes. The Casaba Golden Beauty, a pale-skinned, Crenshaw-type melon in size and shape is popularly called "orange flesh" for having that tropical trait. And tejocote is a small bittersweet fruit, called chokecherry in the United States, which grows on shrubs and small trees. Apricots, which are said to be self-fertilizing and androgynous, are associated with death and timidity by the Chinese. Oranges have, more often than not, a happier connotation. Cox's orange pippin is a popular English apple dessert, red stripes over a smooth orange skin. Orgeat is an orange-and-almond flavoring, and can also be identified as a sweetened punch, but the word is related etymologically *not* to the orange but rather, curiously enough, to the Latin *hordeum,* barley. There are Creamsicles. Across Europe, you can purchase wonderful orange sugar candies made by Troubat. And with chocolates, "O" in Whitman's candy boxes always stood for an orange cream on a square-shaped chocolate (then "P" for pineapple cream, "R" for raspberry cream, and so forth). Andy Warhol loved—*worshipped!*—frozen Sara Lee orange cake. And did you know that Lizzie Borden had a passion for orange sherbet?

Many spices are orange or orange-brown: turmeric, fenugreek seeds, blades of mace, crushed red chiles (yes!) and certain chili pastes, tamarind, achiote (powder of the hard seed of the annetto tree), and saffron powder. Saffron is grown around L'Aquila, Italy, and la cucina Aquilana, which is superb, has as its most famous dish *Risotto alla Milanese con Zafferano.* There is even a saffron festival there called *La Sagra.* When courting, we are told in the *Kama Sutra* to give our lover gifts of saffron. The psyllium fiber of orange-flavored Metamucil, made visually palatable by FD&C Yellow No. 6, is exactly the color of saffron. The perfume of saffron is listed in the *Arabian Nights* as one of the only two things that "corrupt women," the other one being gold. (Not chocolate? Credit cards? Julio Iglesias LPs?) Saffron is the herb of the sun. In Europe it signifies disinterestedness, humility, love, renunciation, magic—and not always joy. The preternatural waters in Silence, a region in Libya in Edgar Allan Poe's *Silence: A Fable,* have a saffron—sickly—hue and do not flow onward to the sea but grotesquely *convulse,* as it were, forever, and, in the midst of all that despair, visitors cannot pronounce a single word!

The variation of hues in egg yolks, incidentally, usually a knockout orange in freshly laid ones, is basically due to dieting differences in chickens—principally by feed—and not genetic causes. If the hen gets plenty of orange plant pigments known as xanthophylls, the result will appear in the yolk. Hens receiving mash with yellow corn and alfalfa meal will lay eggs with medium yellow yolks, those with wheat and barley, lighter yolks. White corn yields yolks that are even paler. According to Tom Parker's *Rules of Thumb,* "If you paint the inside of your chicken coop orange, your chickens will lay more eggs." Yolk, xanthophylls, daybreak, orange coops—the world of chickens, it seems, tends to have a strange orange etiology!

What about orange drinks? Apple juice. Scotch. Carrot juice. And tansy, a tall, hardy perennial with clusters of yellow-orange, buttonlike flowers, was once used in old New England to brew tea. Orangeade is real down-home Americana, like dictographs and Chiclets and coonskin caps. The *New Yorker* cover for January 30, 1995, an oil painting showing half a glass of orange juice, nothing more, seems a perfect anodyne to winter. (A Scottish rock group named Orange Juice, who signed with Polydor in 1981, had a 1983 hit single of—not Little Richard's—"Rip It Up," as well as a thrilling, spine-caressing version of Al Green's "L-O-V-E." King Farouk positively loved *aranciata,* a sweet, fizzy Italian orangeade, and had it corked and chilled as if it were the finest champagne. He attributed his fatness not to food but to the soft-drink sugars of this drink. *Qamer-ad-din* (literally "moon of the religion"), the traditional apricot drink used to break the fast of Ramadan, is soft orange, unlike "bug juice," any solid-colored, very sweet, non-carbonated soft drink usually sold from cheap plastic fountains in various prole-food emporia where on counters, in spilled puddles of it, one can often witness the entomological Olympic games. On *The Andy Griffith*

Show, Wally's service station in Mayberry served Nectarine Crush soda. But Andy's own personal specialty was "Punch Supreme," which consisted of orange sherbet, tomato juice, root beer, and molasses. Yummy. I wonder what color *that* would have been. I once read somewhere that orange soda is of all drinks the roughest on stomach lining.

There is Tang, of course. The Orange Julius, a trademark name for a drink made with orange juice, crushed ice, syrup, and certain powders. (An old and false rumor has it that this egg-based drink includes, among other things, *eggshells!*) "Oranges, preserved in grenadine," a delectable mentioned in Carl Van Vechten's *Firecrackers* (1925), sounds good. Orange brandy is quite delicious. André Simon's recipe for orange brandy goes as follows: Use one gallon of the best brandy, the rinds of eight Seville oranges plus two lemons, all cut very thin, and two pounds of loaf sugar. Put it in a stone jar and cork down. Shake the bottle for a few minutes every day for twenty-one days. Strain it, bottle it, and cork it. *Spremuta di arance rosse,* an Italian orange juice made from blood oranges, is as dark and red as tomato juice. And we can thank Passion Orange Guava—P.O.G.— with its bottle caps for initiating the slammin' craze of pogs that recently swept America. (Pogs is a brand name for cardboard milk caps, it should be pointed out, manufactured by the World Pog Federation.)

A popular drink in the 1920s called Howdy, an artificially flavored orange soda, disappeared when citrus growers got a law passed in Florida that only real orange fruit pulp be used in tonics, whereupon manufacturer

C. L. Grigg came up with a new lemon-lime drink mind-numbingly called Bib-Label Lithiated Lemon-Lime Soda—wisely shortened later to 7-Up.

"I remember that when I first met Giacometti," writes James Thrall Soby in *Modern Art and the New Past,* "it was during a season when André Breton, surrealism's central personage, had decreed that so far as possible, everything he and his colleagues ate or drank should be green in color. Sitting with them, more than a little awed by this flamboyant whim in the romantic spirit, I saw no reason to demur, remembering *crème de menthe* and other delicacies open to choice. But Giacometti ordered something orange. Clearly he was destined for a lonely path." Did Giacometti know something?

At the turn of the century in the salons of Paris, orangeade was *the* social beverage, part of a formalized and traditional rite. Any *salonnard* who knew all the proper rituals, the "do's and don'ts" of dressing, card playing, conversation, everything from wearing monocles to the correct handshake, drank it and expected to drink it. In Proust's *A la recherche du temps perdu,* at the Duchesse Oriane de Guermantes, whose exclusive salon was on the rise, two distinct drinks were served, "in winter a cup of Linden tea" and "in summer a glass of orangeade." Proust points out, "There was no record of anything else, among the Guermantes, in these evenings in the garden, but orangeade. It had a sort of ritual meaning. To have added other refreshments would have seemed to be falsifying the tradition." A virtual paean to the drink follows. "For this fruit juice can never be provided in sufficient quantities to quench one's thirst for it," he writes. "Nothing is less cloying than these transpositions into flavour of the color of a fruit which when cooked seems to have travelled backwards to the past season of its blossoming. Blushing like an orchard in spring, or, it may be, colourless and cool like the zephyr beneath the fruit trees, the juice lets itself be breathed and gazed into drop by drop" (I.1082–83, tr. Scott-Moncrieff).

Mlle. Noémie in the novel serves Morel a glass of orangeade at the Maineville brothel. At one of her dinners, Mme. Verdurin offers orangeade as a preprandial to M. de Charlus, who prefers instead strawberry juice and offends her. Odette serves orangeade to Swann—"not any unknown brew, but precisely that orangeade"—as well as, later in her salon, reincarnated as the fashionable Princesse d'Epinoy, to counts, princes, dukes, and marquesses. And the narrator, Marcel, who has drunk orangeade with the Prince de Guermantes, along with tasting from a small plate of petits fours, a sweet food that is the traditional complement in Parisian salons to orangeade, has a sweeter memory of the drink when he recalls embracing Albertine after she herself had drunk it. "I was thus able to taste with her kisses that refreshing coolness which had seemed to me better than [the drinks] at the Princesse de Guermantes" (VII.192).

The original salon recipe, obviously not the cold and simple orangeade as we know it, as given in Shirley King's *Dining with Marcel Proust,* calls for:

6 oranges
$^{1}/_{2}$ cup of sugar

²/₃ cup water
2¹/₂ cups ice water
1 tsp orangeflower extract

Peel an orange with a potato peeler. Simmer the
peel with the sugar and water (*not* the ice water)
for twenty minutes. Let this syrup cool. Squeeze
the six oranges and strain the juice into a jug or
bowl. Add the ice water, the cooled strained
syrup, and the orangeflower extract. Chill the
orangeade further by adding a handful of ice
cubes. (The peel that has simmered in the sugar
syrup is usually delicious to eat, as it will now
be candied peel.)

What remains a phenomenon to me is the variety of
orange-based spirits and liqueurs there are. Cointreau,
which began life as Triple-Sec; Cordial Médoc, a liqueur
from Bordeaux, reddish in color, a blend of oranges,
cherries, brandy curaçao—did you know curaçao is not a
trade name but a generic one?—claret, and herbs; For-
bidden Fruit, an American citrus liqueur made from
grapefruit, with honey and orange; Mandarine, a Belgian
aperitif flavored with distillate of Spanish mandarins,
the peel of which is first soaked in cognac; Mersin, an
orange-flavored Turkish drink, to be taken with coffee;
Armagnac cocktails—Armagnac could take out a patent
as a perfume; Glayva, a whiskey-based Scottish concoc-
tion flavored with herbs, a whiff of orange, and heather
honey; and Torres, a Spanish blend of pot still brandy,
with extracts of macerated orange, herbs, sugar, and

honey, all aged in American oak. A Harvey Wallbanger, a half measure of Galliano floating on top of a screwdriver, is a popular drink. Southern Comfort, made from a secret formula, supposedly, but surely American whiskey with a flavoring of peaches and oranges. A "fuzzy navel" is a cocktail made with peach schnapps and orange juice. A drink made with peach schnapps and grapefruit juice is a called a "fuzzy pucker." And of course there is the orange fizz, and no end to orange coolers, bucks, comforts, and mists.

A memory intrudes. I remember on many an afternoon when Medford High School let out, I'd walk over to tiny Santoro's Sub Shop on Salem Street, where, entering Mondo Orange-O, I would dispatch an orange-tawny meatball submarine sandwich and talk to the counterman—a brilliant but misanthropic B.U. graduate and ex-playwright named Fred who fueled my dreams to become a writer—while gulping a bottle of Tru-Ade, an orange drink that came in extremely thick bottle glass that was shaped like a spaceship. Orange can be both positive and negative. Burn an orange peel on the stove to dissipate disagreeable odors—the effect is most pleasant. But in 1751, Voltaire, wounded by the insult, said that Frederick of Prussia looked upon him as a "used orange." By the way, I love the Magritte-like line from Thomas Merton's poem "Cocoa Tree" where he mentions in dining rooms how "the wall clock drips/like a half-orange."

The corrupt priest in Robert Browning's poem "Soliloquy of the Spanish Cloister" is drinking "watered orange-pulp." Raggedy Andy in one of Johnny Gruell's wonderful stories—he drew his famous characters as well—lost his smile by drinking orange juice. ("How was she to know that Dickie would feed Raggedy Andy orange juice and take off most of his smile?") In 1957, Pittsburgh Pirates manager Bobby Braga, after a screaming match with the umps, tried to placate them by offering a drink of orange juice—and was thumbed out of the game. In Samoa, Robert Louis Stevenson always had an orange as an aperitif and often used oranges, when hardened, as cricket balls. I own a postcard photo from the 1920s (Underwood Photo Archives) showing, in a PR shot, gorgeous Universal movie star Laura La Plante, star of the 1928 mystery-horror film *The Cat and the Canary,* clearly promoting her career as well as the produce of the young, energetic state of California, holding a giant orange "which made nearly six pints of juice." Red Sox slugger Ted Williams, one of my heroes, the only man to win more than two titles in each of the three hitting categories (batting average six times; HRs six times; RBIs four times), Player of the Year in 1941, 1942, 1947, 1949, and 1957, home run champ in 1941, 1942, 1947, and 1949, eighteen times a member of the All-Star Team, and the last of the .400 hitters (.406 in 1941)—he hit .388 at thirty-nine years old!—has always drunk orange juice. In 1928, on the "Friendship" flight, with a dead radio, Amelia Earhart, the first woman to cross the Atlantic by plane, attached a note to an orange, put both into a paper bag, and aimed it through the hatchway for the deck of the *America,* a ship that was passing below. It failed, twice, to connect. William Verral, author of *The Cook's Paradise* (1759) and

publican of the White Hart Inn in Sussex, was eccentri-
cally famous for using oranges in almost *everything* he
cooked, not merely desserts, but goose pie and par-
tridges, turkey in a braise with chestnuts, and so forth.
In his cookbook, oranges are used in twenty-five recipes
in succession. Were oranges perhaps less sweet then than
nowadays? Not made from concentrate? (Anyone who
stares at a can of orange juice because it says "concen-
trate" is probably wearing a cowboy hat.) In Yucatán,
oranges are called chinos and discounts are given in
Mexico if you buy them by the costal, or gunnysack. Are
oranges hard to digest? As mother used to say, "An
orange is gold in the morning, silver at noon, and lead at
night." I have heard, by the way, that there isn't a single
orange grove left to be found in Orange County, Los
Angeles, an area once rich with them. Could that be one
of the reasons why the sectionalistic but slightly confus-
ing expression "The Big Orange," despite a vigorous
campaign some years ago, became an uncatchonable
name for L.A.?

Do you recall this anecdote? Châteauneuf, keeper of
the seals of Louis XIII, when he was a boy met a conde-
scending prelate who said, "If you can tell me where
God is, I'll give you an orange." Whereupon the boy
quickly replied, "If you can tell me where he is not, I
will give you two oranges."

By the way, in *Oranges,* John McPhee is full of lore on
that fruit. Did you know that vendors on street corners
in Trinidad salt oranges? That in Jamaica, people halve
oranges, go down on hands and knees, and scrub floors
with one in each hand? That in early Europe, oranges

were used mainly for seasoning meat and fish or as ornamentals for their aroma? That Europeans still often eat them with knives and forks? That Norwegian children disrobe part of an orange, jam in a sugar cube, and suck out the juice? Are you also aware that there is for dining, rarely used now, officially an orange *spoon,* a special piece of cutlery, tapered to a point, specifically for eating that fruit? There is even an orange wine, by the way, made in colorful Brazil from fermented orange juice. Blue curaçao, ironically, tastes of oranges, for that matter. And, pray, what color is orange water? Of course. White.

Want more paradox? Botanically, the orange is a berry. (So are tomatoes and chile peppers!) The orange tree is also, ironically, an *evergreen*—with white flowers! ("Feasting beneath green orange-boughs," writes Christina Maria Rossetti in "At Home," "from hand they pushed the wine.") Its wood, furthermore, is not orange but yellow, hard and close grained, excellent for carving and turning. It is often manufactured into small, durable articles. A further curiosity is that commercial oranges are picked green. "An orange can be as sweet and ripe as it will ever be and still glisten like an emerald in a tree," writes McPhee, who points out that coolness is what makes an orange orange and that in Thailand, where oranges are a green fruit, an orange skin of flaring cadmium would surprise them. Most oranges live a month after they are picked but, unlike apples and pears, do not continue to ripen. (Green olives, in contrast, ripen black on the vine.) "The flesh of other fruits contain a great deal of starch," McPhee goes on to say, "and as they go on breathing (all fruit breathes until it dies, and should be eaten before it is dead), they gradually convert the starch within them. . . . Hence, an advertisement for 'tree-ripened' oranges is essentially a canard. There is no other way to ripen oranges."

Oranges, then, are rarely a bright color. No color can be added to the green-skinned orange. They are "degreened" in the coloring room of a plant, shut up airtight "and doused with a gas [ethylene] that removes the chlorophyll from the rind and can leave it anything from a sickly color," according to citrus grower L. P. De Wolf, in Beatrice Trum Hunter's rather pessimistic *Consumer Beware,* "to almost white. While it is being gassed, the fruit is subject to artificial heat and is sometimes held in this room for three or four days. It impairs the flavor and has a tendency to hasten its deterioration and decay," De Wolf goes on to say. "After coming out of the coloring room, the fruit is washed and run through the 'color-added' machine. The color is added by passing the fruit through a vat of hot dye"—tasty— "or else spraying it on hot while the fruit is subjected to steam heat."

An artificial carotenoid pigment emerges in the orange thanks to Citrus Red No. 2—1-(2,5-dimethoxyphenylazo)-2 napthol—"a weird pink bath," says McPhee, "the only orange dye permitted by federal law, in which the orange is immersed." "Color added" must be stamped on all oranges so dosed.

It is a consolation to a city-bred northerner such as I to know that oranges do ripen on the tree, fat and proud and properly juicy. Brightness seems the orange's nature. Painter Egon Schiele in Joanna Scott's novel *Arrogance,* jailed for immorality in 1911, is given an orange by his mistress and model Vallie Neuzil that in his cell "provides all the light he needs." Bermuda's oranges are set against dark foliage, notes Andrew Marvell—who never actually went there—like "golden lamps in a green night." The opening sentence of Lawrence Durrell's novel *Clea,* describing how bright oranges "glowed in their arbours of burnished green leaf, like lanterns," richly characterizes his incandescent prose—very like Scott's—and both recall for me Goethe's line, "Colors are the deeds and sufferings of light."

As to the fruit, Valencias, good juicers, make up half the U.S. crop. They are generally considered the universal orange and, imported in the 1870s, were originally known in California as the Rivers Late orange and in Florida as the Hart's Tardiff. Navel oranges—Thompsons, Golden Nuggets, and Golden Buckeyes—represent about 10 percent of the U.S. crop, while Sevilles, bitter, are generally used for marmalade as well as for liqueurs, like curaçao. (Beatrice in *Much Ado About Nothing,* by using the expression "civil as an orange," is homophonically punning on the town of Seville in Spain.) Temples, a cross between mandarins and tangerines, are tasty. Blood oranges, like Moros, sanguinellos, and taroccos, have bright color and full flavor. ("Blood oranges grow well in Florida," McPhee tells us, "but they frighten American women.") What a bounty! And what evocative names oranges have, as orotund as the fruit: Ruby, Mediterranean Sweet, Osceola, Early Oblong, Maltese Oval, Magnum Bonum, Homosassa!

John McPhee, in whose opinion the Washington navel orange is by far the most beautiful orange of all that are grown in the United States, gives some significant pointers about eating the fruit that might be memorized: the outside fruit on the tree is sweeter than that on the inside; the south-side fruit is sweeter than east or west, and the north side is least sweet; and the blossom end of the orange is sweeter than the stem end. Did you know, incidentally, that a raw pepper contains more vitamin C than an orange?

"What interests me most about food is finding out what a product is all about, knowing where it's from—what the difference is, for example, between a Florida orange and a California orange," says Mimi Sheraton, a *New York Times* food writer who made a choice. "It may take more California oranges to produce a glass of juice—plus the oranges are harder to squeeze—but that juice will have a more intense orange flavor than Florida juice." There are indeed pronounced differences, enhancing the rivalry, between the two sunshine states and their native citrus. In California, for example, the leader in orange production before World War II, plantations are called orchards, there is less rain, and oranges are relatively dryish with a thick albedo or "rag" (the white part of the skin), whereas in Florida plantations are known as groves, rainfall is heavier, which makes the fruit juicier with a thinner albedo, and Florida is now the predominant growing state.

In spite of Florida's current hegemony, the orange does have a sort of Spanish cachet internationally. "Could any image verify a Spaniard's identity," asks

Carlos Fuentes in *The Orange Tree,* "better than the sight
of a man eating an orange?" Did you know people from
Tangier are called Tangerinos? (Tangerines do indeed get
their name from Tangier, for Tangier was the port from
which the fruits were first shipped to Europe in 1841.)
Truman Capote once observed that writer Jane Bowles,
"with her dahlia-head of cropped curly hair, her tilted
nose and mischief shiny, just a trifle mad eyes," was a
"permanent Tangerino," not for any color, for *tangerine*
had long been an English word (first recorded in 1710),
meaning "of or pertaining to Tangier." As regards or-
anges and regional differences, tell me, has "orange
juice" ever been pronounced correctly—or distinc-
tively—*anywhere?* One hears "orance jews," "ah-range
js," "ornch juice," "arn chews," and many other varia-
tions. To my mind, only the words *textbooks* and *Wednes-
day* and *nuclear* beat it for abuse. Forget the word
clothespins, which no English-speaking human being in
conversation has ever pronounced correctly.

I think Rikki Ducornet's phantasmagorical story
"Spanish Oranges" is not only the best fictional tale on
oranges around ("The air fries with the festive smell of
citrus") but easily one of the weirdest and most surreal,
involving hateful and murderous attacks by way of bom-
binating fruit: "However, old man Magot is not satisfied
merely eating oranges, and soon, with fatal glee betrayed
by the fecal glint in his eyes, he throws an orange peel at
one of the customers, a frumpish mother of nine packed
into a rayon housedress." After murdering another
woman, Magot calms down. "He lies as still as Snow

White beneath the glass, shreds of poison fruit caught in her teeth."

"Orange Moll," actually Mrs. Mary Meggs, was a well-known character in the days of Restoration theater. A widow living in the small parish of St. Paul's, Covent Garden, she was granted a thirty-nine-year license by the manager to hawk oranges in the Theatre Royal as a *fruitière*. (An "orange wife"—see *Coriolanus* II.i.70—is a female fruit vendor in Shakespeare.) For this privilege she paid £100 down and 6*s*. 8*d*. for every day the theater was open, which showed it to be a lucrative business. (Dickens refers to the fruit stall area of London's Covent Garden, disdainfully, as having a "damaged-orange countenance.") A contemporary description of the fatal fire in the Theatre Royal in 1672, which completely destroyed it, says it started under the stairs "where Orange Moll keeps her fruit." Perhaps one of the lively orange girls, of whom King Charles II's lovely mistress, Nell Gwynne, by the way, had been one, went searching for fresh supplies with a naked flame. "Let not poor Nelly starve," were Charles II's last words of his illiterate but high-spirited paramour, whose reddish brown hair was as orange as the fruit she once sold. She did not starve, but she eventually did die, and her ghost is said to wander through the Gargoyle Club in London, leaving an uncanny and somewhat preternatural aroma wherever it goes, not of oranges, but of gardenias. Samuel Pepys, by the way, refers to Orange Moll several times and gleaned many items of theatrical scandal from her. Colorful images are somehow always connected to the world of oranges. One is found in Wilfred Wilson Gibson's poem "Color":

> *A blue-black Nubian plucking oranges*
> *At Jaffa by a sea of malachite*

and Salvatore Quasimodo writes in "The Dead Guitars,"

> *Nello speccio della luna*
> *si pettinano fanciulle col petto d'arance*

> (In the mirror of the moon
> young girls with breasts of oranges dress their hair)
> (tr. Allen Mandelbaum)

Whole fables exist about orange trees. Because the tree is evergreen and everbearing, having both fruit and blossoms at all times, it has always been regarded in high repute as a symbol of fruitfulness. They are the only trees that grow and flourish, for instance, on the marble island of Calemplui in Fernão Mendes Pinto's *Peregrinação* (1614). The orange tree was also a symbol of the Virgin Mary by way of a false derivation made by medieval theologians between Mary and the "cedars of Lebanon," a homonym for her in Rogation Day litanies. There is, curiously, no real relation, McPhee points out, however, between the citron tree, the orange's bitter ancestral plant, and the cedar tree—although the Greeks called the citron a *kedromelon* or "cedar apple" (the Romans: *malum citreum* or *citreum*)—except that the greenish yellow cone of the cedar tree in fact resembled the citron. In the eighteenth century, Swedish botanist Carolus Linnaeus officialized the name as "citrus," including in the genus, along with oranges, lemons, limes, grapefruit, citrons, and tangerines. In Voltaire's *La Princesse de Babylone* (1768), the houses of the shepherds in the diamond kingdom of Gangaridia—vegetarians, who consider animals to be their brothers—live in houses decorated with orange tree wood. In André Dhotel's *Les pays ou l'on n'arrive jamais* (1955) and the castle of Never-reachhereland, are orange trees, recalling for me an image from a Salvatore Quasimodo poem: *"Ride la gazza, nera sugli aranci"* (The magpie laughs, black upon the orange trees).

John Stith Pemberton, the man who concocted Coca-Cola—and in empty Coke bottles, the lingering, cloyingly sweet scent of d-limonene, the main ingredient in peel oil, can almost always be picked up—used in the original formula of 1885 not only elixir of orange but an ingredient in perfumes distilled from the flower of the orange tree. (The essential oil of orange flowers, incidentally, is called *neroli,* while that of the bitter orange, *essence de petit-grain,* is used for scenting creams, custards, pancake batter, and so forth.) I would say my favorite poem about orange trees would have to be Edith Sitwell's wonderful "A Bird's Song," part of which goes:

> *Beneath the orange-tree, the sleeper lies—*
> *A bone of fire in a body of thin amber;*
> *The umbrageous tree has changed her to a bird of fire,*

> *Feathered with shade, like me. . . .*
> *Which is the sleeper's long and tangled hair*
> *and which the water-cold gold orange tree?*

And, curiously enough, orange trees are actually mentioned in Irving Berlin's legendary song "White Christmas," the title of which, it should not be forgotten, is the subject of a dream. (Remember, apropos the song's first line, the singer is living in California.) It begins,

> *The sun is shining.*
> *The grass is green.*
> *The orange and palm trees sway.*
> *There's never been such a day*
> *In Beverly Hills, L.A.*

What is there in oranges that invites the antic? A game called Mandarino, orange tossing while quoting from memory alternate lines of Horace's "Odes," usually the same one, is a pastime ecclesiastics of the Catholic Church, mainly in Rome, I gather, often play. Golden verses are exchanged, antiphonally as it were, at ten feet. *"Diffugere nives, redeunt iam gramina campis arborisque comae,"* sings one prelate. And his opponent would reply, *"Mutat terra vices, et decrescentia ripad flumina praetereunt. . . ."* (A classic scene of the game can be found in chapter 5, "The Touch of Purple," in Henry Morton Robinson's novel *The Cardinal.*) At Belgium's four-hundred-year-old Binche festival—from which we derive our word *binge*—hundreds of men parade through the streets to drumbeats during the March of the Gilles wearing weird masks with green sunglasses and toss oranges to the crowds. In Luchino Visconti's film version of Thomas Mann's *Death in Venice,* young Tadzio likewise tosses an orange, but as a would-be cricketer, thus arousing suspicion in writer Paul West, who in his book *Stroke of Genius: Illness and Self-Discovery* complains that the actor does something with an orange "that no Polish boy would do: he imparts to it, as he tosses it to and fro, what a cricketer would call leg spin—and Americans' 'English,' with the hand crooked in a special way." Mr. West is convinced that it was English actors on the set who taught the young Swedish actor Bjorn Andresen that sophisticated pitching maneuver.

Notice how squirrels have orange-tinted fur, or vair, as it is known, which seems to gleam as if the sun is shining on it, as if Constable, say, had given each a touch with an enunciating brush. Garfield the cat is orange—I remember when Garfield dolls started appearing, suction-cupped to car windows, in 1982—as is Orlando the Marmalade Cat, who in one of the many stories by Kathleen Hale actually visits the moon. Did you know that orange is dominant in the molecular genetics of tabby cats? Tigers are orange. And many lizards. So is the golden toad *(Bufo periglenes)*, which, found only in Costa Rica's Monte Verde Cloud Forest Preserve, is brassy orange. An orange-colored reptile is eerily and portentously killed in Hawthorne's tale "Rappaccini's Daughter" by a poisonous drop from a purple flower. Keats writes of orange horses in his poem "Isabelle." The black, or sexton, beetle *(Nicrophorus)* has bright orange "hands" emblazoned on its wing cover. There are copperhead and coral snakes, and Goodfellow's tree kangaroos. Sumatran orangutans are orange, and the Caribbean flamingo, the largest of the six kinds of this bird, is a sort of pinkish orange, due partially to its diet of crustaceans. Isn't there a touch of orange in the russet brown of the nightingale? ("America," observes Ford Madox Ford in *Provence,* "is a vast continent, but it contains no nightingales.") The cock-of-the-rock (male), a South American tropical bird—maybe the most orange of all species on earth—has a brilliant crayon-bright hue, with black wings and tail; the orange feathers on the crown are stiffened to form a permanent crest. The orange-crowned warbler displays its crown only during courtship or when alarmed. Ladybird beetles (the name lady*bugs* is a misnomer) have striking, awning-bright orange wings. And we can find the crepuscular flight of the orange moth, a geometrid, poetically described in Alfred de Musset's well-known lines in *"Le Saule,"* or "Willow":

> *La phalène dorée dans sa course légère*
> *Traverse les prés embaumés*

> (The golden moth in nimble flight
> flits within its perfumed reaches)
>   (my translation)

Orange soils, found throughout the world, are especially evident in India, in the hills of South China (unlike that in the north of China, where one sees only grayish dust and denuded hills of loess), and in much of South America. What about the long, serpentine red-orange roads around Chimayo, Truchas, and Cordova in New Mexico? And red Georgia soils? There are the "orange sands of Egypt," noted by Lady Duff Gordon in her *Letters from Egypt* (1865), in the Great Eastern Sand Sea located in the northwestern Sahara, and in the sunbaked deserts of Namibia, as well as around the Timiman Oasis in Algeria, North Africa. And ultisols, formed on old land surfaces, frequently under forest vegetation, although savannah (even swamp vegetation is common)—located mostly in regions of long growing seasons and of ample moisture—tends to be orange or reddish yellow. When Wallace Stevens wrote "Florida, venereal soil," wasn't he invoking a soil that was orange-red as much as it was ruvid? Of course a good deal of the Australian desert is orange, especially the "Walls of China," around Australia's Lake Mungo. And there are orange rocks in Provence and in Tarascon. A special baseball soil, called Beam Clay, also exists, a clay-and-sand mixture provided to as many as nine major league clubs as well as minor league teams, colleges, and so forth, is made by the Partac Peat Corp. "It's not just whatever comes out of the ground," owner Jim Kelsey has pointed out. "It's a fine mixture that's processed and shredded to the right consistency. And we can even match colors—red, orange, or brown—to suit a particular diamond."

Ask any Vietnam veteran who was stationed in the Mekong Delta around, say, Kan Tho Tan An or My Tho,

Chu Lai or An Kho, Da Lat or Moc Hoa, Phu Bai or Khe San, about his "red boots," constantly muddied, dry or wet, with the orange-red soil of that war-torn, gong-tormented country.

Orange is, as we have seen, a color of exaggeration and fun. It is flagrant and disordered and overripe. It is bold, outrageous, and rarely delicate. There are summer sunsets and sunrises, freckles, the Denver Broncos, basketballs, many pencils, Thanksgiving, people who use "tan-in-a-can," good beer, old pine floorboards, student patrol bands, pencil erasers, Amos and Andy's shoes, rawhide, tobacco leaves—did you know smoking is never once mentioned in Scripture?—fruit crate labels, and monarch butterflies. (Cultivated milkweed, or *Asclepias,* food for the monarch butterfly, is also orange.) It is the color of Italian leather, Lifebuoy soap, and various scourers, like Gojo's Orange, a brand-name hand cleaner ("Cleans with or without water") that, with vitamin E, lanolin, and aloe, and colored with FD&C Orange No. 4—it has d-limonene—has the color and smell of an orange. The color of Syracuse University is orange, of course, as are the University of Georgia's football helmets and uniforms, lighted lampshades, sunflowers, the rickshaws of Hong Kong (if you can't visit, see the movie *The World of Suzie Wong),* fine-grained burnished mahogany desks, New York City garbage trucks, catchers' equipment, Penguin books (the serious ones; green is reserved for detective novels and trash), dead pine trees, old pine needles, rust, sandstone mesas, adobe houses, harvest moons, mountain ash berries, the rubber spouts on bottles of glue, sand *(nafud)* in central Arabia,

and the ironic hair color of many African pygmies—
orange is *chungwa* in Swahili—and various quadroons.

Companies like Asplundh, Inc., makers of earth-
movers and such claw-mouthed and scooping equipment
depend on the utile efficiency of orange. Also, Allied
Van Lines, the Home Depot, Gulf Oil, Dunkin' Donuts,
Union 76, Rexall drug stores, Burger King, U-Haul,
and Federal Express depend on its hailing brightness, as
do Holiday Inns, the designers of which, or so I've
heard, agreed it was not the buildings they should con-
centrate on but rather the sign alone, designed in green,
yellow, and orange, which could be seen for miles—*that*
was what the drivers saw. For decades, the Howard
Johnson chain of roadside restaurants set a precedent for
popularity with the same idea. "Orange roofs," accord-
ing to Jane and Michael Stern in the *Encyclopedia of Pop
Culture,* "were a beacon of civility as well as of disease-
free dependable food." Orange is a comfort. (And to
Neruda, of simple romance, who sang of the *"techos de
teja anaranjada"*—roofs of orange tile—in his *"Serenita
de México."*) Orange Street in lovely Coronado, Califor-
nia, perfectly named, is surely one of the most beautiful
streets in the United States. And as Boston's Washing-
ton Street was once Orange Street in Good Old Colony
Times, the T line that presently follows its course is
called the Orange Line.

The Arch of Orange is a Roman triumphal arch in
southern France belonging to the Augustan period: a
wide main passageway, with two side ones, covered with
relief panels representing military scenes. The Palace of
the Four Winds at Jaipur, an exuberant golden orange,

gets my vote for the most orange building on earth. "Isn't there a lot of orange architecture in Africa?" artist Edward Gorey once asked me, apropos of nothing.

The six Protestant counties of Northern Ireland, or Ulster, as it is called, is "orange country." The Loyal Orange Institute, a society founded and flourishing there, which tends to despise Papists, Papishes, and Popeheads, was established in 1795 to maintain in Northern Ireland the Protestant ascendancy in the face of the rising anticipation for Catholic emancipation. Its name was taken from the family of William, Prince of Orange, later King William III of England, who on his white charger defeated King James II at the Battle of the Boyne. The holiday on July 12 in Northern Ireland celebrates both the victory of the Boyne (July 1, 1690) as well as the Battle of Aughrim (July 12, 1691)—another festival, on November 5, celebrates the day of William's first landing in England in 1688—and all of the locals go about sporting orange-colored flowers and orange sashes and orange hats and join in parades.

The color orange has long been the symbolic color of diehard Irish Protestantism, although the House of Orange has no etymological connection whatsoever with the *naranj* fruit or the reddish yellow color of the peel. Its name derives, rather, from the medieval principality of Orange in Provence, a principality that was centered around the Provençal town of Orange, in what is now the Vaucluse *département* in southeastern France. That town was originally the Roman settlement of Arausio, a prosperous city during the rule of Augustus, named after a god of Gaul, Arausio. The medieval Provençal lords of

Orange, vassals of the holy Roman emperors from the twelfth century on, became involved in Dutch history in the sixteenth century through a marital alliance with the German House of Nassau.

"What does he want to come here for, tooting his Orange flute?" asks Fr. Rolfe of his nemesis, Jeremiah Sant, the Ulsterman in Frederick Rolfe's *Hadrian VII.* "What street corner is he going to bang his Lambeg drum on this time?" I remember once being confronted by three local toughs in the Sandy Row district of Belfast in Northern Ireland in 1966 and almost beaten up—"Air ye Cotholick?"—while taking photos of graffiti on a wall ("Down with Old Red Socks!" "Kick the Pope!" "Pull the Pope's Nose," "We Hate Papists").

In Batavia, New York, the local Irish, in a fit of ethnic intransigence, I've heard, collectively refused to let the green traffic light go below the orange—and by legislation had the two lights reversed.

And who can forget that wonderful scene in Anne Nichols's novel (later a hit play) *Abie's Irish Rose* (1927)? Lovely Rose-Mary Murphy's father, Patrick, with a priest friend visits Solomon Levy's house in New York. Solomon's son, Abie, has just married the Irish girl. In the house, Patrick discovers an orange tree—"Vell, de bride's from California," exclaims Solomon—laden with golden fruit, orange ribbons, and green-and-orange decorations. "Glory be to God, Father! She's not marrying an A.P.A.?" The priest tries to calm him down. "I'm going to get to the bottom of this," says Patrick. "Patrick," begs the priest. "Remember, love has never been a respecter of religion." "Who said love?" roars Patrick

Murphy. "I'm talkin' about oranges! Oh—that color! The A.P.A. divils! How I hate orange. 'Tis the color of them Orangemen!"

The Orange Free State *(Oranje Vrystaat* in Afrikaans), named by the Boers in 1854 and, not coincidentally, after the Dutch House of Orange, is a province of South Africa that became part of the Union of South Africa, now the Republic of South Africa, a country whose largest river, with sandbars that make it useless for navigation, is called the Orange River *(Oranjerivier).* Speaking of areas, when I read that the air in the village of Piura in Mario Vargas Llosa's novel *Who Killed Palomino Molero?* (tr. Alfred MacAdam) smells of "carob trees, goats, birdshit, and deep frying," I cannot help but visualize orange.

It is often the color of fantasy, outspoken and marked by intensity and flash and as bright as Surtus the fire-giant, the flaming angel Sardalphon, and the simmering sun of St. Swithin's Day (July 15). In Francis Bacon's utopian *New Atlantis* (1627), in the Kingdom of Bensalem—where the civic motto is "Things rule men"—men wear orange shoes. In Edward Lear's Bong-Tree Land, a year and a day by sea from a country of uncertain location, and where a pussycat once married an elegant fowl, one can visit the coast of Coromandel, where the early pumpkins blow. All of the inhabitants have orange skin on Cook's Island in Edith Nesbit's *The Phoenix and the Carpet* (1904), a tropical island ruled by a white woman who was once a cook in North London and where all visitors can be cured of whooping cough. And the natives who fix shells to their skin with needles in

Aphra Behn's *Oroonoko, or the History of the Royal Slave* (c. 1678) have orange skin as well. I remember reading with fascination when I was a boy in the *Book of Mountains and Seas* (anonymous, fourth century) of weird and ultramysterious Mt. Kunlun in China being guarded by Lu Wu, a creature with a tiger's body, nine tails, a human face, and, fiercest of all, tiger's claws.

The "Orange Catholic Bible," the religious text referred to in Frank Herbert's *Dune,* curiously incorporates a melange of ancient religions, including the Maometh Saar, Mahayana Christianity, Zensunni Catholicism, and Buddhislamic traditions. Its supreme commandment is considered to be "Thou shalt not disfigure the soul." And in that same novel, a narcotic called Elacca, formed by burning a certain wood—its effect is to remove most of the will to self-preservation—turns the drugee's skin a carrot color. (It is commonly used in the book as a salve to prepare gladiators for the ring.)

The melancholy county of Lituania {sic} in Henri Guigonnat's *Demone en Lituanie,* where it always either rains or snows, has inns that serve an amber drink called *starka,* which will inebriate you immediately. Tiger lilies are aggressive in Lewis Carroll's *Through the Looking-Glass* (1871), where, also, roses are arrogant, daisies prosaic, and violets rude. It has been explained that because the beds in looking-glass gardens are hard, flowers are never asleep and therefore conduct interesting conversations with visitors, though it is part of their etiquette that strangers address them first. The vegetation is orange in the semifascist country of Vril-Ya in Edward Bulwer Lytton's *The Coming Race* (1871), where the people live to be about 130 years old, and when they die, before they are cremated, their coffins are marked "Lent to us [date]/Recalled from us [date]." A Vril-Ya proverb: "No happiness without order, no order without authority, no authority without unity." Who that eats orange vegetation wouldn't be totalitarian?

Orange has many negative—and malevolent—connotations. Satan down through history has often been painted orange. No spiritual significance is attached to it. Weirdly, it is a thoroughly nonliturgical color. Killers in most American prisons, often general prisoners as well, wear orange regulation jumpsuits, which necrophiliac Jeffrey Dahmer wore all through his 1992 trial in Milwaukee. (All of the tarty women in the "camp" film *Caged Heat II* wear orange prison tunics.) It has recently come out that Anna Sage, "The Lady in Red," the Romanian ex–brothel keeper who fingered John Dillinger in Chicago on that Saturday night, July 22, 1934, and caused his death, had worn not a red dress but an orange skirt—it was only the garish lights of the Biograph Theater that night that made it look red. A baby with a copper skull, Belial, tears up the insides of its mother in Isaac Bashevis Singer's horror story "The Black Wedding." On airplanes, the "black box" recorder is actually bright orange. Don't orange lights infect Polaroid photos with abandon? I also think of orange as the color of shotgun fire, cheap Chinese food, fatal mushrooms, poisonous snakes, hideous leisure suits, and orange crepe streamers of the sort, say, used at vulgar bridal showers. It is also the concentrated color of urine, due to high fever, hot weather, lack of fluid, or jaundice, while a dark orange color (or an intense greenish yellow) indicates in beef that the meat is either of an inferior quality or gone west. "To suck the orange" is a colloquial expression meaning to exhaust, to deplete.

Stink bugs are orange. The poison dart frog of the Amazon Basin is a toxic Day-Glo orange. It is also the color of the wicked queen's crown, parody of a halo, in Walt Disney's *Snow White and the Seven Dwarfs.* John Updike in one of his fine short stories, "Broken Grasshopper," delineates to perfection the swift terror of fire: "a few garish, orange seconds," though nothing can match for gravity a contemporary description of the first spark of fire before the dirigible Hindenberg exploded on May 2, 1937, at Lakehurst, New Jersey:

> In the stem of the airship Gas Cell No. IV gave a gasp as if hit in the stomach. A wavering orange flame lit up the inside of the cell like a Hallowe'en pumpkin . . . and then the explosion came.

Poet Anne Sexton in "The Addict" writes of being nightmarishly "hauled away" into druggish stupors by capsules she realistically calls "orange goodnights." The drug LSD in the New York City area is euphemistically called "orange sunshine." In the sixties, psilocybin, a psychedelic, was briefly manufactured by several Swiss pharmaceutical companies and came in the form of tiny orange pills. And actress Florence Lawrence, "the Biograph Girl," committed suicide on December 27, 1938, by, of all things, eating ant paste—deep orange in color.

Orange can be eerie. Bernard Eisenschitz in *Nicholas Ray, An American Journey* is fascinating on the "psychology" of orange as he discusses (and quotes Ray on) *Bigger Than Life,* the fascinating film in which James Mason is treated with cortisone, then touted as a wonder drug, and the subsequent madness he develops after taking too much of it. "Above all, there is the color, dense, opaque, splashed against neutral or even colorless backgrounds: the reds of the schoolchildren's jackets and shirts, Ed's green waistcoat 'against' his wife's yellow blouse or, more especially, the orange dress he buys her, in one of the first manifestations of his mania, at a luxury department store that epitomizes the bad taste of the 1950s (and Fox). He makes Lou try on dresses of increasing garishness, finally settling on the orange. 'I began to feel the need for some extra kick for Barbara Rush,' Ray explained, 'so I had to find one or two significant things ensuring that attention was being paid to her. In that sense, the orange was inevitable. Later, when the highway departments began using orange instead of red for the protection of road workers and for important danger signs, I felt my psychology had been verified. Strange that it took us so long to wake up to that color. Perhaps because of the literary strength of red. No significant orange literature.' " (I suspect this would be a great subject for an academic debate, would it not?) " 'The use of green in *Bigger Than Life* was indicative of life, opposite of the use of green in Party Girl, where it's sinister and jealous, envious.' "

On the Day of the Dead, or *Día de Muertos,* in Mexico in early November, pungent orange marigolds, or *cempasúchil,* the flowers of the dead, along with elate skulls and the smell of burning copal incense with its blue smoke, abound in graveyards and figure prominently almost everywhere during this important festival. *Santísima Muerte* (Most Holy Death) presides, about which writer Carlos Monsiváis wisely asseverates, "Death is still the terrible yet amusing entity that establishes a compromise between memory and the sense of humor, and between the sense of humor and the irremediable."

Kali, the destructive divine mother of Hindu mythology and symbol of anarchic violence—justice in its hardest aspect—is associated, along with red and black, with the orange of fire. In England, Italy, and Sicily, oranges were used in witchcraft as a symbol of the victim's heart. The victim's name was written on a slip of paper, secured to the fruit with pins, and placed in a chimney until the victim died, an activity practiced in Yorkshire as late as 1880. In A. Conan Doyle's short story "The Five Orange Pips," an envelope containing five orange pips provided ominous warnings or threats of impending death to their intended victims by the Ku Klux Klan. The Thing, the alien in that film, is described as a "giant carrot." The black widow spider has an orange hourglass-shaped mark on its belly. The monarch butterfly of orange hue is poisonous. A bird, after eating one of this species, will shiver and, before death, regurgitate, to show its young a lesson that must be learned. Orange rust, a fungus, kills raspberries and blackberries. And James Montgomery Flagg, in his autobiography *Roses and Buckshot,* uses the word *orange* pejoratively, and uniquely, I believe, to describe muck-raking: "At about that time artist's studios were being played up by the orange press as 'dens of iniquity.' "

In Anthony Burgess's remarkable novel of violent, futuristic juvenile delinquence, *A Clockwork Orange* (1963), Alex, the hoodlum protagonist, deprived of anything like a capacity for moral choice by science, himself embodies a "clockwork orange," a mechanical something or other, it seems to mean, which only appears organic, a machine for mindless mechanical violence that exists and functions below the level of choice, although in private Burgess always said it was simply a cockney expression: "queer as a clockwork orange." The dreary socialist England of the novel is in fact also a giant clockwork orange, a challenge to the book mentioned in the novel ("the attempt to impose upon man . . . laws and conditions appropriate to a mechanical creation, against this I raise my sword-pen").

Agent Orange is of course the grim chemical herbicide that afflicted veterans of Vietnam with cancer, skin diseases, and other disorders. A defoliant, it contains minute amounts of dioxin, a highly poisonous substance that accumulated from repeated spraying in the silt of the streambeds and seeped into the ecosystem of Vietnam. (Napalm, on the other hand, is jelly gasoline, and once it gets on your skin, you can throw yourself into a river, the burning will never stop.) It is an iconographic nightmare, a Vietnam jungle suddenly erupting into hot flame, greenery instantly boiling in orange, then turning black. As much as eighteen million gallons of orange rain were sprayed by the U.S. forces over the jungles and forestland of that beleaguered country. "After the war," according to Neil Sheehan in *A Bright Shining Lie,* "scientific tests indicated that the Vietnamese of the South had levels of dioxin in their bodies three times higher than inhabitants of the United States." As Edith Sitwell almost prophetically writes in her poem "The Youth with the Red-Gold Hair,"

> *Fear only the red-gold rain*
> *That will dim your brightness, O my tall tower of the corn*

Warnings and the color orange are often close cousins: Intergovernmental Maritime Consultative Organization shipping labels for explosives and fireworks are orange, as are the markings for the dangerous parts of machines on energized equipment that can cut, crush, and shock. It is *the* construction and maintenance warning color, of men at work, of all road and bridge signs (merge, detour, and so forth). You will often see orange metal balls spaced out along electrical wires in high-wind areas to keep the wires from swinging. After the Oklahoma City bombing in April 1995, before the shell of the building was razed, the part where two immured bodies, unreachable, still remained was sprayed bright orange for later identification. Who that ever heard of it can forget the fatal "nuclear tan" suffered by the victims of the Reactor Four explosion at Chernobyl on April 25, 1986, or the convulsions that immediately followed? And I suppose the orange light in darkroom photography serves as much for warning purposes as well as a utility. The U.S. Postal Service uses deep orange for "priority" mail bags, orange-and-blue bags for the faster Express Mail. A bright orange that can be seen at farther distances than any other color is often used on arctic and antarctic equipment, much mountain-climbing gear, and a good deal of rescue equipment, including helicopters. It is the color of highway lights (halogen), rockets, flashlight beams, and the flare path of light. "And then the flash of orange; an inpho beam shining out from the shadowcop's eyes," writes Jeff Noon in *Vurt* (1993), supposedly the first cyberpunk novel. We can include boat life preservers and jackets, ships' "donuts," phosphorescent hunters' doublets and hats, most bandoliers of school-crossing monitors and the Day-Glo orange safety garments of traffic cops and bicyclists at night, highway lines, snow plows, and the uniform stripes on NHL referees. Sports photographers and reporters at college basketball games often wear orange vests to identify themselves. I have seen miners in Welsh collieries, with helmets and oxygen, wearing orange overalls as they descend into dark seven hundred meter holes. Are not most border crossings replete with orange warning signs? The U.S.-Mexican border at San Ysidro–Tijuana is incoherent with all sorts of ramps, passageways, and official signs, all a minatory orange. And an orange flag with a blue center—orange's color complement, as we have seen—is officially waved in the sport of auto racing when one car is trying to pass another.

The particular species of staphylococcus called *s. aureus,* a microbe infection or toxin that causes food poisoning, toxic shock syndrome, and so forth, is golden orange, unlike *s. epidermis,* which is white.

There is more than a hint of orange in the skin of the Japanese *fugu,* or "blowfish," which is flooded with poisons. (Red, yellow, and orange are the most common warning colors in the animal kingdom.) The death adder is a reddish orange, as is the red-headed krait and the Sinaloan milksnake, which, although it is reputed to suck on cows' teats, does not in fact drink milk. The orange-and-black pitohui bird—its name actually sounds like an expectoration—also called the "rubbish bird" (it can't be eaten), from the rain forests of New Guinea, is deadly poisonous in its feathers, skin, and flesh, its poison being the same as that found in the arrow-poison frog. Orange is a warning color in many other manners and morphs. Scorpios, whose stone is topaz, are considered to be blunt, argumentative, and natural fighters. Those born under that sign are bold and persistent, but also malicious and jealous and should control their tempers. It is the constellation that is the symbol of fighting and quarreling and strife of all kinds. It controls the genital organs and the womb. Many wounds and gashes in the human body gape orange, as is often shown in crucifixion scenes in painting and sculpture, Mexican retablos and bultos, and so forth, where Jesus, ripped in hands, feet, and side, hangs in agony.

Question: what is the only man-made thing in heaven? *Answer:* the nail marks in Christ's body and the spear mark in his side.

It is not a color everybody likes. Wendy MacLeod's man-hating play *Sin* (1994), in which is advanced the

rather comic if not fatuous idea that the modern coun-
terpart to Everyman in the fifteenth-century morality
play would be a feminist Yalie yuppie living in San
Francisco. (Anything closer to a more graphic concep-
tion of hell I couldn't imagine.) Avery, the sanctimo-
nious protagonist, confronts all of the Seven Deadly Sins
in this updated allegorical farce, and when Gluttony of-
fers her a sack of Cheetos, she sneers and rejects them,
saying, "They're so orange. I hate orange." So much for
postmodern theology. As to hating orange, it was the
entrepreneurial pooh-bah Harley Earl, the first person to
put food in spray-on aerosol cans and the man who de-
signed both Fig Newtons and roll-on deodorant, who
also pioneered (drum roll) the use of orange Naugahyde
on chairs and couches. And remember all of the tacky
seventies burnt orange decor—curtains, chairs, rugs, so-
fas, and so forth—in the film version of Neil Simon's
crude New York Jewish comedy *Plaza Suite*? What per-
mutation of a single color could possibly get worse than
that? In spite of it all, there is an elegance to certain,
perhaps subdued, shades of orange. In *The Children of the
Sun*, Martin Green, visiting Sir Harold Acton at La Pi-
etra, his estate in Florence, speaks of that "dim, old
various brown-and-gold harmoniousness that the aes-
thetes favored." Did he mean fawn, which is often de-
scribed as reddish yellow? Or sandalwoodesque?
Wandering the bazaars of Egypt in 1850, sexually tour-
ing and looking for *almehs*, or, as he said, "professional
singers," Gustave Flaubert evocatively describes inhal-
ing "the odor of sandalwood," which piqued his passion.

In the adulterous film *Double Indemnity*, the seductive, somewhat kinkily atonal song "Tangerine"—with its unhealthy languor—is playing in the last hideous scene where Fred MacMurray shoots Barbara Stanwyck. It may seem passing strange, but there *can* be found even in the relatively simple and uncomplicatedly Barnumesque color orange a quality of the erotic. The garb of Greek harlots was orange. A penchant for falsity and corruption was symbolized by the color orange during medieval times. According to *The Rainbow Book,* "orange and saffron also symbolized avenged adultery, by combining red, or vengeance, and yellow, adultery." In that book we also read, "Homer describes Helen as wearing saffron clothes because of her adulterous affair with Paris. The marigold is the characteristic flower of deceived husbands even today." As mentioned, prostitutes in ancient Greece wore orange. Men's togas were always white. During the Imperial period of Rome, however, colors were much more varied—women during a later time can be seen on the frescoes of Pompeii and Herculaneum wearing garments of many bright colors—but Seneca the younger in his *Naturales Quaestiones* (vii, 31) says, "We men wear the colors used by prostitutes, in which respectable married women would not be seen." In the performance of *Le Pavillon d'Armide* in Paris in 1908, when Nijinsky took the stage in his famous pas de trois with Alexandra Baldina and Tamara Karsavina—at which supreme moment, according to Richard Buckle, "the conquest of Europe by Russian dancing and the reign of Diaghilev as Director of the Ballets Russes, can be said to begin"—he was erotically clad in orange, white, and gold. Orange can be vulgarly sexual as well. Isn't there a libidinous connotation to No 5 Orange, the Vancouver strip club on 205 Main Street—Aerosmith and Guns N' Roses love the place—where Courtney Love supposedly once stripped? Gays refer to a thing called "golden showers." ("He was pouring orangeade all over the fire hydrant" is one of a number of vulgar homosexual expressions.) And at least according to Philippe Sollers in *Watteau in Venice, orange* is a term used, at least in France, to denote the female genitals. Jazzy orange in women's underwear, according to novelist Alison Lurie, is worn "less to give erotic information" than "to express a mood," motives that I have always thought were more or less dynamically parallel. A lot of eye-staring orange clothes (rust, brick dust, earth orange, and others), orexigenically worn in the slouching sixties by hippies and hoopoes who were sartorially and simultaneously half draped and sexually open, because they were orange, either tamed or made facetiously harmless the entire "gear" of the wearer, no? Maybe that is what Lurie means.

Orange befriends and is almost accommodating in its visible comfort. As Wallace Stevens says in "Esthetique du Mal," a poem documenting the approaches to the reality of evil,

> *And it may be*
> *That in his Mediterranean cloister a man*
> *Reclining, eased of desire, establishes*
> *The visible, a zone of blue and orange*
> *Versicolorings, establishes a time*

To watch the fire-feinting sea and calls it good.
The ultimate good.

Orange *is* invitation—at the same time there is a connotation to it of brainless easiness. When Rhett Butler visits Scarlett, hard upon her having spitefully asserted she will henceforth lock her bedroom door, Belle, the prostitute in the film *Gone With the Wind* is wearing a garish orange dress, along with bell earrings. "You've got a heart, Belle, and you're honest," Rhett says to her, but she, childless, scorned, alone, looking garishly sad in orange, appears forlorn. Incidentally, she wears a purple dress in a later meeting with Melanie Wilkes, as if somehow, even if self-consciously, trying to look a bit more worthy, if not royal, as indeed she manages a tad to be. Orange is also the vivid color of the carpet on the sweepingly elegant main stairway of Tara.

Lovers wash in flower water in Boccaccio's *Decameron,* where we also discover a courtesan sprinkling her sheets with orange perfume. Pomander balls, oranges stuck with cloves, are often given to sweethearts as keepsakes. Oranges are tender Christmas presents or gifts at any time, and as such doubtless have their origins in deep affection. Noël Coward made epexegetic hay out of such a gift when in the spring of 1913 he fatefully first met Gertrude Lawrence: "She then gave me an orange and told me a few mildly dirty stories, and I loved her from then onwards." In Germany, girls used to toss oranges to suitors from their balconies as love tokens, and in the seventeenth century, oranges, like limes, were even used provocatively, to redden girls' lips—the acidic d-limonene stinging them alive, showing the same tartness that slightly burns the lips of children after sucking an orange.

There is to the flesh and juice of the color orange a sensuousness. In its burning insistence can be detected the irresistible. It tempts, it entices, it insinuates. In his poem *"Au Lecteur,"* Baudelaire mentions how we squeeze our clandestine pleasures *"bien fort comme une vieille orange."* And in his wild, passionate, almost electrically erotic poem "Les Bijoux," his mistress, *"un tigre dompté,"* a tamed tigress, *"polis comme de l'huile,"* shiny as oil, perches by a hot fire completely naked, that *"inondait de sang cette peau couleur d'ambre"* (drenches that amber skin with blood). Even the sheet music to the 1933 hit "Temptation" (lyrics by Arthur Freed, music by Nacio Herb Brown) is a lurid orange. In Carlos Fuentes's *The Orange Tree,* we read of "the hidden flesh of the orange, her flesh, the woman-fruit, the feminine fruit." A young fellow says, "I finally had a garden of perfect breasts, suckable, edible, renewable . . . I was a boy without the shame or nostalgia of being one. I could suck oranges until I died." As to physiological "oranging," anyone exposed to someone with meningitis is immediately given the drug rifampin, which turns all body fluids and mucosa orange (tears, urine, and so forth). Phenazopyridine, an azo dye for urinary tract infection, turns the urine orange. And of course hepatitis can make a person look positively carrotlike.

Speaking of decadence, Des Esseintes, the protagonist of Joris Karl Huysmans's *A Rebours,* chooses of all colors for his private rooms, *orange*—a color described as a "hot-headed fellow which often blazes out into a crimson or a fire-red," a color that would be strengthened under artificial light, no small consideration for Des Esseintes, who has virtually lived his entire life at night. It was a choice, Des Esseintes's, about which Huysmans meant to be complimentary neither to his protagonist nor to that man's color preference. He went on to say dismissively, "As for those gaunt, febrile creatures of feeble constitution and nervous disposition whose sensual appetite craves dishes that are smoked and seasoned, their eyes almost always prefer that most morbid and irritating of colors, with its acid glow and unnatural splendor—orange." But his antihero had other things in mind. "Every room has its gloom," said Gertrude Stein. "The great thing is to find the color that will cut that gloom."

Would Edith Wharton have approved? Quite possibly. It was her fixed and distinct belief that the fewer colors used in a room, the more pleasing that room would be. "It is well, as a rule, to shun the decorative schemes concocted by the writers who supply our newspapers with hints for 'artistic interiors,' " she writes in *The Decoration of Houses* (1902). "The use of such poetic adjectives as jonquil-yellow, willow-green, shell-pink, or ashes-of-roses gives to these descriptions of the 'unique boudoir' "—a place in which, when married to Teddy, she found scant happiness—"or 'ideal summer room' a charm which the reality would probably not possess."

Amber, a fossil resin—derived from extinct coniferous trees—with its high brilliance, reflects the reddish yellow of orange. It is well known for its translucent quality and high polish, especially Baltic amber, which has been called "congealed light." (True amber will always float when put in saltwater.) In China, amber represents courage: "the soul of the tiger." It was sacred to Apollo and Helios. Freya's tears for Svipdag fell as amber. Amber dust was often mixed with honey and oil of roses and given as a medicine to those suffering from earache or failure of sight in certain cultures. And in others the smell of burned amber helped women in labor. A model of an amber phallus was regarded as powerful protection against the evil eye in southern Italy. A heavy amber-colored, "indeed almost amber-scented champagne"—Dagonet, 1880, specifically—was Lord Alfred Douglas's favorite wine, as Oscar Wilde sadly recalls in the *De Profundis,* of the many bottles he bought his catamite ("All have still to be paid for," he later laments). There is, oddly enough, an amber-colored raven in *Love's Labour's Lost* (IV.iii.86). Electrum, a compound of metal and gold and silver mentioned in the *Aeneid* (VIII.402), probably derived its name from its resemblance to pale amber. An ambivalence attaches to amber. There is an amber stream in Milton's heaven (*Paradise Lost,* III.359), and Dalila smells sweetly dangerous in *Samson Agonistes* (I.720) for its aroma ("An amber scent of odorous perfume/Her harbinger"). Its orange, more often than not, has a soft hue. Tennyson writes in his poem "Margaret":

> *Like the tender amber round*
> *Which the moon about her spreadeth,*
> *Moving through a fleecy night*

Charlie Chan, the detective, had amber eyes. Amber often describes an orangeaceous complexion. Cecil Beaton once described tall and chic Gertrude Lawrence as having "shining apricot skin and a fruity pout." Pitiful, shapeless, gray Mattie Silver in Edith Wharton's novel *Ethan Frome,* whose "eyes had the bright witchlike stare that disease of the spine sometimes gives," had a bloodless and shriveled but amber-tinted face. The subject of Robert Louis Stevenson's poem "Dark Woman" was none other than his own older, gypsyish orange-brown melanodermic American wife, Fanny Osborne, of whom a maid once said, "He merrit [married] a black woman."

> *Dark as a wayside gypsy,*
> *Lithe as a hedgewood hare,*
> *She moves a glowing shadow*
> *Through the sunshine of the fair;*
> *And golden hue and orange,*
> *Bosom and hand and head*
> *She blooms, a tiger lily,*
> *In the snowdrifts of the bed.*

"But beware of the girl tourists from the Bronx and Brooklyn," advises Weegee (Arthur Fellig) in his somewhat dated introduction to *Greenwich Village.* "They make the rounds of the Village in wolfpacks, tightly corseted and copiously petticoated, flashily dressed in tailor-made suits from the Thrift Shoppe and $20 shoes. You can tell the immigrants by their orange pancake makeup and purple lipstick . . . they usually chew chlorophyll gum and carry a copy of *Confidential.*"

Regarding amber, what about the theft by the invading Nazis during World War II of the Amber Room? It had been a gift for King Frederick I of Prussia to Czar Peter the Great, an elegant present that was an actual chamber of twenty-two lustrous amber panels, Venetian glass, and intricate bas-relief. Now valued at upwards of $160 million, it had stood in Catharine Palace near St. Petersburg, Russia, since 1755. Hitler, who had wanted to use it as a centerpiece for a museum honoring the Third Reich, had it dismantled piece by piece in 1941 and shipped, according to one theory, to Konigsberg (now Kaliningrad). Some even say it was shipped to the United States. It has been hunted for decades but to date has never been found.

In Botticelli's *St. Augustine in His Study* (c. 1490), the saint wears a celestial bright orange robe, with blue trim, as does the younger version of Augustine (c. 1480) painted by Botticelli, who iconoclastically seemed to favor that color for spiritual raiment, using it repeatedly on the women's robes, for example, in the fresco *Young Woman with Venus and the Graces* (1483) and for the magnificent angel's rich robes in his *Madonna of the Pomegranate* (1487). Then there is the orangeade color and drooling smiles of Il Rosso's sticky canvases and that of other Mannerists who relied on two-toned colors—

orange turning yellow, flame turning red, lavender turning rose—found nowadays, as a somewhat nettled Mary McCarthy points out, chiefly in sleazy taffetas popular with home-dressmakers for girls' first formals. Poussin defines the beautiful as delectation, by which presumably he means what delights and diverts, and nowhere is the sentiment better realized—or embodied—than in the fluid and extravagant possibilities of the color orange. Watteau's *Harlequin and Columbine* is a canvas virtually on fire with orange, teasing up in passionate sympathy a whole spectrum of reds, pinks, and beiges. And how the bright torch, blazing orange, illuminates the circled figures in his *Love at the Theatre Italian,* burnishing everyone and everything in an amorous glow.

Speaking of art, Paul Cézanne's *Pommes et Oranges* is alive with the splendid orange fruit, as is Giorgio de Chirico's *Florentine Still Life* (1923). And in Paul Klee's *Ad Parnassum* (1932), where the color scheme in a grid of mosaiclike fragments or tesserae moves between poles of light and dark, colors seem to increase in intensity toward the top right-hand corner, where the brightest part of the work, offset in blue, is that orange circle. The orange sun! Aren't ants eating the orange pocket watch in Dalí's *The Persistence of Memory* (1931)? And isn't the hat on the singing boy in Georges Seurat's *Bathers, Asnières* (1883), a bell dome of rich, raw sienna and alizarin red, also singing? F. G. Cowper's *La Belle Dame Sans Merci,* one of my favorite paintings, shows an orange-gowned, triumphant bare-armed beauty in a poppy field, delicately fixing her long hair—what has she just done?—while a knight in armor lies dead at her feet.

And in Gustave Klimt's *Danae* (1907), the virgin who lies in a swoon is draped in orange. The orange and ochres used on the bed of the railroad track in Edward Hopper's *House by the Railroad* (1925) quote almost exactly the orange of the chimneys in sunlight of that solitary Victorian house. Much orange-yellow was used in the chair of van Gogh's *Chair with Pipe* (1889). In Monet's *Effet d'Automne à Argenteuil* (1873), the orangy green tree and rough country foliage is autumn itself! Renoir loved to use orange accents, as in, say, the background of *Young Bather* (1892), *Girl with a Blue Ribbon* (1880), and *Young Girl Combing Her Hair* (1894). Henri Matisse's *Woman in Front of the Window* (1905) is a study in orange, with that almost cartoonlike woman in an orange dress and hat, emerging out of the orange background. It has always been a saturated color for halos, crowns, hair, and decorative medallions to frame a figure.

How the orange hair of the voluptuary in the foreground of Edouard Manet's *Déjeuner sur l'herbe* (1863) makes the picture! Eugene Delacroix's *Taking of Constantinople by the Crusaders* is a virtual study in orange and its variational hues. Titian used orpiment (yellow) and realgar (orange-red) on Diana's robe in *The Death of Actaeon* (c. 1560), maybe even for her lovely burnished knees, hands, and cheek. And look at that softness of nap on the tunic worn in *The Water Seller of Seville* (1620) of Diego Velázquez, who loved soft hair brushes—has a richer orange, a more subtle painterly definition of that color, ever been seen?—and the orange in the guitar of his *The Guitar Players* (c. 1660). In Frederic Leighton's

Flaming June (1895), that exquisite woman with the pre-Raphaelite hair, asleep, wears a tangerine gown. The orange sponge in Degas's *The Tub* not only fixes the painting but echoes the reddish gold of the copper pitcher and the surrounding furniture, as well as the woman's body and her own red hair. There is in the solitary reverie Picasso's *Girl Reading* (1934), beautiful Marie-Therese Walter in repose over a book, a warm, sensuous coloring of orange in various hues in all the melting organic shapes, especially the phallic orange arm of the chair. Speaking of orange, the sculptor Christo, at a cost of $750,000, suspended a bright orange curtain 1,350 feet—it weighed four tons—above and across the Rifle Gap in Grand Hogback, Colorado. It blew completely apart in a fifty-mile-per-hour gust of wind a day later.

Monet discovered that by putting a stroke of pure red next to a stroke of pure yellow, the side-by-side vibration of the two notes—a technique, later picked up by Pissarro, Seurat, and Paul Signac, called "visual mixing"—results in a richer and more vibrant orange. "All colors are the friends of their neighbors," as Chazal wisely once noted, "and the lovers of their opposites." Cadmium Orange is commonly used today for the color orange, when a pure tube isn't squeezed out, or Cadmium Scarlet, which is an orange-red.

To me, Edvard Munch, the only Scandinavian painter and printmaker of modern times to have achieved a major world reputation, is *the* orange painter. *Sunbathing (Woman on the Rock)* (1915) is an explosion of orange suns, the passionate woman on her back, hands behind her head, merging with, into, the rock itself. *Melancholy (Laura)* (1899)—his sister, mentally ill—is terrifying with its orange walls, turbulent, almost kinetic table, and poor Laura's rigid apprehension. Also, the sky of another *Melancholy* (1896), a doleful man pondering space, shows an almost psychopathic orange sky, oppressive and relentless in its mania. That very same sky can be seen in Munch's *Fear* (1896) and in *The Scream* (1895), with its sunset of coagulated blood and waving skies, undulating with noisy brutality and screaming waves of swirling lines, all acoustic vibrations of the scream: panic itself. It is of course the case that baleful rain warnings are attached to a morning sky, especially of altocumulus clouds, which are often an orange or Indian red, and stratocumulus clouds at sunset, when accompanied by winds northeast to south, often a weird, unsettling orange or smeared red—read Mat. 16:2–3— usually forecast rain within a day.

Horribly, Munch feared women, and what he felt was their murderous possessiveness. One wealthy young woman in particular remorselessly pursued him, making him drink, enter a sanatarium, and even make, or stage, a suicide attempt—he shot off part of his finger. A woman in an erotic orange dress often appears in Munch's work. Consider *Girls on the Jetty, The Dance of Life,* and *Jealousy,* showing a lewd woman propositioning a man while Munch peers, lost, into our eyes. "Illness, insanity, and death were the black angels that kept watch over my cradle," writes Munch—tuberculosis killed his mother when he was only five—"and accompanied me all my life."

The painter Francis Bacon's *Triptych, Studies from the Human Body* (1970) is a roaring orange, memorable for the mad action in the central panel of two figures on a bed. ("I wanted them in a sense either to be copulating or buggering," said the artist.) The outrage, as is so often the case with Bacon, is in the mouths of his figures. Is color implied? More specifically, orange? "I like . . . the glitter and colour that comes from the mouth, and I've always hoped in a sense to be able to paint the mouth like Monet painted a sunset." Grace Hartigan did an *Oranges* series of gouaches in New York in 1960. She had been a friend of poet Frank O'Hara, whose own favorite colors were orange and blue—he once painted his refrigerator orange, it was the color of his book *Lunch Poems,* and so forth—and who surrealistically observes in "Radio,"

> *Well, I have my beautiful de Kooning*
> *to aspire to. I think it has an orange*
> *bed in it, more than the ear can hold.*

As a matter of fact, O'Hara himself in 1949 began working on eighteen pastorals entitled "Oranges," his attempt to write, according to his biographer, Brad Gooch, "in the style of Rimbaud's *Illuminations,*" a series of prose poems, antipastorals, as it turned out, about his life growing up in Grafton, Massachusetts, years that had been particularly painful for him. And now that I'm thinking of orange and the antipastoral mode, why shouldn't Antony Gormley's astonishing *Field,* a sculpture made up of thirty-five thousand terra-cotta figures, come to mind?

Orange, by the way, greatly lends its vitality to stained glass. The most remarkable surviving window of Dutch expressionist Johann Thorn-Prikker (1868–1932)—his real name—is in fact his magnificent *Orange,* designed in 1931, a rich, bright orange arranged in horizontal zones that make you feel as if you are walking east into the orange sun, a great medallion rising in the sky. It can be seen in the Kaiser Wilhelm Museum in Krefeld. He also fashioned the brilliant figurative windows in the Hagen Railway Station. A masterpiece of orange stained glass can be found in Evreux Cathedral. Executed by Canon Raoul de Ferrieres around 1325, the artist can be seen offering the Virgin and Christ a small model of his window—a popular fourteenth-century device. Mary's robe, a unique touch without liturgical precedent as far as I know, is an earthy orange, a favorite color, along with leafy green, of English glass painters. Also orange is the robe of the very human thirteenth-century Madonna in a window at Eaton Bishop in Herefordshire. As far as churches go, I love the small church of St. Bartholoma on the Konigsee in Bavaria, which has a beautiful orange dome.

Nowhere in art, however, can orange find the vast multifariousness of color that nature presents in its spectrum of lights and darks, from bright blooms to the bracts of tiny flowers to Chinese lantern perennials, those hollow orange inflated fruits used in winter bouquets. There are perennials, like orange larkspur, heliopsis, Olympic poppy, trolius; and many beautiful wildflowers, such as turk's cap lily, Carolina mallow, scarlet pimpernel, spotted touch-me-not, hoary puccoon, orange milkwort, butterfly weed, flame azalea, trumpet creeper, climbing bittersweet, and, of course, orange hawkweed ("devil's paintbrush"); an orange iris called wayside sunset, some impatiens, and many others of subtle hue. And many annuals are orange: zinnias, calendula, pansies, chrysanthemums, cosmos, gaillardia, rudbeckia, strawflowers, Iceland poppy, portulaca, celosia, and snapdragon. Tiger lilies provide a yearned-for orange in the spring, and Emily Dickinson often carried lilies about, not white ones but orange-red ones, like her hair. (Sniffing tiger lilies, according to legend, is believed to give a person freckles.) Marigolds love sun and will open to its rays with joy. And sunflowers light up fields with their sunny visages. Thomas Carew observed in his "Boldness in Love,"

> *Mark how the bashful morn in vain*
> *Courts the amorous marigold*
> *With sighing blasts and weeping rain,*
> *Yet she refuses to unfold.*

There are orange lilies. As Amy Lowell noted in her wistful "The Garden By Moonlight":

> *Ah, Beloved, do you see those orange lilies?*
> *They knew my mother*
> *But who belonging to me will they know*
> *When I am gone?*

Orange blossoms, the symbol of fertility and fruitfulness, are the conventional decoration for the brides at weddings. It was introduced as a custom into England from France around 1820. Symbolically, the orange is said to indicate the hope of fruitfulness, as few trees are more prolific, while the white blossoms are symbolic of innocence. Hence the phrase, "to go gathering orange blossoms," to look for a wife. A song called "When It's Orange Blossom Time in Loveland (I'll Be Waiting at the Church for You)" was big in 1915. The Chinese see in orange blossoms immortality and good fortune, while to the Japanese it denotes pure love. They were worn by Saracen brides as signifying fecundity. The lovely orange blossom is also an emblem of Diana, chaste goddess of the hunt. A bright orange veil, symbolizing dawn, furthermore, was worn over the hair of brides in ancient Rome. Many scholars believe that oranges were in fact the golden apples of the Hesperides. According to myth, Zeus is supposed to have given Hera an orange at their wedding. It is also thought that orange blossoms from a wedding must be discarded before the end of the first month—before they wither—lest they cause barrenness. "What is this craving after orange-blossom?" asks Enid in Ronald Firbank's play *The Princess Zoubaroff*. "They would persuade us, it seems, a woman's chief aim is a march to the altar."

What about an orange dye? In vegetable dyeing, yarns that have been dyed yellow can be dyed with red in order to obtain orange (and rust shades). Yellow and red dye baths can be combined. Raw materials, such as goldenrod blossoms and scarlet sage blossoms, can be cooked together to make orange and rust dye baths. Annatto is also a good source of orange, and chrome mordant can be used to make orange and rust out of a yellow dye material. As to nature, Osage orange, a rough-and-tumble shrub, was planted as living fences in northern Texas, Oklahoma, and Arkansas before barbed wire was introduced. It was called *bois d'arc* by the French because the Indians used its tough, springy wood in making bows, but it got its English name from the round, baseball-size seeds that look like green oranges. Osage orange was promoted out west as both low-cost fencing and cattle-tight hedging by an old Yankee named Jonathan Baldwin Turner, who tried to spread its usefulness with zeal in order to "democratize" the prairie. Its bark yields tannin; boiled chips yield yellow dye. The magnificent orange flower of the crane-headed Streitlizia plant, the "bird of paradise," is all over southern California. And trifoliate orange, an imported shrub with red buds, bell-like and bitter, became popular and was often planted as a hedge in the South.

Orange is audible, loud and singing, borderless, ego-free, wayward, and, shot through with cheery reinvention, easy with tropic nonchalance. It has amplitude and brass and unduplicatable sass, a cabochon color and shape, fiery with fun and sweet as hesperidene, never shy in what of force and fire it connotes. But it can be soft as well.

"Warm red, intensified by a suitable yellow, is orange," writes Wassily Kandinsky in *Concerning the Spiritual in Art.* "This blend brings red"—and he stresses the warmth of that color—"almost to the point of spreading out towards the spectator. But the element of red is always sufficiently strong to keep the color from flippancy. Orange is like a man, convinced of his own powers." As a color of high aspiration, with the drive of vivid red chanting in its aura, it may stumble, be deficient on the sensual side, cause mistrust, at times even show a lack of warmth, even want of intelligence and logic, and yet like other colors of hot hue ambiguity it badly wants success and deeply yearns to please. It is perhaps there in the unreconstituted and rewarding pleroma of that conviction, a "red brought nearer to humanity by yellow," as Kandinsky says, making a marriage of one strong color with a less highly pronounced but supportive and nurturing one, that orange, blushing with youthful charisma, finds its singing life.

Purple

PURPLE IS THE MAGISTERIUM. It is a color combining blue (spirituality and nobility) and red (courage and virility), and symbolizes, among other things, wit, intelligence, knowledge, religious devotion, sanctity, humility, temperance, sobriety—amethysts (from *a-* plus *methyein,* to be drunk) were once worn as an anti-alcoholic—penitence, and sorrow. It can seem, on the one hand, sad as a sunless twilight, in which, as a hue, it invariably predominates, or startlingly strong on the other, for it encompasses dusk ("When purple-colored curtains mark the end of day," sang the Platters) and dawn ("Iris had dipt the woof," writes John Milton of the celestial robe of the archangel Michael, the colors of the goddess of dawn), as well as old age, venerableness, love of truth, and revered memories. It is an elite, at times histrionically pious, severe color, a hue, like blue, that, absorbing light, is passive, retreating, and cold. There is nevertheless a dignity to the color that is as formal and fastidious and as fine as the Faubourg St. Germain. Mountain ranges are purple ("purple mountain's majesties"), and so are molehills. In psychology, vanity is purple, as is hauteur—Shelley refers to "purple pride"—and of decadence, as well. Purple ranks eighth as a child's color preference, an adult's sixth, stands for foundation in the Hebrew Kabbala, and possesses of all other colors the highest frequency in the visible spectrum. Law wears a purple doctoral hood, and lilac is worn for dentistry. Virtue and faith in Egypt are purple. It is the color traditionally worn when reciting the *Odyssey* to signify, with respect, the sea wanderings of Odysseus.

It imbues solemnity, always, and ingrains a tone of majesty, of the imperium, in whatever it colors. As black gospel singers might put it, purple has a lot of "church" in it. We choose to call the color purple, of course, not violet. Shakespeare never once uses the word *violet* as a color, only *purple* (confer Sonnet 99 to see the distinction); nor, for that, matter does he ever employ the words *heliotrope, mauve, lilac,* or *fuchsia.* Burgundy was a place, a duke, and, by extension, a wine. Purple is *the* color, violet a color—it should be noted but not made into a big deal. It merely recalls in the distinction a cartoon I remember having seen once, which showed the adjoining business offices of a veterinarian and a taxidermist, where the poignant if humorous caption read: "You get your dog back either way." Or as novelist Katherine Ann Porter, fastidiously quoting the words of her favorite proverb, often liked to repeat, "There is no such thing as an exact synonym and no such thing as an unmixed motive."

As a secondary color, the cool red that purple borrows—Aunt Leonie's back kitchen in Proust's *A la recherche du temps perdu* with its red-tile floor gleams "like porphyry"—is redeemed by the nobility of blue, which nevertheless undergoes its own suddenly married transformation.

It is hue of show and shadow, both. Shadows have color, as the impressionists (who avoided black, considering it not a color but rather an absence of light) well knew. Notice the rich flesh shadows, for example, in Renoir's *The Theatre Box* (1874), a pure pale blue not even Rubens or Gainsborough would have dared attempt. They made shadows, not of black or gray, but of the complementary colors, blue or violet. (What did the great Billy Strayhorn mean by his composition "Multicolored Blue" if not the magic of perceiving an intrachromal swirl of colors in what to the dull seems only one?) It was John Ruskin in his *Modern Painters* ("Of Truth of Chiaroscuro") who taught Proust that shadows are not monotonous areas, mere black and nothing else, but rather surfaces or planes of many colors. Proust observes in *Le Côté de Guermantes*, "*la route . . . où bleuissaient les falaises*" (along the course . . . where cliffs were turning blue), and in *Du Côté de chez Swann*, "*Les grandes ombres des arbres donnaient à l'eau un fond que parfois . . . j'ai vu d'un bleu chair et cru, tirant sur le violet*" (Long shadows of the trees gave the water bottomlessness at times . . . I have seen flesh blue and raw, approaching the color violet).

But isn't this precisely what poet Rainer Maria Rilke is getting at when, writing to his wife Clara, who had been a pupil of Rodin, he observes, "then he [Cézanne] doesn't let up but fetches out the so-to-speak wrapped up violets, just as some evenings do, autumn evenings especially, that address the graying of facades directly as violet, so that it answers them in every tone, from light, floating lilac to the heavy violet of Finnish granite" (letter, October 24, 1907).

An old Chinese saying goes, "It is so red, it is purple," meaning something is so hot, it cannot be hotter— it is the best that can be, out of this world, and so forth. In China, the color is proudly worn by literary and educated figures. (A purple button on a Chinese cap indicates an official of the third rank.) "If someone has a purple *ch'i,* this indicates a high nobility, a powerful, rich, and fortunate individual," according to Lin Yan, master of color concepts and the world's leading authority on *feng shui,* or the art of placement.

Purple is the royal color, the tinct of imperial and sacerdotal power—pomp, justice, truth, pride.

> *The purple pride*
> *Which on thy soft cheek for complexion dwells*
> *In my love's veins thou hast too grossly dyed,*

writes Shakespeare, apostrophizing the "forward violet." "The Purple" is a synonym for the rank of Roman emperor, a term derived from the color of his dyed woolen robe. Phrases such as "born to the purple"—an expression coming from a Byzantine custom that ordained that the empress should be brought to bed in a chamber whose walls were lined with porphyry—or "raised to the purple" are common in histories of the Roman Empire. (Oscar Wilde wanted all of the actors playing Romans in his play *Salomé* to be dressed in purple.) Romans often paid a thousand denarii for a pound of double-dyed Tyrian wool. Tibullus refers to the *"fulgentem Tyrio subtemine vestem"* (the garb of flaming Tyrian tissue) found on the consul's *toga praetexta* and notes romantically in "Sulpicia's Garland," *"urit, seu Tyria voluit procedere palla"* (she fires the heart if she chooses to appear in gown of Tyrian hue [tr. J. P. Postgate]). "Purple in Israel, as in Roman Carthage, was a sign of [overly authoritative] power," writes Henri Daniel-Rops in *Daily Life in the Time of Jesus*. "The evil rich man in the parable was dressed in purple and lawn. And the faithful were warned by their teachers against this pagan color." There is the military masculinity of purple. Decoration; also substance. And it *flows*. We read in Milton's *Paradise Lost*,

> . . . *over his lucid Arms*
> *A military vest of purple flow'd*
> *Livelier than Meliboean, or the grain*
> *Of Sarra, worn by Kings and Heroes old*
> *In time of Truce; Iris had dipt the woof;*
> *His starry Helm unbuckl'd showed him prime*
> *In Manhood where Youth ended . . .*
>
> (XI.240 ff.)

And yet the empress Josephine, like Napoleon, wore the heavy traditional mantle of power—in her case a mantle of Tyrian purple twenty-three yards long, adorned with embroidery and lined with Russian ermine and gold bees. (Like the emperor, she also had the right to a ring.) Nobility and honor were invariably won on the battlefield. It was Julius Caesar's insistence on wearing robes of purple, usually reserved for kings—after the Tarquins, Roman citizens despised the whole idea of monarchy—as much as his ordering a statue of himself to be erected on the capitol, along with the presence of Cleopatra and Caesarion in Rome (Caesar's living with his wife, Calpurnia, did nothing to stifle rumors of his marrying Cleopatra and uniting their empires) that led to his assassination. According to Appian, when Brutus struck him, Caesar ended all resistance, crying out in Greek, *kai su teknon*—"you, too, my child?"—drawing that same robe over his face, submitting to the blows, and falling at the foot of Pompey's statue. Later, fighting Antony at Philippi in September 42, Brutus, upon seeing that all was lost, suicidally threw himself upon the sword of a friend and died, whereupon Antony, coming across the body—they had once been fast friends—covered it with his own purple robe. Purple was always the royal hue of the Caesars—the color of Jupiter at Rome—but it meant majesty and sovereignty to the Aztecs and Incas as well. To the Chinese, it is a superior color; graceful connotations and nobility adhere to purple in Japan, where it signifies position and wealth. Purple, one of the tinctures *(purpure)* in heraldry, indicates royalty and rank and in engravings is always shown by lines running diagonally from sinister to dexter (that is, from left to right as one looks at it).

Cleopatra in Shakespeare's *Antony and Cleopatra* is vividly described with requisite pomp:

> *The barge she sat in, like a burnish'd throne*
> *Burnt on the water. The poop was beaten gold,*
> *Purple the sails, and so perfumed that*
> *The winds were love-sick with them . . .*

(II.ii.191–94)

(Reviewing Tallulah Bankhead in *Cleopatra,* critic John Mason Brown somewhat less than favorably wrote, "She barged down the Nile and sank.")

The Nile itself, in fact, in literature is often said to be purple. Gibbon uses the great word *porphyrogeniture,* born to the purple. The place name *Canaan* probably came from the Hurrian word *Kinahhu,* meaning purple, from the dye made from the shellfish. Purple was also used for coverings for the seats of princely palanquins (Song of Sol. 3:10), drapery for idols (Jer. 10:9), and awnings for the decks of luxurious ships (Ezek. 27:7), the richest cloth of the ancient world. Isn't it always, at least theoretically, the color of baby bunting: royal purple, for royal foundlings, like Moses, Tom Jones, Heathcliff? Aren't there even purple seats in Madison Square Garden for posh ticket holders? It is the luxurious color, extravagant, given to excess. Oddly enough, it denotes temperance as well. Take the amethyst, a purple or violet gem of the quartz family, which, according to legend, serves to prevent and cure drunkenness. Many were convinced of this because it was the color of violet wine, but Pliny in his *Natural History* (xxxvii.40) states that they had no connection. He does mention that magicians believed that if the magic names of the sun and the moon were written upon an amethyst and tied to the neck with peacock feathers, it would protect one against sorcery. Wine drunk from an amethyst cup is said never to intoxicate. It is supposed to control evil thoughts, quicken the intellect, make a man shrewd in business matters, put a sobering check on the passions, and when worn on the third finger of the left hand, protect sailors, doctors, and hunters.

Amethysts to the ancients also improved memory, gave a person immunity from poison, and when placed under a pillow, allowed a sleeper pleasant dreams. The presence of an amethyst in a bishop's ring blessed both the wearer and the devotee who kissed it. The amethyst is mentioned in Exodus as one of the stones in the high priest's breastplate, and in Revelation as one of the foundations of the New Jerusalem. St. Valentine is said to have worn an amethyst ring engraved with a Cupid. (To test the authenticity of amethysts or topazes, place them on a sheet of white paper: genuine ones should have only two shades within the stone.) Purple is almost always a healing color. "Stories that the glovers of Grasse, who used lavender oil to scent their fashionable leather, were remarkably free of plague, encouraged others to carry lavender to ward off pestilence," observes L. Bremners in *The Complete Book of Herbs.* Egyptian warriors always carried amulets of purple as a preparation for death. It is February's birthstone. I think of purple as the color of dreams and fantasies—isn't that why diaries and photo albums are often a sort of commemorational purple?—suggesting the oneiric and the occult and the out of the ordinary in everything from Batman's lavender hooded cape and trunks to exotic Duke Ellington hits, like "Lady of the Lavender Mist," "Azure" (very purple), and "Purple Gazelle," to the parchments of Byzantium.

> *Books of learning from Byzantium*
> *Written in gold upon a purple stain*
> (W. B. Yeats, "The Gift of Harun Al-Rashid")

A shellfish *(Purpura, Bucimum, Murex)*—or mollusk—provided the dye, the color from *Murex* being bright and from *Purpura,* dark. The mixture of the two shades produced the famous "Tyrian purple." Tyre was the main center of the dyeing industry. Discovered by the Phoenicians and doubtless well known in Homer's time (see *Iliad* IV.44), the purple dye was extracted from the cyst or vein near the head of the mollusk. The thin liquor of purple was called "the flower"—large shells were broken open to get at the gland, smaller ones pressed in mills—and, as the amount taken from each shell was very small, with much labor required to collect it, the subsequent price was correspondingly great. It took 250,000 shellfish to make one ounce of dye, for each mollusk secreted only one drop. Murex had a very sharp shell, with pointed projections—in the *Aeneid* (V.205), a ship actually strikes one—and could be found in abundance throughout the Mediterranean. Shades of color varied from coast to coast, but, whatever distinct shade, one of its values was that it was one of the very few dyes that retained its richness of color even under the effect of water or hot sun.

The best dyes, used for garments of a distinctive nature, such as the mantles of the noble archons at Athens and the purple stripes on the togas of Roman magistrates, were made in Tyre specifically and were very expensive. ("Dives . . . lived in purple," notes Shakespeare in *Henry IV, Part I* [III.iii.32].) Why, lovely Europa herself, borne away by taurine Zeus across the waters to Crete, his own island, clung with one hand to the bull's great horn and with the other caught up her purple dress to keep it dry. A large portion of the Phoenician population devoted itself to making the purple and linen so admired by the ancients. According to Pliny, pigments made from it were used principally as glazing colors. A bluish shade was also known as "Graecian purple," "ostrum"—the Latin *ostrum,* the purple dye prepared from a shellfish, and *ostrea,* an oyster, are cognates—and "Byzantine purple." We read of embroidered trappings *("ostro . . . pictisque tapetis"* [VII.277]) and purple dyed garments *("Ostro perfume vestes"* [V.111]) in the *Aeneid.* It is even significantly mentioned in the *Aeneid* (IV.262), quite dramatically, as if to sanction its power, its force, that Triton himself in the way of warning blew a murex shell.

The art of dyeing was derived by the Greeks from Phoenicia. Although the Greeks called these people Phoenicians, which some derive from the Greek φοινός ("blood-red" or "purple") and not from φοίνιξ ("date palm"), which does not grow readily in that country, the

Phoenicians were in fact called Sidonians by neighboring peoples. The Greek word *porphyra,* which would later become Latin *purpure,* comes from the mollusk and was a color between primary blue and red, like the Hebrew word *bahat,* which denotes a purple red. But the purple of the ancient world was a somewhat indefinite color, as often a shade of crimson as it was purple, thus the seemingly conflicting references to the shade of Christ's chiton. There is nothing contradictory about its being described by Mark and John as purple, while Matthew speaks of scarlet. The one distinction that should be made is that of the one between Christ's inner and outer garments. The difference is made manifest in the Lord's commandment in Matt. 5:40: "If any man would go to law with thee, and take away thy coat [chiton], let him have thy cloak [himation] also." When the soldiers had crucified Jesus, they took his garments (himation, in the plural), that is, they took both his outer garments, the long flowing outer robes, as well as the coat, the chiton, the tighter-fitting inner garment, which was without seam, woven from the top throughout (John 19:23). The outer garments were easily divisible among the four soldiers, but they could not divide the purple, or purplish red, chiton without splitting it, and so they proceeded to cast lots for it, as was prophesied.

It should be mentioned here that vegetable dyes also existed at that time. There was a guild of dyers in Greece who made an especially famous purple called "Turkish red," named from the madder root of the region rather than from the shellfish, the source of Tyrian purple. But the classical Hebrew and Greek words for purple were probably also generally used for the color we commonly call crimson.

Speaking of dyes, it should perhaps be noted that the very first aniline or synthetic dye was purple. Although the dyeing of cloth by means of vegetable and other naturally occurring dyes such as indigo was known from ancient days, the development of synthetic dyes to be used in the modern textile industry stems from one basic event: the discovery in 1856—by ingenious eighteen-year-old William Henry Perkin (1838–1907)—of the synthetic dye aniline purple or "mauveine," as he termed it. A student at the Royal College of Chemistry, Perkin inadvertently discovered the dye by trying to synthesize quinine from the by-products of coal tar. Mauvine dye became a basic feature of the high fashion of the day, incidentally, and its popularity made Perkin rich. (His teacher at the Royal College, August Wilhelm von Hofman, an organic chemist, would himself later create the reddish purple we now know as magenta, the particular name he gave it in celebration of a French victory over the Austrians at the Italian town of that name in 1859.)

Has there not always been a crucial connection between blood and purple—or between sadness and purple? Violetta in Verdi's *La Traviata,* so wounded and rejected by society, is not misnamed. There is something depressingly and hauntingly mournful in the color purple, wistful and bleak, and the mere chromocantillation of the various hues by which it goes has a synagogal and dirgelike sound, like the summoning echo of a shofar. Ralph Waldo Emerson believed that after the age of

thirty, a man wakes up sad virtually every morning—
what else would he have but a purple coverlet? But
purple in its somberness has always been a color reserved
and highly controlled. As Garry Wills points out in *Lincoln at Gettysburg,* "Restraint deepens passion by refusing
to give it easy vent." Tyrian purple, the "highest glory"
in Pliny's words, was the color of congealed blood. In his
epics, Homer refers to "blood of purple hue." But in the
matter of sacrifice, all soldiers are brave, and no one
should ever forget Henry David Thoreau's words in
Walden: "When the soldier is hit by a cannonball, rags
are as becoming as purple." What of the Purple Heart?
A U.S. military decoration awarded to those wounded or
killed in action, we all know, consists of a silver heart
bearing the effigy of George Washington, suspended
from a purple ribbon with white edges. (Rambo only
had *four!*) Purple is commemorial. Curiously, it is a very
rare color in flags, making the Welsh flag—on which
more than half the field is purple—somewhat unique.
Shakespeare everywhere writes of purple blood (for example, "Our lusty English, all with purpled hands/Dyed
in the dying slaughter of their foes," *King John*
II.i.322)—and even of purple tears *(Venus and Adonis,*
1054). And John Dryden writes,

> *I view a field of blood*
> *And Tiber rolling with a purple flood.*

As noted, it was a color known to Homer. In the
Odyssey, he uses the expression ἁλι-πόρφυρος, sea
purple, or purple as the sea. He also employs the

word πόρφυρω, meaning the boiling or the surging of the ocean, which extends to the idea of "mental disquiet," "being troubled." (King George III of England, who often became unhinged, was one who suffered from porphyria, a mental disturbance many associate with lycanthropy and hairy palms!) Vergil in the *Georgics* applies the same adjective to a sea swept by oars or disturbed by a heavy storm: *"quo non alius per pinguia culta/In mare purpureum violentior effluit amnis"* (IV.372–73) ("with more fury than all floods flows through fertile lands into the purple sea"; my translation). Another Homeric word, ἰοδνεφής, meant dark as violet. The sheep of Polyphemus were so described, as a matter of fact. Their prized "dark purple-black" wool, which as a commodity would have been highly valuable in ancient markets, was a visible sign of his wealth. We read,

ἄρσενες οἴες ἦσαν ευτρεφεες δαϲύμαλλσι
καλοί τε μέγαλοι τε, ἰοδνεφης εἶρος ἔχοντες

(Odyssey, II.285–86)

(The rams were well-grown, large and fine,
with coats of rich dark wool)

(my translation)

There is an original idea in Vergil's *Eclogues* that sheep feeding on rich pasture will soon naturally assume in their fleeces those rare colors most sought after and that men are at pains to dye their clothes.

> *Nec varios discet mentiri lana colores*
> *Ipse sed in pratis aries jam suave rubenti*
> *Murice, jam croceo mutabit vellera luto.*
>
> (IV.43–45)

(But the ram will, of his own accord, change [even while] in the meadows, the hue of his fleece, now with delicate purple, now with saffron-colored wool.)

(my translation)

Is this surprising? Tinting *dogs,* a fashion in the fifties, was big among New York matrons, Hollywood starlets, and, among others, deputations of what Noël Coward called "nice young men who sell antiques." There is no end to what people would color, and I am reminded that Jerry Garcia of the Grateful Dead once wanted to write songs, evoking the experience, about "colored silence" and "thick air." Singer-actress Doris Day, wearing a peekaboo shirt, actually appeared on the cover of *Collier's* (August 9, 1952) holding the leashes of six poodles—one dyed green, two blue, one orange, and two a glorious purple! That's not decadent enough? One can get one's pubic hair cut and colored—purple, not surprisingly, is a popular request—at Kaiserschnitt, a Berlin salon, for seventy-five dollars.

In the *Eclogues,* the lovely word *purpureum* means "beautiful," in the general sense that this adjective is used: *"Hic ver purpureum; varios hic flumina circum/Fundit humus flores"* (IX.40–41). We also find it used that way in the *Aeneid,* when we read, *"Purpureosque jacit flores"* (V.79). And what evokes the majesty of the color more than when in the *Aeneid* stricken Aeneas, gazing on the dead body of Pallas, son of Evander, who, having followed his friend to war, was, in Aeneas's absence, slain by Turnus, covers his body:

> *Tum gemines vestis auroque ostroque rigentis*
> *extulit Aeneas, quas illi laeta laborum*
> *ipsa suis quondam manibus Sidonia Dido*
> *fecerat et tenui telas discreverat auro*
>
> (XI.72–75)

(Then Aeneas brought forth two coverlets stiff with gold and purple, which Dido had wrought for him by hand, in other days, delighting in the work, and had streaked their webs with threads of gold.)

(my translation)

Of the ancient Argonaut story, a legend older than the *Odyssey*—Aeschylus wrote no fewer than six plays based on various Argonaut themes, most of which are lost, and Sophocles five or six as well (Euripides' *Medea,* the most famous one, survived)—Simonides in the sixth century B.C. says that the Fleece, the object of Jason's famous voyage to rob Aetas, king of Colchis of the fleece, was not gold but rather sea purple, which to many later interpreters became the symbol of a thundercloud. "In Greece, clouds could be seen heading east in summer towards Colchis, returning in spring and autumn, bearing rain," observes Tim Severin in *The Jason Voyage*. According to this imaginative interpretation, the intrepid Argonauts were "descended from watery spirits, such as water nymphs, river gods, and Poseidon himself." Cambridge don Janet Brown in her *The Voyage of the Argonauts* (1925), however, reaches the scholarly, and perhaps more likely, conclusion that Jason was a Minyan of Thessaly, an adventurer, and that his was "a real quest for real gold."

Violet, mauve, heliotrope, puce, burgundy, gridelin, lilac *(lilla,* after lilac, is the Estonian word for purple). How many names exist for how many variations of the color! Cranberry bogs in November are fuchsia, which, strictly speaking, is always reddish purple. Maroon is said to have a hint of yellow in it. Women's eye shadow tends toward lavender, which, like verbena violet, is reddish blue in hue. Vladimir Nabokov found on an arctic spring morning in St. Petersburg the slush in the streets "a rich purplish-blue shade," a color, he adds, "I have never seen anywhere since." Had he never heard of mallow, a particular color bluish red in hue? Or would it be mauvine, or mauvette? Magenta is a purplish shade of red, sort of amarinthine. Amy Lowell loathed magenta—no magenta flower was ever allowed in her garden. So how does one explain the fact that her custom-built Pierce Arrow limousine was maroon? Or that her chauffeur and footman wore the same matching livery? "Peacock ore" (bornite) is a mineral that tarnishes to an iridescent purple. *Aubergine* is French slang for the nose of a full-blown drunk. Wisteria is a delicate

light purple. Photographers, I'm told, commonly con-
sider yellow, cyan, and magenta as primary colors. Odd,
is it not? These three can be combined, additively, to
produce white. One type of sweet pea exhibits a striking
hue change; the flower, which is blue-purple in daylight,
appears red-purple in electric light, a change of approxi-
mately five hue steps. And there's a green bean, too, that
is purple until cooked.

A dying hydrangea leaf in fall, with its mortal
wound, becomes a glorious black or bisterlike purple,
very like poison ivy, like vines, like waters and wines,
like many of the purple lipsticks Lancôme puts out, such
as Ombre, Rose Taffeta, and Grappe Mystique. Or the
cheek colors Elizabeth Arden makes, like Woodrose,
Foxglove, and Rhubarb. Poppy lipsticks come in deep
purples, with wild names like their red-red "Courage"
and blue-red "Lust." It is a very protean color, with
multiple personae. That is the thing about purple. It
goes under more names than James James Morrison
Morrison Weatherby George Dupree. I mean, don't
snobbish and woosishly overfussy interior decorators, for
example, almost always try to avoid the common and
direct word *purple* and choose instead to refer to it
pretentiously as something like "raisin" or "garnet" or
"monsieur," "dahlia mauve" or "bellflower," "bouquet"
or "full wine," "frou-frou" or "cerise," "crepe iris" or
"paradise bird"?

"Over the years I've painted my rooms to match my
mood, my *mode de vie,* my passions and vicissitudes," my
friend writer Karen Elizabeth Gordon with characteris-

tic style and exuberance once wrote to me, "always nam-
ing the colors myself, after mixing the paints and the
metaphors: my carefree, tawny twenties in Tiepolo;
Dusting the Credenza; Steals Some Cookies; then Calva-
dos on the Double; the lovelocked room of Under My
Rhinebeau; the misted mauve I called Maud Gonne, Get
Out of the Sun; a frisky violet wing-tip that went by
Zephyr Laughing Gently at the Canterbury Pilgrims;
and the latest lavender of them all, Mirror Murmuring
On The Wall—a spirit summoned from the Coast of
Sorrows, Cracking The Windows and Flooring My Ceil-
ings: Life Is Too Big Without You."

Rimbaud regarded the letter *i* as purple. In his book
Provence, Ford Madox Ford admits to getting depressed
by "a purplish phantom of sunlight." The sounds of
names of cities appear to Proust in various combinations
of color. The city of Parma, for instance—for its soft
light, its uniform streets?—appears to him in *Du Côté du
chez Swann* as *"compact, lisse, mauve, et doux."* It stands for
bad taste for Thomas Beer, who in his book *The Mauve
Decade* chose the ten years of American life at the end of
the nineteenth century—he quotes Whistler's (some say
Wilde's) remark, "Mauve is just pink trying to be pur-
ple," for a motto of the lost elegant world of Emerson
and intellectual strength—symbolized by foibles, the
proliferation of Irish oafishness, bad manners, and so
forth, and women with attitudes of moral superiority
trying to dominate literature, art, and the stage. And
Ernest Dowson, who felt the letter *v* was not only the
most beautiful of all letters but could never be used too

often, once confided to Arthur Symons that of all the verse ever written, his ideal line was Edgar Allan Poe's "The viol, the violet, and the vine."

Purple to Emily Dickinson meant dusks and dawns and dreams, for the most part—her consistent choice for the magical, the marvelous, the "mystic," along with white, was purple—but there was a touch of melancholy and a presentiment of sorrow in it as well: "the purple well," "the purple territories/On Pizarro's shore," the "purple host," and of course death ("None can avoid this purple"). And in places in her poetry it evokes passion. I confess I myself have always loved too intensely, if intensely means inordinately, with the extended sense of having romantic overexpectations—in a purple way, I think—like other otherworldly and misguided rhapsodes, if I may put myself in such proud company, such as Hector Berlioz and Vincent van Gogh and Edgar Allan Poe and Emily Dickinson, certainly, Purps and Mauvets and Lavendricals who, having loved not wisely but too well, waited out many a dreadful night, bereaved, sleepless, in rumpled beds, for only yet Another Dawn. (Incidentally, *Another Dawn* is a wholly fictitious generic movie title used for years in Hollywood on the marquee of a cinema in any film when one was needed. Then in 1938 it actually became the title of an Errol Flynn flop.) To Marie Louise Shew, one of Poe's many affections, he wrote passionately of "one whose loveliness and love enveloped [his] existence in the purple atmosphere of Paradise," an echo perhaps of Keats, who in his sonnet "When I Have Fears" wrote:

And thrilling as I see . . .
Amid empurpled vapors far away
*To where the prospect terminate—*thee only.

Keats, by the way, along with Poe and Tennyson, was a very purple poet. His "The Eve of St. Agnes," almost a stained-glass poem, is filled with such color imagery ("and in his pained heart made purple riot," "and on her silver cross soft amethyst," and so forth), and of course the hero's name is Porphyro.

Gerard Manley Hopkins in his poem "Henry Purcell" describes a beach this way: "The thunder-purple seabeach plumed purple-of-thunder." And in his incomparable "The Blessed Virgin Compared to the Air We Breathe," he calls upon Mary to be "his atmosphere," assuring us of the beauty and holiness of the air and the sky, and indicates power in the richness of a purple sky: "Yet such a sapphire-shot/charged, steeped sky will not/ stain light." Purple rain, according to Edith Sitwell, is a reality: "The mauve summer rain/Is falling again—/It soaks through the eaves/And the ladies sleeves." D. H. Lawrence speaks of the wonder of "purplish elms" in his poem "Tommies in the Train." Ogden Nash never saw a "purple cow." There is no purple license plate, either, except for Idaho, with its touch of purple on the mountains (remember in Nabokov's *The Eye,* "I paused and looked up at a milk chocolate advertisement with lilac alps"?), but Volkswagen did make a purple car, as well as an orange one. Film star Olga Petrova once drove around Hollywood in a purple Packard touring sedan.

And the Lincoln Premiere—Elvis Presley owned one in 1956—had a wisteria purple bottom and a white top, like a lot of those dated hats he wore at the time. And as Pleasant Gehman, in her poem "White Trash Apocalypse" from *Señorita Sin,* rather fluorescently pleads,

> *When the end comes, honey,*
> *PLEASE*
> *put me in a lavender Earl Scheib $99.95 paint-job Pinto*
> *with home-made dingleball fringe around the headliner . . .*

There is purple soil, at least in Tahiti. Gauguin observes in his journal *Noa Noa,* "On the purple soil, long serpentine leaves of a metallic yellow make me think of a mysterious sacred writing of the ancient Orient" (tr. O. F. Theis). I have often seen purple sand. There are purple whelks, of course, seashells, and conches. (Oliver Wendell Holmes in "The Chambered Nautilus" refers to "its irised ceiling.") *And* there is distinctly "the purple light of a summer night in Spain," according to Cole Porter in "You're the Top," who rhythmically adds, "You're the National Gallery,/You're Garbo's salary,/You're cellophane." In 1929, when Libby Holman delivered a resonant and sexy rendition of "Moanin' Low" in *The Little Show, New York Times* critic Brooks Atkinson described her sultry contralto voice as having a "deep purple flame." And Vergil even speaks of a purple soul, or movement, or tide of life *("purpureum animam"* [*Aeneid,* IX.349]). Purple seas are not found only in Homer. Marianne Moore mentions "a sea the purple of a peacock's neck" in "The Steeplejack." (She also says of a jellyfish: "an amber-tinctured amethyst inhabits it," an odd image, no, for something so fluctuating?) And Alice Corbin writes in "What Dim Arcadian Pastures,"

> *What dim Arcadian pastures*
> *Have I known*
> *That suddenly, out of nothing,*
> *A wind is blown,*
> *Lifting a veil and a darkness,*
> *Showing a purple sea—*
> *And under your hair the fawn's eyes*
> *Look out on me?*

It is revealing that Eustacia Vye, "the proud girl from Budmouth" who celebrates—indeed, appreciates— very little in Thomas Hardy's *The Return of the Native,* prefers only the heath of penitential color. "I cannot endure the heath," she cries, "except in its purple season." Could it have been for the same dramatic reasons, one wonders, that Wilfrid Wilson Gibson gives of such a desolate world in his poem "On Hampstead Heath," when he describes how the heath

> *Sits tight-lipped, quaking, eager-eyed and pale*
> *Beneath her purple feather*

Henry James saw Italy as picturesquely violet. He remarked several times on "the great violet Campagna" in Rome and wrote to his sister, Alice, of the "beautiful views of Florence lying in her circle of hills like—like what?—like a chiselled jewel in a case of violet velvet," although at one juncture, traveling from Florence to Rome in 1878, he made angry note on the irksome innovation of an express train stopping in Orvieto at the base of the "horrid purple mountain" there. He admired the pale purple cyclamen in Roman neighborhoods, the "long-armed" violet flowers in Sienna, and even the details of porphyry in St. Mark's in Venice.

It is the color of transmission fluid, borscht, Easter and Resurrection, the old dimpled windows on Beacon Hill in Boston, political ribbons, lavender pastilles, orchids, Lent, shadows, carbon paper, razor blades, birettas, dung beetles, *boudin* (slang in France for an "ugly girl") or blood sausage, stamp pads and stamp pad ink, mussels, Irish passports, the "color added" punch on orange skins, and an angry wave smashing its lilac foam on the sand. Bears' tongues are purple. So are the vinous noses of drunks, oil in water, nipples and aureolae, seaweed, liverwurst, shrunken heads, bug lights, and the eighth ribbon in equestrian three-day eventing. In Judaism it is the color of God, and for the French government, the circular stamp mark *(violet de bureau),* in the center of which sits two capital letters, R.F., means *République Française.* It is the color for the direction east in Ireland, the power supply in chassis wiring, twilight— what else did Browning mean in "Love Among the Ruins" when he wrote of "the quiet-coloured end of evening"?)—and on maps in weatherfront markings the color of an occluded front. Maori tattoos (a.k.a. *moko* or *whakairo)* with their beads, spirals, curls, and so forth, are purple. As are grapes, gum, quartz, hives, tuna fish, hand stamps, printer's ink, black lights, red wine stains on white linen, leeches, the seats in many opera houses, and the purpurescent five-piastre note in Egypt. It is the irresistibly deep and beckoning color of leather, heather, feathers, sagebrush, winter slush, Tibetan mush, age, sage, shade, grapeade, a forest glade, mince pies, winter skies, a harlot's eyes, a baby's cries, vicious lies, butchers' dyes, and purple drifts of evening snow.

Aren't Weimaraner blue dogs purple? And, oddly, guppies and goldfish? ("Their scaly armour's Tyrian hue/ Through richest purple to the view/Betrayed a golden gleam," we read in Thomas Gray's "Ode on the Death of a Favorite Cat, Drowned in a Tub of Gold Fishes.") Isn't there also a hint of purple in such things as milk chocolate? Crow black? Roasted woodcock? Pine boughs laden with snow? The *interieur* of vinegar? Smoke? Rain? Doesn't the "environmentally friendly aqueous coating" used on a lot of modern postcards have the faintest patina of purple? And what about Henry Higgins's mother in the film *My Fair Lady*? In the words of Wendy Lesser in *His Other Half,* she wears "a grey satin-and-lace outfit in which the grey is so warm as to be almost lilac." Isn't there also a tint of purple in mahogany, shale, and rhubarb, or "pie plant," as old Cape Codders call it? Used carbon paper? Old shiny antiquated "ditto" sheets that teachers, before the age of copy machines, handed out to classes, usually in the form of exams? (They always smelled like alcoholic drinks to me.) The hides of rhinoceroses? Sponge stone, or volcanic rock? Certain slates? Wet stone scree, the kind, say, found along the

Rio Grande on the high road between Taos and Santa Fe? Metal caskets? Plastic videocassette boxes? Elvis Presley's pompadour?

Speaking of the pompadour, it is not only an elaborate, unusually high coiffure, but also in fact a shade of purple—"a color between claret and purple," according to Rosie Boycott in *Batty, Bloomers, and Boycott: A Little Etymology of Eponymous Words,* who adds, "the Fifty-Sixth Foot Regiment (now part of the Third Battalion Royal Anglia regiment) were nicknamed *Pompadours* from the use of this color in their uniforms. There is even a tropical South American bird with brilliant crimson-purple plumage named after her [Marquise de Pompadour]."

There is also a strict and distinct concordance of purple, at least in my mind, to high-rise windows, gin, and the flesh of a fat person's palm (Sen. Ted Kennedy, I once noticed up close, has fat, purplish, meaty hands), as well as to Cordovan leather, severe shock, oyster shells, gasoline, varicose veins, clay mud banks, the Liebestod of Wagner's *Tristan und Isolde,* and the sun shining through a person's paper-thin ears. It is also the color of Taco Bell uniforms. And I remember a girl who made love *a pioggia,* as they say in Italy, like a gentle rain, which in my memory will forever be violet. It is also the hopeful color of youth in Jack Kerouac's novel *Maggie Cassidy.* (One of Kerouac's all-time favorite songs, by the way, was "Deep Purple," which is also the name of a late-sixties English rock band, who loved to trash their guitars and smash up the stage.) As to music, Scriabin considered both D-flat and A-flat to be purple. Goethe believed that the French horn had a distinctly purple sound, while Kandinsky heard in purple the acoustic shadow both an English horn and the deep notes of wood instruments. (Personally speaking, I hear purple, *not,* as might be expected in the contemporary grunge group Hole's song "Violet," but in the tympany, for instance, at the beginning of Beethoven's Violin Concerto in D Major and in the "Intermezzo" of *Cavalleria Rusticana,* which by the way, along with Mozart's Fugue in C Minor for Two Pianos [K426], the most beautiful of all his compositions for piano, I would like to have played at my funeral.) A purple (or green or orange) dancing bear is a symbol of the Grateful Dead. And did you know that there are colored musical instruments? The G. Leblanc Corporation of Kenosha, Wisconsin, makes a lilac clarinet—"Dazzlers," they're called—as well as those colored red, yellow, blue, green, or white.

"Violet corresponds to a shrill note of high pitch," says Maitland Graves in *The Art of Color and Design,* noting that of all the colors, purple has the highest frequency and shortest wavelength. Since we know that beyond the ends of the spectrum are the "invisible" colors, infrared and ultraviolet, can't one legitimately say that violet light is an octave higher in pitch than red light? The spaceship *Endeavor* went into orbit on March 2, 1995, with the specific mission to try to determine the nature of ultraviolet light in space emitted from stars and quasars. Do you recall, by the way, that the "Purple Staff for Distinguished Music-Making in the Line of Duty" was a medal hung around Sgt. Pepper's neck in the 1978 movie of the Beatles' *Sgt. Pepper's Lonely Hearts Club Band?* And then there is Prince, whose color is purple, and his song "Purple Rain."

What about the human body? George Gissing, who frequented prostitutes—his first wife, of an early marriage, was one—was disfigured in his face by a purple syphilitic scar. After her miracle recovery from a suicide attempt, Laura Riding, theatrically referring to herself as "Finality," according to her biographer Deborah Baker, took to wearing a shawl with a "representation of her damson-colored surgical scar on it." The forehead of Mikhail Gorbachev is of that portwine color. Lady Annamaria Oliovino, the pittrice, in Bernard Malamud's story "Still Life," from *Idiot's First,* has a "violet mouth." Singer Sheena Easton wears purple lipstick on the 45 rpm picture sleeve of her song "Do It for Love." "His bald purplish head now looked for all the world," writes Melville of the harpooner Queequeg in *Moby-Dick,* "like a mildewed skull." *Moulinyan,* from *melanzane,* eggplant, is the contemptuous slang Italian term for an idiot, a fool, or a black person. "His nose swelled up like a big white grape and turned violet inside," writes Walker Percy in *The Last Gentleman* (1966). A cop in William Styron's *Lie Down in Darkness* chastises tipsy Peyton Loftis, who, preoccupied with her own thoughts of suicide, is almost hit by a car in New York City but in a daze sees only "the sweat run purple underneath his shirt." William Hazlitt says of his friend S. T. Coleridge, " 'A certain tender bloom his face o'erspread,' a purple tinge as we see it in the pale thoughtful complexions of the Spanish portrait painters." And the subject of John

Singer Sargent's famous portrait *Madame X* has subtle lavender skin, which was supposedly a feature of that intriguing woman, Madame Virginie Avegno Gautreau, as she appeared in real life.

Prune Face, a character in the Dick Tracy comic strip, has a purple face. So does the vintner and distiller in Charles Dickens's *Barnaby Rudge,* Old Langdale. Dickens had a highly purple palette. Mrs. Bloss, a fat, red-faced boarder at Mrs. Tibbs's in *Sketches By Boz,* wears a pelisse "the colour of the interior of a damson pie." A certain foppishness is almost always suggested by purple habiliments. In *Little Dorrit,* young John Chivery is always neatly attired in a plum-colored coat, "even though Dorrit refused his suit." And Mr. William Guppy, clerk to Kenge and Carboy in *Bleak House,* sports lilac kid gloves. (He too is spurned by Esther Summerson.) There are also purple breasts, if we believe Baudelaire, who writes in his poem "Femmes Damnées," from *Les Fleurs du mal,*

> *Saint Antoine a vu surgir comme des laves*
> *Les seins nus et pourprés de ses tentations*

> (Saint Anthony saw the naked purple breasts
> Of his temptations rise up like lava)
>
> (tr. William Aggeler)

As an altar boy, I remember seeing a plethora of purple tongues, and even purpler papillae, when people knelt at the railing as I served for priests at Communion time at St. Francis of Assisi. And did you know our hearts are purple? "A purple stone in a red forest," as one physician described it.

The Purple Island (1633)—also called the "Isle of Man"—by Phineas Fletcher, is an odd poem in twelve cantos that describes the human body as an island. Bones are the foundation; veins and arteries, rivers; and the heart, liver, and stomach are goodly cities. The teeth are "twice sixteen porters, receivers of the customary rent." The liver is the arch-city, where two purple streams (two great rivers of blood) "raise their boil-heads." The eyes are watchtowers, the sight, the warder. And taste and tongue are man and wife, with the intellect a prince whose five senses are his counselors.

The "punk generation," with its greasy spikes and Technicolor quiffs, is by no means the first to have garish purple hair. In Andrew Marvell's "A Poem Upon the Death of Oliver Cromwell," a tonsure of Eliza, the protector's daughter (Lady Claypole) is succinctly memorialized: "And now Eliza's purple Locks were shorn." The allusion may go back to another well-known rape of a lock and the story of Nisus and Scylla in Ovid's *Metamorphosis.* Nisus, king of Megara, was beseiged by Minos. Scylla, daughter of Nisus, fell in love with Minos, and in order to win his affection cut off her father's famous locks of purple hair, on which his life depended: "This [a city] Nisus held; whose head a purple haire/ 'Mong those of honorable silver bare." As opposed to the deliberate, puritanical simplicity adopted by proponents of the French Revolution, later indulgences and self-adornments by ladies under Napoleon included colored wigs, at twenty-five louis each—shaped à la Minerve or à la Liberté—and a very popular color was purple. The dark Italian beauty, photographer Tina Modotti, was described by Mexican art critic Lolo de la Torriente as having "plum-colored hair." Mavis Gallant speaks of Colette's "mop of mauve-tinted hair." The people of the sea in the fantastical submarine world of World's End Island, in C. S. Lewis's stories, have dark purple hair. In Edith Wharton's morbid ghost story *After Holbein,* a once regal New York hostess—supposedly modeled, it is said, on Lady Astor herself—continues in her senility to receive nonexistent guests at her Fifth Avenue mansion, always wearing her jewels and a purple wig. Wigs, yes. But it's mostly Mother Rit and Father Tintex! Andy Warhol vestal Ultra Violet—Isabelle Collin-Dufresne, when she was home—predictably had purple hair and a French accent. St. Catherine of Siena in William T. Vollmann's *The Rainbow Stories* has violet hair, "almost translucent in the sunlight . . . persistent and inescapable," and in this tale with its Heideggerian ontifications we are told that her thought "traveled like bullets along the violet beams of her gaze." Miss Pennycandy, Krusty the Clown's secretary on *The Simpsons,* has purple hair. Aren't trolls reputed to have purple hair? And in his poem "Before Parting," Swinburne writes,

> *I know not how this last month leaves your hair*
> *Less full of purple color and hid spice. . . .*

As far as real life goes, the Copacabana girls of 1940s and 1950s New York–nightclub fame, with their upswept tresses—as well as mink panties and fruited turbans—often dyed their hair green, orange, and purple to match their flamboyant, sequined costumes.

A friend of mine, Julie Jones, once told me that in Cuba, people told her mother that if she rubbed Russian Violet cologne on her baby daughter's bald head, her hair would grow in curly, and she did, and it did!

Does Liz Taylor have violet eyes, as is constantly reported? I doubt it. The one time I saw her, being chauffeured regally down Mass. Ave., Cambridge, through Harvard Square, in a Hasty Pudding parade, she *was* wearing a purple turban. As a first wedding anniversary to his wife, Eddie Fisher, the husband she would later publicly jilt, gave Liz a complete set of all of her movie scripts, including photos and memorabilia, which were all bound in lavender leather, with the endpapers done in lavender paisley. And I remember reading that Malcolm Forbes gave her a purple Harley-Davidson sportster. I would have an easier time believing violet eyes of lewd and sultry Hedy Lamarr when in the film *White Cargo* she lickerishly whispered, "I am Tondelayo." According to Lady Colin Campbell in her book *Diana in Private,* "vulgarizing her appearance by heightening the colour of her eyes with a blue eyeliner pencil on the inside rim of the lower lid," Lady Di picked up this trick of the makeup trade from none other than Elizabeth Taylor, whose so-called violet eyes probably owe less to God than to an Estée Lauder "automatic" pencil. Alla Nazimova, the Russian actress, we are told by Miss Mercedes de Acosta, had "large violet eyes"—the two women had once met after a large benefit in Madison Square Garden, at which time Nazimova, wildly dressed as a Cossack and draped in a Russian flag, was running madly around the arena and leaping up every few steps. Oscar Wilde wrote to Lily Langtry in late 1883, "I am going to be married to a beautiful girl named Constance Lloyd, a grave, slight, violet-eyed little Artemis." And one of Cecil Beaton's worshipful notes on Greta Garbo went: "The eyes like an eagle's of pale mauve."

In *Billy Budd,* we have an example in Claggart's violet eyes of the moronism of hatred: "Meanwhile the accuser's [Claggart's] eyes, removing not as yet from the blue dilated ones [Billy's], underwent a phenomenal change, their wonted rich violet color blurring into a muddy purple." And Melville adds the ghastly detail: "Those lights of human intelligence, losing human expression, were gelidly protruding like the alien eyes of certain uncatalogued creatures of the deep." Within seconds, Claggart will be a corpse, lying dead, those eyes glass, useless as marbles.

Virginia Woolf, describing the young hero of her novel *Orlando,* writes that he had eyes "like drenched violets, so large that the water seemed to have brimmed in them and widened them." Miss Wonderly in Dashiell Hammett's *The Maltese Falcon* has eyes "of blue that was almost violet." In 1850, Gustave Flaubert describes the Egyptian dancer—he much preferred Oriental women over Western—as having a "dark violet gaze." The lovely Madonnina in Baron Corvo's *In His Own Image* has "truthful, peacock-purple eyes." Malcolm Cowley's Roxane in a poem from *Blue Juniata* is "Flatbush born, was twenty six,/had lavender eyes and frizzly hair." The A-ha kachina doll, which is used in Hopi Indian bean dances, has bright red shoes and purple eyes. "Shrinking Violet," a cartoon character from the sixties who went on to become a fat little cloth doll (my sisters owned one) with a flat bum and woolly yellow-yarn hair that parted in the middle—she was one of the first string-pull talking dolls, I believe—had violet eyes. And do you remember in Lawrence Durrell's mysterious and polychromatic novel *Justine,* the energetic character Little Mnemjian, "a dwarf with a violet eye that has never lost its childhood"?

Speaking of eyes, aren't phosphenes purple, what we see after rubbing our eyeballs when our lids are closed, those luminous impressions, explosions of photoma, afterimages like %#*~^*@! brought up like fireworks? And when sunbathing, don't our lids retain a purplish bejeweled impression of the sun in lively sparkling mosaics?

Purple makes its appearance at choice moments in the oddest little places. Little Black Sambo, for instance, in Helen Bannerman's famous story, wears purple shoes. Melanoids, who have purple gums and a blue-black, almost auberginesque skin, like the Watusi, seem to love purple clothes. Ronald Firbank found their blackness touched by mauve. "Little mauve nigger boy," he writes in *Prancing Nigger,* "I t'ink you break my heart." Who can forget Ornita, the slim thirty-year-old black woman in Bernard Malamud's short story "Black Is My Favorite Color"? The narrator worshipfully observes, "That was the night she wore a purple dress, and I thought to myself, my God, what colors. Who paints that picture paints a masterpiece." Preceptors and Trollopean rectors and English prebendaries of old wore purple soutanes, didn't they, and violet socks? "For example, I said that the violet legs of my college-rector were formed like little Jacobean communion rails," says George Arthur Rose in Fr. Rolfe's novel *Hadrian VII.* Mr. Verity, Peter Anthony's detective in novels like *How Doth the Little Crocodile* (1952) and *Withered Murder* (1955), who is also fond of black Cuban cigars and swimming, relies on an old purple bathing suit he had bought thirty years before. There is Miranda the Purple Bird of Paradise, one of Dr. Doolittle's adoptees. And Violet Beauregarde in Roald Dahl's *Charlie and the Chocolate Factory* (1964) turns purple after chewing experimental gum, which brings us to the subject of purple in matters of food.

Purple restaurants turn people off. No one wants to eat purple food—the rarest color in foods. Imagine a purple sauce, purée, or *salpiçon!* It is rare even in food packaging, to which, whenever it should appear, only kids seem to respond. In Spanish, ironically, the expression "to turn purple" *(ponerse morado)* means to stuff yourself with food! Sauerbraten, when marinating, is real purple. And aren't most *abats*—tongue, liver, kidney? Trout is a bluish purple. (The fish in Lucian of Samosata's *True History,* for that matter, have "the color of the taste of wine.") Salami, I suppose it could be argued, is purple. And maybe mince as well. What pâté isn't purple? As to vegetables, what do we have, eggplant and purple cabbage and asparagus ("finely stippled in mauve and azure," observes Proust [bk. 1, p. 2], "through a series of imperceptible changes to their white feet . . . a rainbow-loveliness that was not of this world"). "Violet Queen" is a cauliflower. (I once ate a delicious *piatto del giorno* of purple cauliflower in Paterno, Sicily.) There is definitely a purple onion. There also exists a purple Old World potato, and many sweet potatoes *(camotes)* in Mexico are purple. Burgundy beans are purple, and there is a purple snap bean called Purple Teepee. The patzcuaro chile, of fairly medium heat, is an oxbloodish purple. But it is as if somehow nothing in nature, as regards food, quite dares to declare itself fully purple, so powerful is its chroma. Much in natural food is of course *touched* with purple—the tops of turnips, a mild Japanese mustard green called Osaka Purple, whose leaves are tinged that color, the Cherokee Purple tomato, a dusky pink with purple shoulders, and purple perilla (or red shiso), a popular herb in North Vietnamese cooking. Beets, I suppose, are a sort of magenta—Einstein loathed both the vegetable and the color—though they really have their own mixed tint. Amaranth plants are a kind of mauvish pink. So is rose-leaf jam. Queen Elizabeth I had a fanatical craving for lavender conserve. And Concord grapes are purple, of course, along with a good many other kinds of grapes, although grape-seed oil is yellow. (The grape leafhopper, whose delectable main food is grapes, is also, not surprisingly, purple.) Alexander Pushkin, in his carpological tribute to this special fruit, "Grapes," writes,

> *I shall not miss the roses, fading*
> *As soon as spring's fleet days are done.*

> *I like the grapes whose clusters ripen*
> *Upon the hillside in the sun. . . .*
> (tr. Babette Deutsch)

There is granadilla, a purple passion fruit. *(Granada* is pomegranate in Spanish.) Prunes. And plums. ("You should have had plums tonight,/In an eighteenth-century dish," writes Wallace Stevens in "Floral Decorations for Bananas.") Lao Tzu was born under a plum tree. Many exotic fruits from South and Central America and Asia have rinds that are purple and largely wet, like the mangosteen, which has a juicy, white, raspberry-flavored pulp and a thick purple skin. (I will forego here expostulating on my theory that everything is better when it is moist.) Nor should we forget artichokes. I wonder if Robin Robertson's poem "Artichoke" is definitive, the first stanza of which goes,

> *The nubbed leaves*
> *come away*
> *in a tease of green, thinning*
> *down to the membrane*
> *the quick, purpled*
> *beginnings of the male*

"It is always allowable to ask for artichoke jelly [!] with your boiled venison," observes Lewis Carroll in his essay "Hints for Etiquette; or, Dining Out Made Easy," "however, there are houses where this is not supplied." *Artichoke jelly not supplied? Whither grace?*

What else as to purple foods? Raisins? Grape jam or

jelly? Grape Pop-Tarts? Candied violets? ("Candied violets are the Necco Wafers of the overbred," observes Fran Lebowitz.) Bad baloney? Actually, the water that black beans have been soaking in—ironically?—is purple. But I mean, forget it, it's all downhill from there. There are no purple drinks. Well, grape juice. Certain rare violet grappas. And of course wine. Thyonian juice! Persephone's grape! Plonk! Keats's "blushful Hippocrene" ("With beaded bubbles winking at the brim/And purple stained mouth") may qualify as being purple, but who knows anyone who has ever *tried* blushful Hippocrene? Lord Byron in his notebooks praises gin as his own personal Hippocrene because of the boldness he says it gave him. Needless to say, most red wines are actually purple, just as "white" wine is actually yellow, most of the time. Have you ever heard of a cloyingly sweet, violet-colored liqueur called *parfait d'amour?* It is made from violet water, which in turn is made from an infusion of flowers. Speaking of foods and flowers, there is a restaurant in Rousillon where I once ate pale lavender ice cream. There is also a fake coffee called Roma, a drink, along with cereal, chicory, molasses, and maltodextrin, that is purply—a legitimate adjective—that is actually made from beets. *Beets!* Novelist Paul West in *A Stroke of Genius* bravely admits to having tried Roma, while recovering from a mild stroke. Many breads made without eggs, by the way, using canola oil for fat, get their moist crumb not from sugar but from the addition of grated beets, which, have no fear, disappear in the batter.

Marcia Madhuri Acciardo in her 1977 vegetarian cookbook, *Light Eating for Survival* ("More Than 450

Raw Food Recipes"), writes, "Purple is inspiring and spiritual food for the mind. It is for meditation and quiet. It is etheric, electric, and full of light." Maybe when we dine we should always use purple bowls and eat in purple rooms?

There are no purple M&M's—and in any given bag only 10 percent are the secondary colors orange and green, as opposed to 20 percent of yellow and red ones. Brown, the most popular color in that candy and the *only* color when the candy was first made in 1940, is more than healthily represented by a full 30 percent. In a recent M&M contest for a new color, purple and pink lost out to blue in popularity; in 1943, purple *was* made for a while, but it proved so unsatisfactory, it was replaced by tan in 1949. As far as desserts go, "Andy Warhol once created a TV ad for Schrafft's," Paul Dickson discloses for posterity in *The Great American Ice Cream Book,* "featuring the Warhol Sundae, portrayed in wavering notes of puce, magenta, chartreuse and mauve." Was Warhol, who adored sweets and who once said, "Sex is the biggest nothing of all time," sublimating in the process other, more immediate, but complicated, drives?

Overwriting, like purple food, is to be eschewed. It is, in Augustan terms, almost as if there is something immoral or ersatz in it. Only the truly brilliant manage it well. (Didn't Oscar Wilde, whom the ornate never challenged, once say, "We cannot go to war with France because her prose is perfect"?) The allusion to "purple patches," highly colored or florid passages in a literary work that is (generally speaking) otherwise undistinguished, goes back to Horace's *De Arte Poetica,* where this trenchant observation is made:

> *Inceptis gravibus plerumque et magna professis,*
> *Purpureus, late qui splendeat, unus et alter*
> *Adsuitur pannus*

(Often to a work of grave purpose and high promise, one or two purple patches are sewed on to give the effect of color.)
(my translation)

When Henry James refers to Violet Hunt as his "Purple Patch," one still wonders if it was because of her name or her writing or her labored company.

And there are lush, bombastic, grandiloquent, orotund, turgid, sesquipedalian ranters and gum-beating *speakers* as well—they love synonyms and lists—like Euphues and Mr. Micawber and Nestor and Dick Swiveller and Sir Piercie Shafton and Calhoun the lawyer and Jack Falstaff and Pistol, who are undoubtedly purple people-eaters. And I believe that D. H. Lawrence, who wrote some of the worst and most misguidedly overenthusiastic passages in all of literature, actually uses the word *purple* in several of them!

"I know my prose is touched with plum pudding but then all the prose belonging to the poetic continuum is; it is intended to give a stereoscopic effect to character. And events aren't in serial form but collect here and there like quanta, like real life," writes Lawrence Durrell in *Balthazar.* And he is of course correct. Purple writers are invariably daring. Often brave. Electric. There are far worse. There are "white" writers, for instance. Cliché-meisters. Tin stampers. *Evirati.* Hacks. I know a man who is fifty-five, has written about twenty-five books, assorted novels and travel books, dedicates them, not to cats, but to just about everyone else, and yet not a single one of his books, isomorphic and literal, takes a narrative chance or shows any originality. They are predictably all the same. Pale. Poached. Undermedicated. Middle-brow. Strictly white bread. You know what I think: *Why bother?* Wasn't it Eugène Delacroix who said, "Without the masterpiece, there is no artist"?

"He is very sad," someone once said to me of this person, picking up one of his junket-white books and idly dropping it on top of a remainder pile. "Shouldn't he try harder than—"

"Rearing turkeys?" I asked, for I couldn't help but agree with him.

Speaking of writing, Ford Madox Ford thought that poet Christina Maria Rossetti was deprived. "And we may say that her whole life of writing poems on the corner of her Bloomsbury wash-stand was one long obsession of longing for [Provence], that South that begins after you have passed Valence—*entre La Mer et la Durance,*" he writes of Rossetti, with whom, together with Henry James and exactly no one else, he rates as "the only significant figures of London Literature in the XIXth century" and who, he was convinced, pined with the obsession of an exile for the land of the contests of the troubadours, for the courts of love, for the sun, in short, for the violaceous. He may have had these lines of hers in mind:

> *Raise me a dais of silk and down,*
> *Hang it with vair and with purple dyes,*
> *Carve it with doves and pomegranates*
> *And peacocks with a hundred eyes . . .*
> *Work it in gold and silver grapes*
> *In leaves and silver fleur de lys*
> *Because the birthday of my life*
> *Is come, my love is come to me.*

But Rossetti never dissembled. Can Ford have forgotten her poignant line from "The Royal Princess," recapitulating the poet's dream life, no doubt, "For all I shine so like the sea, and am purple like the west"?

Purple is the color for repentance, contrition, endurance, and suffering, symbolizing the Passion of Christ, who wore battered purple before the Crucifixion. There is an almost Xenophontic piety to the closed and hermetic stateliness and beauty of the color. A priest's stole, during confession, is purple—as are gilded dalmatics, funeral copes, lenten veils and coverlets, and velvet confessional kneelers and those of many prie-dieux. It is the color, liturgical purple, of vimpa and burse and a bishop's zucchetto or skullcap (abbots wear black, cardinals red). "Kissing the Sacred Purple, I am Your Eminence's most obedient servant" is the fustianate closing paragraph of a letter to the late William Cardinal O'Connell of Boston. Pope John Paul II's book *Crossing the Threshold of Hope* (1994) was symbolically issued in purple cloth. It is the liturgical color of Lent and Advent, from vespers on the Saturday before Advent Sunday to vespers on the eve of the Nativity; from vespers of the day before Ash Wednesday, throughout Lent (excepting Good Friday), to vespers on the eve of Easter. The joyous feast of Christmas, ironically, is a penitential season. With purple vestments, the coming of the Holy Infant is celebrated by a reflective church, ever mindful that the Incarnation leads to the Crucifixion. No more beautiful lines, I feel, can be found relating to the holy day of Christmas, with that significant touch of purple, than Martin Adan's "Nativity":

> *Y en la penumbra*
> *los bosques de ocaso*
> *las frondas moradas*
> *tu caballera mulle sus pajas*
> *para el Dios niño*

> (And in the half-light
> the groves of sunset
> purple foliage
> your hair spreads its straw
> for the infant God)
>   (my translation)

In the Christian liturgy, purple symbolizes, as well, sacerdotal rule, penitence, humility, fasting, sadness, remorse, temperance, martyrdom, and authority. (Look at Raphael's *Pope Leo X with His Nephews Giulio de'Medici and Luigi de'Rossi* [c. 1518] if you want a good idea of the full authoritative force of ecclesiastical purple.) I once attended Ash Wednesday services at the Cathedral of Our Lady of Guadalupe in Tijuana, Mexico, where in mystic pedigree, purple veils covered crucifix and altar and statue like a thunderstorm of purple vespers, and it seemed to rain in the cavernous darkness within like the anguish of this world. It is the color for the second period of mourning, black being the first. Ribbons at funerals are purple. Sar Peladan, the Rosicrucian mage— a former bank clerk—wore a flowing violet robe for his pageants. The stage curtains of evangelist and adept Aimee Semple McPherson *Hoffman's* (she was married *three* times!) garish five-thousand-seat Angelus Temple in Los Angeles—Charlie Chaplin advised her on the sets—were purple, as only a full-fledged ecclesiastical drama queen would have them. ("The wildest night-life I encountered [on the West Coast] was at Aimee McPherson's tabernacle," wrote H. L. Mencken in a 1927 *Photoplay* article. "I saw no wildness among the moviefolk.") As a color, purple in the chromomorph of chaste remorse is often associated with the passionate sinner St. Mary Magdalene, whom Ronald Firbank (or better, Mrs. Creamway, his mouthpiece) ludicrously, but prankishly, insists in his play *A Disciple from the County* "was actually engaged to John the Baptist!" In Leonora Speyer's poem "Mary Magdalene" we read,

> *I think that Mary Magdalene*
> *Was just a woman who went to dine;*
> *And her jewels covered her empty heart,*
> *And her gown was the color of wine.*

Angels can also be purple, as Nancy Campbell demonstrates in "The Apple Tree":

I saw the archangels in my apple-tree last night,
I saw them like great birds in the starlight—
Purple and burning blue, crimson and shining white.

Regarding depravity, Jezebel, the cruel queen who tried to replace the worship of God in Israel by Baal, was, in my opinion, not so much a "scarlet" woman as a classically purpureal one, which in those days, chromatically speaking, amounted to virtually the same thing. A princess of Tyre, which was then the center of dye making, Jezebel was foreign born. Her father had even been a priest of Astarte, the voluptuous Phoenician goddess associated with luxury and fleshly intemperance. More than any of the other famously lewd women in Holy Scripture, Jezebel is associated with lasciviously having made up her face and eyes—"She painted her eyes, and adorned her head, and looked out the window" (2 Kings 9:30) remains, iconographically, the very portrait of temptation—and she would almost surely have used violet on her eyes and crushed cochineal as lipstick, to say nothing of wearing purple robes. (A woman *can* be dressed as a harlot [see Prov. 7:10], and Jeremiah even inveighed against the harlots of Babylon wrapped in purple clothing [see Baruch 6:11].) It is also possible that, as was the habit with many Roman women, Jezebel might have gone so far as to trace the veins of her temples with delicate amarinthine lines of blue or purple, a quaint cosmetological practice at the time that somehow never managed to survive the ancient world.

According to legend, Salomé's seven veils, lewdly shed one by one as she danced before Herod Antipas—a man who had the unique maldistinction of being personally singled out for criticism ("that fox") by Jesus Christ—were purple. Although she bore the shame of marrying her great uncle, Herod Philip II (it wasn't bad enough that her father, Herod Philip, was also her uncle, whose own half-brother, Antipas, also later married Salomé's mother, Herodias?), Salomé is never once mentioned by name in Scripture but rather is identified only as the "daughter of Herodias," which theologians have ascribed to the Evangelists' desire that it be her wicked mother's name, and not hers, that goes down in history in nefarious disrepute.

Israel of course got its valuable purple cloth from Phoenicia, using it almost exclusively for curtains and hangings for the tabernacle (Exod. 26:1; 27:16) as well as for the temple (2 Chron. 2:7). Linen, along with purple, is often mentioned in the Old Testament as a symbol of wealth and position. In Esther, we read about Mordecai: "And Mordecai went out from the presence of the king in royal apparel of blue and white, and with a great crown of gold, and with a garment of fine linen and purple" (Esther 8:15). And in Luke 16:19: "There was a certain rich man, which was clothed in purple and fine linen, and fared sumptuously every day."

We read in Scripture of Lydia, the seller of purple. Paul and his companions witnessed to this businesswoman, a merchant (*porphuropolis,* or πορφυρόπολις) who earned her livelihood buying and selling purple dye and dyed cloth, and it is thought by many that she was Paul's first European convert. *"And a certain woman named Lydia, a seller of purple, of the city of Thyatira, which worshipped God, heard us: whose heart the Lord opened, that she attended unto the things which were spoken of by Paul* (Acts 16:14). (As it was not a name used in ancient days, the woman in all probability was not named Lydia but rather came from a region of Lydia.) The hospitality she extended Paul and his companions *("Come into my house and abide there")* suggests that because of her trade, her house was no doubt spacious and there were many servants in the household. It is possible that Lydia, or the Lydian woman, had been carrying on the trade of her deceased husband, for she was living in Philippi at the time she met Paul, which probably means that she would have moved there only with her husband from Thyatira, a northwestern suburb of Sardis, capital of Lydia, which had a thriving trade in purple dye, since in that day and age women almost never traveled alone. Even in ancient Greece, where wisdom flourished, women were not allowed to walk abroad except under surveillance. "Twice in Greek tragedy (Sophocles' *Electra* and *Antigone)* girls are brusquely told to go indoors, which is their proper place," says H.D.F. Kitto in *The Greeks.* Great openness toward women, however, was shown in early Christianity. It was a distinctly innovative aspect of the ministry of Jesus, who flouted Jewish tradition by speaking freely with women. The wife of Herod's steward even supported Jesus. Lydia happened to be a merchant, but many women of the early church, not unlike her, served as teachers, apostles, even prophets. It goes without saying that Lydia, who also offered her house as a sanctuary and refuge to Paul and Silas even at a later date, when they returned from prison (Acts 16:40), had no small role in establishing the Christian church at Philippi.

There is an easy progression from the holy to the remote and exotic. Arnheim, Edgar Allan Poe's mysterious city, is surrounded by a vast amphitheater of purple mountains. And in the *Decameron* of Boccaccio, certain heliotrope stones worn in the arc of Bengodi make whoever wears them invisible. In Ursula LeGuin's novel *A Wizard of Earthsea,* all of the houses of Hort Town have purple tiles. The sun resembles a purple flower, out of whose center streams forth the light of the world, in Marie Anne de Roumier Robert's *Les Ondines* (1768). In James Barrie's *Peter Pan, or The Boy Who Wouldn't Grow Up* (1904), boy fairies wear mauve in their nests in the treetops in Never Never Land. The dominant color of Gillikin Country in L. Frank Baum's *The Wonderful Wizard of Oz* (1900)—with unique towns with names like Rith metic, Catty Corners, and Squee-Gee Villa (where the winged monkeys come from)—is purple. And Old Mother West Wind and her Merry Little Breezes in Thornton W. Burgess's bedtime storybooks always "come down from the Purple Hills." What occult link exists between the color purple and islands? On Homer's Ogygia, an island in the Mediterranean, where Calypso the nymph lived, the soft meadows are thick with violets. Purple Island, which lies in the Pacific Ocean at latitude 45, is inhabited, ironically, by the Red Ethiopians, a tribe of unknown origin, so called because of the color of their skin. The island of Her in Alfred Jarry's *Gestes et Opinions du Docteur Faustroll, Pataphysicien* (1911) is ruled by a cyclops who can see things that are visible only in ultraviolet light. And the lovely, faraway, mysterious island of Bali-Hai shimmers amethystine in the misty distance in the film version of Rodgers and Hammerstein's musical *South Pacific,* which calls to mind, as far as exotic places go and the way they beckon, the fortress of Shahr-i-Zohak, built by the Turks in the sixth century A.D., above the Bamian River valley in remote Afghanistan, near the Kulu River. "A purple mountain rears up," writes Arnold Toynbee in *Between Oxus and Jumna,* "crowned by this purple fortress, line above line of purple curtain-walls and towers."

What about purple spiderwebs as fashion? The temple altars on the Island of the Blessed in Lucian's *True History* (2d c. A.D.), which are used for human sacrifices, are made of amethysts, and around the city runs a river of exquisite perfume, fifty feet deep, and dwellers there dress in beautiful purple spiderwebs ("In spite of being bodiless, they can move and talk as mortal beings. They resemble naked spirits, each covered with a web that gives it the shape of a body"). The purple flower of the bachkou plant in Raymond Roussel's enigmatic *Impressions d'Afrique* (1910) has razor-sharp thorns: if a traveler pierces a finger with one of these thorns, he has only to press the flower's petals in order to obtain a juice that is both antiseptic and coagulant.

Threats and dire fears are often linked to the color purple. The Zhar-Ptitza bird, the oldest and wisest creature in the world, which inhabits the vast forest of Acaire in James Branch Cabell's *Figures of Earth* (1921)—where each creature of the many who live there is unique and therefore very lonely—is purple. There are bloated purple spiders in the waste plateau of Leng, incidentally, in H. P. Lovecraft's eerie "The Dream Quest of Unknown Kadath" (1943), whom the inhabitants of that dying and remote but strangely unforgotten land have to fight. In Edith Nesbit's *Uncle James* (1899), a purple dragon terrorizes the kingdom of Rotundia. By magic, it is later transmogrified into a small purple newt. Fred T. Jones's *The Violet Flame* (1899) tells of a mad scientist who invents a flame that disintegrates all it touches in his loony effort to make himself dictator of England. And in Angela Carter's *The Loves of Lady Purple,* the protagonist is a murderous puppet, part Kali, part Lizzie Borden, made monstrous by the voracity of others.

There is much in purple that is negative. It is the color of bad magic, instability, vampires' capes, edemas, and uncontrollable anger. A furious person "turns purple with rage." To go through a bad time in Spanish idiom is to *"pasarlas moradas"* (or *"negras"),* and *"una morada"* is a bruise. Kaposi's sarcoma leaves a whole series of purple—and fatal—nodules on AIDS victims. Dr. Seuss's Grinch has "purple spots on his heart." "Purple scale" blights oranges and other citrus. Birthmarks ("port wine stains") are purple. Poison ivy is a black purple in the fall. An old proverb goes, "In the year when plums flourish, all else fails." Lilacs are often looked upon as flowers of illness. The Jewish surname *Veilchenduft* (scent of violets) was a mock-genteel one assigned to them in Austria in the late eighteenth century. The Reverend Jim Jones in Ghana forced his flock of

913—of them 213 were children—to drink grape Fla-Vor-Aid laced with potassium cyanide and liquid valium (some were actually injected with it), then he shot himself, making sadly real Sheila Kaye-Smith's phrase, in another context, "the dim purplescent mass of the twilight people." It is not only the color of caution against wastes but, with yellow, of radiation hazards. During the Trinity test of the Manhattan Project, the initial seething white-hot brilliance of the exploded bomb of 20,000 tons was followed by a sudden purple radioactive cloud glowing over Alamogordo, New Mexico—"As it rose in the air it became predominantly purple," said Neils Bohr—which instantly called to mind, as Robert Oppenheimer dolefully confessed later, a phrase from the Bhagavad Gita in Hindu Scripture when Vishnu, taking on his thousand-armed form, fatally pronounces, "I am become Death, the destroyer of worlds."

It is the color of evil-tinted dyes and defoliants. The desolate Coketown in Dickens's novel *Hard Times* has a river in it "that runs purple with ill-smelling dye." Sybil, blindfolded and shut in the wheat bin by her abusive mother, repeatedly marked with a purple crayon the inside of the box so that someone would know she was there. She would later refer to this abusive period, hideously, as the "purple" or the "purple anger." How vastly different from small Harold's felicitously drawn purple line in Crockett Johnson's children's story *Harold and the Purple Crayon,* a "thread" that led him into and out of many adventures.

As a packaging color, it is uncommon and generally

avoided. A curious design mistake is cited by Thomas Hine in *The Total Package,* whose assertion that "color is the fundamental language of packaging" is surely correct, when he points out that "a California design firm's prominent use of purple—an Easter color in Catholic areas of Europe—in the graphic design system for Euro Disney provided fodder for those who argued that the theme park was an insensitive imposition on Europe, 'a cultural Chernobyl.' " Designers working on packages for international use, Hine points out, are often oddly counseled "to stay away from white in Morocco, violet in Egypt, black in Greece."

Have you heard it asserted that pregnant women and people with thyroid malfunctions tend to prefer purple? It was also the color generally adopted by the suffragettes as their signature, and no doubt illuminates Leon Edel's comment in his biography *Henry James* on the slashing of John Singer Sargent's portrait of James: "The peaceable-looking lady was wielding with vigor a meat-cleaver she had concealed beneath the purple cloak." In Maria Edgeworth's curious moral tale "The Purple Jar," the protagonist, Rosamond, neurasthenically prefers a gaudy jar to a new pair of shoes. And cannot there be found in dim enervated and semimanqué "menopause mauve" the dried-blood hue portending for women barrenness and oncoming old age? Or something in that base pale blue–violet liquid creme hair rinse of Wella's "True Steel," covering dead yellow strands, that hints of embalming? On the other hand, what was the closeted Victorian woman's grim purple bombazine but a shroud?

Lepers, who centuries ago were considered already dead even though they were living, terrified people with their often-purple bodies and faces. During the twelfth and thirteenth centuries, the ravages of the plague reached to monstrous proportions. "It is estimated that at one period at least a quarter of Europe's population were lepers," writes John Farrow in his biography *Damien the Leper.* A formal act of proscription, banishing them, also allowed them by way of issue a black cowl to wear, a wicker basket, special gloves, a barrel, and a long stick upon which was a rattle—to wag and warn men of their unclean presence (cf. Lev. 13:45). A document was then read aloud to each one, which goes in part: "We sworn physicians have examined this man by order of the authorities to disclose if he be leprous. We report as follows: we have found, particularly, his face to be pimply and of a violet color. We pulled a hair from his beard and another from his eyebrow, and at the root of each hair a minute fragment of flesh was attached. We found small tubercles around the eyebrows and behind the ears. The expression is fixed and immobile. The breath is evil, and the voice hoarse and nasal. . . . From these and other unmistakeable signs we solemnly declare that he is a leper." An ancient and forgotten disease? Not quite. There were six thousand cases of leprosy diagnosed in the United States in 1995.

Purple is the color of grief, dead leaves, merciless pride, prison complexions, coffin silk, acne, funereal trappings (vestments, cortege, and so forth), ruin, the mark of hypodermic drug injections, wheals, varicose veins, oral lesions, blood blisters, welts, collapsed lungs, oxygen deprivation, and inevitable, enveloping death in a dying—or dead—body. Gregory Corso's "Italian Extravaganza" goes in part,

> *Mrs. Lombardi's month-old son is dead.*
> *I saw it in Rizzo's funeral parlor,*
> *A small purplish wrinkled head.*

Thrombocytopenic purpura is hemorrhaging into the skin, with mucous membrane bleeding, anemia, and low platelet count. After death, blood turns a dark purple from lack of oxygen. ("I found bright drops of purple blood/Beside a dying fawn," we read in John Cowper Powys's poem "The Blood.") Poisons empurple the skin. "And purply did the knot/Swell with venom," observes John Crowe Ransom in "Janet Waking," where Janet's pet hen Chucky is killed by a bee sting. (What is hinted at, I wonder, in the liquid of "Poison" perfume being purple?) Burns scorch skin purple. Sumner Redstone, president of Viacom, who was caught in a Boston hotel fire in 1979 and, to save himself, clung by his fingertips from a third-floor ledge, later underwent sixty hours of skin grafts; his right hand is now a bright purple-red. The tiny fingernails on starving black children and babies, ironically, turn a weirdly beautiful yet ghastly purple. Purple shadows or pouchy rings under the eyes often prove in older people that circulation is sluggish, usually from fatigue or convalescence, and it is common in those who have had malaria. A mauve or purple complexion can often be a symptom of emphysema, methemoglobinemia, probably from a sulfa drug, heart difficulty (obstruction to veins returning blood to heart), or, in a child, congenital heart disease ("blue baby"). And don't I remember some lurid type of gentian violet athlete's foot medicine some quack podiatrist—not an oxymoron?—once used on me?

Artist Larry Rivers's searing—and tasteless—eulogy read in front of all the mourners on July 28, 1966, for poet Frank O'Hara, who had been run down by a jeep on a Fire Island beach at three o'clock in the morning, included a grotesque rehearsal of the episode as well as the dying man's final state: "He was purple wherever his skin showed through the white hospital gown. He was a quarter larger than usual. Every few inches there was sewing . . . he looked like a shaped wound." And who that knows them can ever forget the ghoulish lines from Swinburne's nightmarish "A Ballad of Death":

> *By night there stood over against my bed*
> *Queen Venus with a hood striped gold and black,*
> *Both sides drawn fully back*
> *From brows wherein the sad blood failed of red*
> *And temples drained of purple and full of death*

And as Richard Aldington writes in some of the bleakest lines of "Choricos,"

> *For silently*
> *Brushing the fields with red-shod feet,*

> *With purple robe*
> *Searing the grass as with a sudden flame,*
> *Death,*
> *Thou hast come upon us.*

Cecil Beaton, in his diary, describes his nose turning "mauve with cold." Claire Quilty in *Lolita* dies "flapping and heaving . . . in a purple heap." (The purple robe he is wearing, a priap's in both cases, matches one that Humbert also wears in certain scenes.) Barney the purple dinosaur, I'm convinced, is a character that appeals to children only for its fetal attraction. It is the color, purple, of preciosity and artifice. There is an unhappy fellow who is dissatisfied in his hotel with the wasted violet night on his lover in Wallace Stevens's poem "Two Figures in Dense Violet Light." Jehovah's Witnesses were forced to wear purple badges in Nazi concentration camps, just as Jews had to wear yellow. NKVD officers who carried out the secret arrests under Stalin's Reign of Terror—they drove black sedans called "ravens" and their favorite calling hours were between 11 P.M. and 3 A.M.—always carried purple identity cards. A notorious Detroit cadre of bootleggers in the 1920s was called "The Purple Gang." The purple death adder is a large, venomous Australian snake. Purple mites, only one-fiftieth of an inch long, infest the leaves of fruit and citrus trees. And isn't there something violet in the tattered inky onset of a thunderstorm? In the screaming of Francis Bacon's mad cardinals? In the flesh tints of his grim cadavers of meat? It is the color of regret, sublimation, loss, mourning, resignation, futility, and fading. As Alice Corbin writes in "Juan Quintana,"

> *Old Juan Quintana's coat*
> *Is a faded purple blue*

Purple has always had resonances of mystery and the inscrutable. Take the "Purple Code," for example, the Japanese secret code during World War II that was broken by U.S. Army cryptographer Col. William F. Friedman. Herbert O. Yardley had broken the Japanese code in 1920, and it had been changed before World War II. (Friedman, by the way, was equally fascinated with Joyce's paronomasiac novel *Finnegans Wake,* as a cryptographic phenomenon—he did not interpret; his work he called "decipherments"—as well as the famous Voynich Manuscript, 235 vellum pages supposedly written by Elizabethan essayist Francis Bacon.) As to Japan and the war, William Laurence, a reporter for the *New York Times* who had been selected to accompany *Bock's Car* on August 9, 1945, for the dropping of the atomic bomb over Nagasaki—Kokura was the original target, but clouds obscured that city—writes these eyewitness words: "Observers in the tail of our ship saw a giant ball of fire rise as though from the bowels of the earth, belching forth enormous white smoke rings. Next they saw a giant pillar of purple fire, ten thousand feet high, shooting skyward with enormous speed. . . . It was a living thing, a new species of being, born right before our eyes." A concentration of ultraviolet light can be damaging to the eyes and lead to solar retinitis, as with snow blindness, but photophthalmia can take place in *deserts* as well, which can reflect as much as 80 percent of the light that falls. There existed in China, finally, the Purple Forbidden City *(tzu chin ch'eng),* a walled secret enclosure in old Peiping—closed to the public—that was riddled with old pavilions and winding halls and mysterious corridors and secret passageways.

A vaporous beauty adhibits to so many hues of purple, smokiness and soot notwithstanding. Samuel T. Coleridge writes to his friend Robert Southey from Edinburgh in a letter on September 13, 1803: "I stood gazing at the setting Sun . . . then all at once turning my eyes down upon the City, it & all it's *{sic}* smokes & figures became at once dipped in the brightest blue-purple—such a sight that I almost grieved when my eyes recovered their natural Tone."

Purple is also the color of enchantment. The "silken, sad, uncertain rustling" curtains in Poe's *The Raven,* terrifying him, are purple. Incidentally, Poe borrowed the line from Elizabeth Barrett Browning, who in her Gothic poem "Lady Geraldine's Courtship" had her own purple curtain in the line, "with a murmurous stir uncertain in the air the purple curtain," and so forth. Angelica Garnett thought purple had a sad quality; she wrote of the "sad-purple gooseberries" she remembered seeing in her aunt Virginia Woolf's home, Monks House. The ghostly moon in Noyes's "The Highwayman," who wears a wine red velvet coat, shines over the purple moor. And according to critic and cabalist Perle Epstein, the low purple foothills in Malcolm Lowry's masterpiece *Under the Volcano* mysteriously stand for

Yesod, "a probationary sphere," the first plane leading out of Malkuth (the kingdom) into higher worlds, the magical sphere whose color is purple. I am certain in the subfusc worlds of creatures like Dracula, Vampira, the Phantom of the Opera, and all such chthonians who never come out in the daytime, who never see sunlight, who wait in the dark all day long, month after month, totally blacked out, derive their night vision from what inevitably grows out of the penetrating black darkness like cancer, "visual purple." Visual purple lets men see at night like fish and squid, but only to a degree. Humans only see the *presence* of light, whereas owls' eyes, unlike humans', are packed tight with rods that contain the chemical visual purple, which converts even the faintest glimmer of light into a chemical signal. Remember, rod cells yield no clues to color. It is the cone cells that provide the basis for color vision in vertebrates whose nervous connections allow hue discrimination. An owl at night, in terms of sight, has a hundred times the acuteness of humans.

Cold is often evoked by the color purple, not standard chilliness, but that terrible, whit-flawed, brutalizing antarctic subzeroness that empurples and freezes the heart—or any other appendage. One recalls Robert Browning's complaint, for instance, in "Time's Revenges,"

> *Tonight when my head aches indeed*
> *And I can neither think nor read*
> *Nor make these purple fingers hold*
> *The pen; this garret freezing cold*

It is a color found in icebergs and ice floes and in unforgiving, ongoing, desperate, almost embalming gelidness, the color of shivering, teeth-shattering, bone-chilling cold. Ivan Bunin's story "Henry" begins, "On a winter evening like a northern fairy tale, with lilac-colored hoar-frost spread over the gardens. . . ." Purpling in plants occurs when they are deficient in phosphorus—the leaves turn dark green, then purple—which often happens in early spring, as phosphorus is neither active nor available in cold, wet soil. But don't all leaves and flowers revert to purple in the chill of autumn, as with crabapples and King Crimson maples and Chinese smoke trees? "The Tyrian would not come," succinctly writes Emily Dickinson, "until the North evoked it." Edith Sitwell to a degree captures this in her poem "The Song of the Cold," the second line from the following snatchet of which, no doubt, some aimless, crackpated, self-promoting plagiarist hunter—I'm not thinking of any bamboo-brained snirt in particular—might want to take note, is borrowed from Rimbaud's poem "Metropolitan": "Huge is the sun of amethysts and rubies/And in the purple perfumes of the polar sun/And homeless cold they wander." And Wallace Stevens speaks of the same insistent cold in "The Man Whose Pharynx Was Bad":

> *The malady of the quotidian.*
> *Perhaps, if winter once could penetrate*
> *Through all its purples to the final slate*
> *Persisting bleakly in an icy haze*
> *One might in turn become less diffident*

There is a weirdness, a vagueness, an otherworldliness—a kind of lunar numinousness—to the color purple, from pounce paper to the violet-tinged nimbus of gaslight to the closed, hothouse vibrations of Prince's "Purple Rain" and Jimi Hendrix's "Purple Haze," a street-hip phrase, along with "windowpanes," "microdots," and "blotter acid," for LSD *(lysergic acid diethylamide)*. The poster for Roger Corman's LSD opus *The Trip* (1967) promised audiences that they would "Feel purple! Taste green! Touch the scream that crawls up the wall!" The color suggests limpid dawn, long shadows, faraway tones, the horizontal last sight of distance itself. And isn't smoke a marriage of purple and burned umbers? I belong to a secret society at UVa., the Society of the Purple Shadows: they left a purple feather on my desk on the West Range late one night in 1967, their mystic communication; I have never heard from them again. There is a violet shine to rain and misty climates and ungainable mountain ranges. I saw in the Outer Hebrides in 1966 wet foggy sheets of violet mist, which reminded me, as a vaporous parallel, of the shades of violet water, "like shot silk," drinkable—yet able to be cut!—running through the mysterious polar island of Tsalal in Edgar Allan Poe's *The Narrative of Arthur Gordon Pym* (1838). Peyote visions are delicate floating films of color, usually neutral purples, "color fruits," Dr. S. Weir Mitchell called them in 1896 after drinking an extract of peyote. He writes, "All the colors I have ever beheld are dulled as compared to these." There is the *flou* of photisms where one sees colored spots, "the stab of an afterimage," as Vladimir Nabokov writes in *Speak,*

Memory, where, among other images, he sees "a mauve remoteness melting beyond moving masts." Nabokov, a true synesthete, always associated the letter *w* with violet, combined with dull green. The "purpills" Humbert lecherously administers to Lolita in that novel are composed, he says, of "summer skies, and plums and figs, and the grapeblood of emperors." "Purple hearts" is slang for speed. And infamous "purps," or purple pills, several recognizable kinds of which induce drowsiness and dizziness, are almost generic as a color for those used as aphrodisiacs, purple as vetch and eerie as violet in "black lights."

As to the world of drugs, Huysmans in *A Rebours* begins happily discussing colors, then ends ominously by taking refuge in the possibility of hallucination. *Interior painting!* "Nor again was it any use considering the various shades of purple," he writes, "which with one exception lose their lustre in candlelight. That exception is plum, which somehow survives intact, but then what a muddy reddish hue it is, unpleasantly like lees of wine! Besides, it struck him"—hypersensitive and erethic Des Esseintes, his antihero, who "suffered much from a morbid acuteness of the senses" (the odors of all flowers were oppressive, faint light, and so forth)—"as utterly futile to resort to this range of tints, in so far as it is possible to see purple by ingesting a specified amount of santonin, and thus it becomes a simple matter for anyone to change the color of his walls without laying a finger on them." Psychokinesis!

Then there is purple and death. I remember reading how Marilyn Monroe, after Johnny Hyde's death in December 1950, made her first suicide attempt. Her coach Natasha Lytess wrote how she found her with "an ooze of purple paste in the lip corners and forced my fingers into her mouth. . . . It was crammed full of this purplish paste—there must have been about thirty Nembutal capsules wadded in her mouth. Enough to kill five people." It was Nembutal pills, about fifty of them, along with chloral hydrate, that Marilyn would take in her bedroom on that fateful Saturday, August 4, 1962, that finally killed her. And it may be mentioned here that in Egypt the traditional uniform of the condemned criminal, when being hanged, is a black shirt, red trousers, and a purple cap. No, purple seems never even at its best a natural color but rather one that indicates "closing time," as Cyril Connolly says (in a different context) "in the gardens of the West."

Who can forget the poison plant in Hawthorne's story *Rappaccini's Daughter*? "There was a shrub in particular, set in a marble vase in the midst of the pool, that bore a profusion of purple blossoms. . . ." So toxic is it that Dr. Rappaccini, who has cared more for science than humankind, has to wear a mask whenever he goes near it. It is described as "too luxuriant." It glows like a nuke. "It is fatal!" Its beauty conceals a deadly "malice," just as young Beatrice does, who grows up "nourished" by the plant, her "sister," she calls it, and even whose actual *voice,* we are told, evokes the deep hues, the fatal color, of purple. Jimsonweed, or "angel's trumpet," purple-tipped and often lethal when eaten, smoked, or brewed, is impossible to ingest without being poisoned. And didn't young Lord Krishna's skin change to purple when, before killing the snake, it blew its fetid breath on him? No, the color is often unreal and eerie and dangerous. Isn't the bright carpet Clytemnestra's handmaidens spread out between Agamemnon's chariot and his door, like his "prophetic robes," a crimson purple, like his blood, soon to be shed?

In his novel *Purple* (1886), Ozaki Koyo, who was always able to analyze emotions and psychological confusions, especially sexual and amorous ones, writes very insightfully of a medical student's neurotic anxieties—never a great creator of character, Koyo nevertheless manages to deal brilliantly with violet, violent anxiety—and the purple cushion his teacher's daughter presents him with for use as an elbow rest is fraught with sexual connotations.

I never fail to connect the color purple with sex, Easter, bad dreams, the country of Algeria, sweet gum, secrecy and darkness, fruity concoctions, bad headaches, lying, women's garter belts and nylons, Aubrey Beardsley drawings, neurasthenia, the sound of bass drums, hothouse flowers, closed windows, the plot and music of Puccini's *Tosca,* madness, chain mail, Vienna, blindness, illicit meetings, entropy increasing, night skies in Java, Chekhov types, that is, people who live in the past, thin glass, the name Charmaine ("I wonder why you keep me waiting, Charmaine, Charmaine"), all thoughts of fantasy, poison, wasteful extravagance, strangulation, the American West, fish, the jungles of Paraguay, bleak outerspace, and, along with Duke Ellington's "Magenta Haze," recorded on the Musicraft label in 1946 and featuring an incandescent solo by the great Johnny Hodges, as well as his "Lady of the Lavender Mist" the following year, the song "Lush Life," part of which goes,

> *I'll forget you, I will*
> *while yet you are still burning inside my brain.*
> *Romance is mush, stifling those who strive.*
> *I'll live a lush life in some small dive*
> *And there I'll be, while I rot with the rest*
> *Of those whose lives are lonely, too.*

Few fail to find connotations of the erotic—of the languorous and unhealthily erotic, one might add—in the colors purple and mauve. Keats writes of the "purple-lined palace of sweet sin." Purple is in fact a word used nowadays for something really pornographic, worse than blue. There are livid bruises and welts from pleasure spankings, swollen lips, and purple love bites on the throat. Doesn't Swinburne's poem "Laus Veneris" actually begin with a purple love bite (". . . her neck/ Kissed over close, wears yet a purple speck/Soft, and stung softly. . . .")? The phallus, engorged, is purple. Whatever is purple and darkly swollen seems to one degree or another to indicate such. "Purple as an Iris and half the length of a man's arm! Pulsating, gigantic, ugly!" cry the male orderlies in a hospital ward of Python, poet Charles Bukowski's flattering nickname for himself in his short story "Purple as an Iris," as they try to pull him off his lewd partner, Mary. And in Thomas Pynchon's *Gravity's Rainbow,* we read of Captain Blicero wearing "a false cunt and merkin of sable both hand-crafted in Berlin by the notorious Mrs. Ophir, the mock

labia and bright purple clitoris molded of—Madame
had been abject, pleading shortages—synthetic rubber
and Mipolam, the new polyvinyl chloride. . . ." It was
a color Marlene Dietrich particularly loved and that, for
some reason, I always think of in the movie *Shanghai
Express* when she pronounces, "It took more than one
man to change my name to Shanghai Lily." Purple—
inordinate—is corrupt. "He and his brother are like
plum trees that grow crooked over standing pools," we
read in John Webster's *The Duchess of Malfi.* "They are
rich and o'er-laden with fruit, but none but crows, pies,
and caterpillars feed on them." I'm convinced that the
Dutchman Thoroop, in his mauvish and libidinous can-
vases, reveals a touch of necrophilia. Purple lips seem
lascivious. They are always Dionysian. Hesketh Pearson
describes Oscar Wilde as having "thick purple-tinged
sensual lips." And in 1789, the Duke of Devonshire
passionately wrote in his erotic apostrophe "To Lydia,"

> *Let thy lips, that breathe perfume*
> *Deeper purple now assume*

Wistful, pale, the chromopassivity of mauve has
something of postpassion. "Mauve is the more insouci-
ant, the less confessedly sin-laden aspect of purple,"
writes Brigid Brophy. It is the very hue of faded or dried
blood, one good definition of mauve (Latin *malva,* mal-
low). Linguist Morris Swadesh in *The Origin and Diversi-
fication of Language* (1971) finds in something even as
remote as the Torres Trails language of New Guinea the
words *kulka-dgamulga* (red, purple) from *kulka* (blood)

and *dgamulgna* (it looks like). Dried blood suggests a hue far different from vigorous neo-menstruative purple. Don't many, if not most, postmenopausal women with Mary Worth hair, tinted, say, with something like Matrix "Eggplant" or Redken "Amethyst" no. 94, tend to wear mauve clothes and sport lavender handbags and spray themselves with exotic, orchidaceous perfumes? I recall attending several outdoor brunches and parties on the island of Nantucket with several groups of venerable old ladies, lavendrical at a thousand points, sitting about like rare but wiltable plants, foliaceous, ramified, and umbelliferous and all giving off such heady intoxicants that the mere fumes alone of what they wore could have perfumed the Augean stables. It all brought to mind Wilhelm Reich's theory that repressed people develop noticeable "character armor"—frown lines, worry furrows, blotches, and so forth. Although we sat there in the sunshine—odd, because purple is sun-sensitive— there was ironically more than a touch of the funereal, and at certain increasingly crucial intervals I often felt that I was, not at a wake, although that had occurred to me, or a cattery, but was rather captured, like one of those Victorian butterflies, in an elaborate, overscented boscage. *"Son yacht"*—(pronounced "i-ak")—*"porte bien sa toile,"* one faded Mme. Rhoubarbe said to me, pointing a terrible thin finger adorned with a huge synthetic alexandrite to a middle-aged male gay twanker walking arm-in-arm with another mother image. And one thinks, of course, of the aptly named Violet Venable, the rich, husbandless, desiccated, if genteel harridan in Tennessee Williams's *Suddenly Last Summer,* who wants her niece to have brain surgery in order to silence her. Apparently, purple can also connote passion, being a versatile and multifarious color. "Never trust a woman who wears mauve, whatever her age may be, or a woman over thirty-five who is fond of pink ribbons," Lord Henry Wotton advises his young friend in Oscar Wilde's *The Picture of Dorian Gray.* "It always means that they have a history." Dame Edna Everage, the comic television matron ("something called Lalique, which I believe is French for dead people's wedding presents") is extremely fond of mauve. The empress Alexandra, Czar Nicholas II's wife, kept a mauve boudoir in the old ocher-washed Alexander palace at Tsarskoye Selo. "Violet," Spengler writes, "a red succumbing to blue, is the color of women no longer fruitful and of priests living in celibacy." A lifelessness adheres to it. In Gabriel García Márquez's *One Hundred Years of Solitude,* Mrs. Fernanda Segundo carries a calendar with the dates of venereal abstinence—allowing her, after "Holy Week, Sundays, holy days of obligation, first Fridays, retreats, sacrifices, and cyclical impediments," only forty-two carnal days in the year!—marked by her spiritual adviser in purple ink. And isn't something wistfully symbolic being said in Edith Wharton's *The Age of Innocence* when we read, "Miss Archer's brown and purple poplins hung, as the years went on, more and more slackly on her virgin frame"?

There is something of the all-washed-up about mauve, of the twilight, the depleted—"of a want of moral energy," as Edgar Allan Poe says of the House of Usher—even the eunuchoid. It is settled in and sober.

"He had known her," Leon Edel writes of Henry James and the arch, high-tempered Mrs. Frances ("Fanny") Kemble—she would never read or perform during the Civil War years in the bigoted southern states—"since their meetings in Rome in the 1870s when she had appeared in purples and mauves [like many stylish conservative older *grandes dames*} and possessed in her voice the manner, the style and grandeur of the Kembles." Considered a color generally out of favor after the turn of the century, when it was popular, it periodically makes a comeback in fashion. Only very rarely, as in the 1980's *Maverick in Mauve,* a memoir of a young woman in Victorian times, does mauve denote youth and energy. "Mauve as a hue attracts light, according to the House of Guerlain, which created "Météorites," a woman's finishing powder that comes in little spheres or balls. It can have fussy, overprecise connotations. H. L. Mencken in his book *The American Language* cites a British newspaperman who essentially believed that everyone, including his own posh countrymen, spoke dialects, and who paradoxically hated the fact of his own country's being singled out, with its plummy pronunciations, as having the lock on Standard English, when he himself found it had "a mauve, Episcopalian, and ephebian ring." Purple has connotations of dopey overconsideration and preening. Scobie in Durrell's *The Alexandria Quartet* uses the word *mauve* as meaning "silly." ("He was just plain mauve when it came to . . .") It is invariably a delicate color. Humbert Humbert in *Lolita* declares he wants to "mauvemail" Mrs. Haze, considering "blackmail" too strong a word. It is also a precious color, a self-conscious and vain and fussified color, almost always swishy and effeminate when worn by men.

But purple, or mauve or lavender, as a color, has always had "gay" connotations and seems to be historic as a gay indicator—even little yappy dogs favored by big yappy men wear mauve or puce collars. It is surely the universal color, with pink, for homosexuality. "He's a dash of lavender" is the way someone once referred to a gay fellow to me. (Lavender water, used by fops in the thirties and forties, is a period cologne.) Those men or gossoons who are homosexual before arriving in prison are known in the clink as "lavender boxes" (or "pink-tea freaks"). A "lavender rectory" indicates an abode of gay priests or ministers. Bruce Rodgers in *Gay Talk,* a compendium of gay phrases and handbook of terms, gives us a great grouping of such phrases. "Have your neighbors burned a lavender cross on your lawn yet?" A "lavender boy" is a faggot. A group of gay men, especially if large, is often called "a lavender convention." "Well, your trip to Marbelle certainly brought out your deeper tone of lavender." "Purple passion in the ovaries" is an elaborate phrase for saying that someone is gay or has the wild, irrepressible urge to rut. Flamboyant, fussy, plump Carl Van Vechten, a married gay who in the twenties, like Cole Porter, who shared this taste, had affairs with Negroes—a patron of black artists, like Robert Mapplethorpe, one of whose late commercial assignments, in the words of Peter Conrad, "propped a high-heeled shoe, sleek in purple satin, on the cushionary mound of a black man's buttocks," Van Vechten wrote a novel of

Harlem life called *Nigger Heaven*—and "kept a growing collection of photographs of nude black men," according to Ann Douglas in *Terrible Honesty: Mongrel Manhattan in the 1920s.* He "sometimes affected the elaborate and cerise and gold Mandarin costume of (in a friend's words) 'the Dowager Empress of China, gone slightly berserk.' " And Nijinsky often wore pinkish purple leotards, with limp silk petals of pinks, reds, and purples "merging into each other," in the words of Richard Buckle in his *Diaghilev,* "like the colors of Galle or Tiffany glass, abolishing contours and camouflaging sex."

The *New Yorker* cover for June 13, 1994, showing a cartoon of two gay men, one dark-haired, the other blond and holding a bouquet of purple flowers, is laid out entirely in lavender with a mauve border. In the Castro district of San Francisco, one sees orchids everywhere, which gays seem to love and "drama queens" tend to send each other in drenching emotional moments of either apology or appreciation, epiphanizing in a rather elaborate if not ostentatious way, at least to my mind, what in grand opera is called "illustration" or in Italy the *bella figura.* Venturing into color photography toward the end of his young life, Robert Mapplethorpe, confined himself, rather tamely, to floral arrangements, making dye-transfer prints of lilies and roses against backdrops of velvety purple and magenta. Peter Conrad observes, "Predatory, erectile plants—calla lilies with prongs or lush, labial orchids—became his 'flowers of evil.' " Many lesbians sport purple ribbons in public to show togetherness and solidarity. Fifties bohemian and Harvard-educated black eccentric Dorothy Dean, the self-described "Spade of Queens," for a while published a low-camp newspaper called the *All-Lavender Cinema Courier.* The gay Castro Theater's seasonal film program, "Castro," has a purple masthead, while the San Francisco Bay *Times* Gay/Lesbian/Bi/Trans Newspaper and Events Calendar dots the *i* of the word *Times* with a mauve triangle. Rococoa, a chocolate shop in San Francisco in the district with a display of glittering fairies in the window, has a pink-and-mauve decor. Hitler forced gays and various marginal groups and so-called *secta nefaria* in his concentration camps to wear patches of a pink triangle. Gayness *is* lavendrical. The tiny toy town of Provincetown, Massachusetts, at the farthest tip of Cape Cod, has a predominantly gay population, as purple and pungent as the juniper berries that grow along the bogs. Walk along quaint Commercial Street, the main drag, so to speak, sometime during summer, and you will find example after example of rows of quaint, overdeliberate houses with roof finials and rococo gingerbread work whose front gardens are flirtatiously and fussifiedly asprout with purple flora: lavender mums, lilacs, columbine, blue flag lilies, purple sage, skunk cabbage, dusty miller, and so forth.

"The Purple Hand," as a symbol of gay liberation, was codified, as it were, in San Francisco. In 1969 a band of gays picketed the San Francisco *Examiner* because of an antihomosexual editorial, an occasion when antagonists from above windows cruelly drenched the demonstrators below with buckets of purple printer's ink. One of the gays responded by angrily imprinting the side of the building with his ink-stained hand. Others repeated the gesture, each one stamping his or her disapproval on the offending walls of the newspaper. " 'Purple hand' seems to be a play on words on lavender," notes Bruce Rodgers (q.v.), "[a color] often associated with male homosexuals, and the 'black hand' death notice of the mafioso during the '20s." Decadence tends to be purple, incorporating the lush, the eerie, the overripe, the overblown, the nocturnal, even the introverted. Anna Ahkmatova, who would later take her own life, as a member of the "Stray Dog" circle of poets in prerevolutionary Petrograd, wearing purple-black silk, read her famous call to decadence: "We are all winners, we are all whores. How sad we are together."

A hedonism, in short, is attached to purple, or at least the bias implied in it that there are no certainties, no lasting meanings, no restrictions. (Should we not ascribe it to her libido that sex legend Mae West acquired a lifelong passion for lilac?) It is much less a cerebral than sensual color and forever asks the question Wallace Stevens does in "The Greenest Continent,"

> *Why think,*
> *Why feel the sun or, feeling, why feel more*
> *Than purple paste of fruit, to taste, or leaves*
> *Of purple flowers, to see?*

It was supposedly the color of Salomé's veils, as we have seen, and in *La Tragedie de Salomé,* a production of Diaghilev's in 1913 with no Herod, Herodias, or John the Baptist, ballerina Tamara Karsavina, wearing long, false eyelashes—an embellishment she claimed to originate—and a red rose on her bare knee painted afresh at every performance, danced her long solo in front of elegant, Beardsley-esque stage designs by Serge Sudeikine of purple, black, and silver.

Copies of Oscar Wilde's own play *Salomé* were expressly bound in purple, as he himself noted, "to suit Bosie [young Lord Alfred Douglas, his catamite] and his gilt hair." And Wilde wrote to Frances Forbes-Robertson in 1893, "A copy in Tyrian purple and tired silver is on its way to you." Wilde, who was once actually, and ludicrously, photographed dressed as Salomé— "I always say you're born naked, and the rest is drag," says RuPaul, a well-known contemporary drag queen— tended to reckon forbidden pleasures in purple terms. "In the mortal sphere I have fallen in and out of love, and fluttered hawks and doves alike," wrote Wilde to Robert Ross on May 14, 1900. "How evil it is to buy love, and how evil to sell it! And yet what purple hours one can snatch from that grey slowly-moving thing we call time." A purple-gold coverlet, remember, is, rather like a mask, always kept draped over the portrait—the decadent, corruptible portrait—of Dorian Gray, while he himself, always "exquisitely dressed," goes about wearing in his buttonhole a spray of Parma violets. And somehow I am always put in mind of Wilde—along with his wife, Constance Lloyd—when in the *Aeneid* (bk. 10, p. 722) I read the line, *"purpureum pennis et pactae conjugis ostro"* ("all bright with plumed crest and with a purple robe [the work] of his betrothed wife"). Purple was always used to indicate an aspect of daring and shocking excess. In Huysmans's *A Rebours,* Des Esseintes had printed for himself "in violet ink, Bishop's violet, within a border of Cardinal purple on an authentic parchment which the church officials had blessed, a copy of the *Diaboliques* [by the profane Barbey d'Aurévilly] set up in 'letters of civility,' whose outlandish serifs and flourishes, twisted into horns and hoofs, affect a Satanic contour." Wilde, by the way, claimed to hate mauve, which he (or Whistler) described as "pink trying to be purple." But decadent writer Ronald Firbank loved it. He wrote in purple ink. The fifteen manuscript notebooks in which he wrote his novel *Vainglory* have long sections in that vivid color. And it was "in violet ink," according to Siegfried Sassoon, that Firbank always "wittily inscribed" copies of all books. (He always sent *blue* postcards through the mail, however.) It was Firbank who also wore mauve trousers to meet Oscar Wilde's friend Ada Leverson, the "Sphinx," although on that occasion she hautily sent a servant to say she was not at home. All of his work, from his fey dream play *The Mauve Tower* ("I have a dagger in my hair") to the highly stylized comedy *The Princess Zoubaroff* ("Let me admire your heliotropes"), is highly purpureal, its style lush, mannered, and hyperbolic. One of the schoolgirls in his novel *Concerning the Eccentricities of Cardinal Pirelli* says, "I can't explain; but I adore all that mauvishness about him." Even Mme. Mimosa's Pomeranian pup in *Valmouth* is named "Plum Bun."

But isn't the habit of writing—or painting or dreaming or even wearing clothes—in one chosen color singularly a way of seeing? Why isn't what preponderates in an obsession not, at least for that person, epistemologically needful and therefore sound? I know someone who insists he *thinks* in violet. And aren't we told that men taste shapes? St. Francis of Assisi was in the habit of praying to God in the language of Provençal, his mother's tongue, simply because Italian seemed too debased by common use for such a holy purpose.

Speaking of purple ink, Dr. Ferdinand C. Lane in his classic *The Story of Trees* mentions how the naturalist John Muir, who so ardently admired California's ancient redwoods—in one of them he is said to have once counted four thousand annual growth rings!—actually wrote a letter to a friend, ingeniously, by using the actual sap of that hugest of all trees as a kind of purple ink, saying, "Do behold the king in his glory, King Sequoia. Where are such columns of sunshine, tangible, accessible, terrestrialized . . . the King Tree and I have sworn eternal love . . . there is a balm in these leafy Gileads."

I have always thought it luridly apt that Mary Miles Minter, movie star of the 1920s, wrote on what would later be her notorious violet-colored stationery (with purple butterflies on the letterhead) to her lover—her initialed "step-ins" were found on the scene, while actress Mabel Normand's love letters were also discovered in his riding boots—William Desmond Taylor, an English expatriate director, who was found shot in the back in his bungalow court apartment in Hollywood on February 1, 1922. The murder has never been solved.

Jean Cocteau, who was gay, described decadent and vain Count Robert De Montesquiou, *exquisite* and supposed model for Proust's unsavory Baron de Charlus, in the precious line: "white-gloved, grey-coiffeured, violet-clad, hydrangea full." Like many old inverts in *A la recherche du temps perdu*, Charlus, more than Montesquiou, was part of a subgroup that Proust, who was himself a homosexual, mockingly and pitifully caricatured in that masterpiece of his, built so much on the ironies of un-equal love, as *"La Race des Tantes"* ("The Race of Aunts"), creatures very much like Webster's crooked plum trees. "They prattle and chatter," he satirizes, "magnificently dressed and ridiculed. The aunts! The word alone conjures up their ceremoniousness and their whole manner of dress; this word-in-skirts calls forth visions of a society reception and of the plumage and chirping of a different kind of bird" (tr. Scott-Moncrieff).

And do you recall that last look we have of Charlus? The narrator Marcel sees, meandering around the ram-parts of bleak, wartime Paris in *Le Temps retrouvé* and walking behind two Zouaves, "a tall stout man in a soft hat and long ulster, whose purplish face made me hesi-tate whether he was a certain actor or a painter, both of whom had been involved in countless notorious cases of sodomy." It is M. de Charlus, vice-ridden, and bloated, lonely, a dissociated and pusillanimous invert who "had gotten as far away as possible from his real self," living an unsavory, isolated life, debased and disgraced and diseased.

But does not the color purple in fact often describe an extra-real zone, a separate reality, a locus or midworld, so to speak, inhabited only by artists and dreamers and marginalists and hipsters and sexual sub-cultists?

The late gay Episcopal priest, the Rev. Robert Williams, who died of AIDS in 1994, in his book *Just As I Am: A Practical Guide to Being Out, Proud, and Christian,* describes gays as "by nature a highly *liminal* people," people living "on the limits, on the cusps, between two realities or alternatives," in the liminal space "between society's perceptions of 'masculinity' and 'femininity.'" He notes that "even the colors associated with the queer nation, lavender and pink, are the colors of the liminal periods of change between night and day." Was not this idea prefigured in Huysmans's *A Rebours,* where we read, "it appeared to him to be an undoubted fact that the eye of that man amongst them who has visions of the ideal, who demands illusions to satisfy his aspirations, who craves veils to hide the nakedness of reality, is generally soothed and satisfied by blue and its cognate tints, such as mauve, lilac, pearl grey"? I have often thought of purple as vaguely the sort of subjective-correlative color of dreamscape, of the lunar world, of the twilight-zonish quality of unreality—dreams, premonitions, melancholy, bouts of daydreaming, even shock—a color presence or telepresence to which a person is delivered up, "immersed" in cyberspace or VR jargon, to a synthetic reality, where the wetware of the brain is, as it were, dyed an uncanny lavender or a kind of crocus-colored mist.

The famous "knocking on the gate" scene in Shakespeare's *Macbeth* brings the suddenly shocked murderer back from vaporous purple to the unavoidable reality of red blood. Isn't that what makes *The Purple Rose of Cairo* purple in Woody Allen's 1985 film, with Cecilia and movie star Tom Baxter outside of—and opting for a solution to—reality? ("It has been said that if I have one big theme in my movies, it's got to do with the difference between reality and fantasy," Woody Allen once said. "It comes up very frequently in my films. I think what it boils down to, really, is that I hate reality. And, you know, unfortunately, it's the only place where we can get a good steak dinner.") Ruminating alone in his upper room, Raskolnikov the murderer abides in neither a realistic St. Petersburg nor in a realistic novel—and only when he descends the stairs do we recognize a common, quotidian world, and even there Porfiry the detective—observe the name—literally becomes his liminal purple shadow. Neither are Fagin in his thieving aerie in *Oliver Twist* nor Heathcliff darkly brooding at Wuthering Heights—or even Anne Frank with her family, hidden for twenty-five months in that Amsterdam garret—in identifiably circumscribable worlds. They too are on the cusp, sequestered from reality, veiled from hard fact, as it were. There are certain souls who need to be embraced by mystery, to be saved by some midnight beyond reason, to cope, to endure, to live, at least to try to live, beyond the logic of daytime. They have in a strange and highly liminal way gone into the purple.

Was that the case with the flamboyant Vita Sackville-West? In a letter written to her lover on February 3, 1926, composed at the height of their mutual infatuation—about the time when Vita left England for Persia with Harold Nicolson—Virginia Woolf said, "Mrs. Woolf has 2 long novels to read; and should be at it now instead of scribbling to Vita, who's much too happy and excited to attend, and looking divinely beautiful too (I say, what do you wear—the purple dog's hair dress?)." What could be more decadent? Or outré? Or marginal! *A purple dog's hair dress!* It all rather reminds me in its decadence of a line from aesthetician Harold Acton's early collection of poems, *Aquarium,* specifically "Violincello," part of which goes,

> *Voluptuously blatant in my greed*
> *I am the woman garbed in heliotrope,*
> *Whose bustle panics peacocks in the park*

The color is daring. Anna Magnani, who plays Pilar ("She has a tongue that scalds and that bites like a bull-whip"), wears a purple shirt—defiance!—in the film *For Whom the Bell Tolls.* It can be too daring, in fact, too extreme. "When the heroine of E. M. Forster's *A Room with a View* becomes engaged to the wrong man, her mistake expresses itself in the language of clothes," observes Alison Lurie in *The Language of Clothes.* "Lucy's new cerise dress has been a failure and makes her look tawdry and wan—her own mother compares her to a flamingo." It is also stylish. It was one of writer Anatole France's literary affectations to wear a violet dressing gown when he worked. Voltaire and Diderot had always worn theirs, so did Flaubert, and it is impossible to think of Balzac dressed any other way. I don't doubt that most of Noël Coward's signature matinee-idol Charvet dressing gowns were purple. And his friend Elsie April's hats. And Ivor Novello's socks. And the same probably goes for Edith Sitwell and that great Risorgimento cape of hers. One of Sherlock Holmes's three dressing gowns was purple, by the way. (The others were blue and mouse-colored.) Frank Lloyd Wright had his own way of self-projection, and the purple cape he wore to match his blue-violet hair was a totem that, swirling imperially around his own self-conception, fostered his self-regard. There is always with purple a lingering hint of regality and pomp. "The man in the lavender shirt, the woman in the lilac hostess gown," says Lurie, "appear to have (or to claim) finer perceptions and more refined tastes than their peers in blue or pink."

Miss Gloria Swanson had something of a yen for purple turbans, which she of course wore with style and pluming self-regard. I haven't the slightest doubt she planned to be wearing one on the day of her forthcoming appearance, after acquiring the third of her five husbands, Henri, Marquis de la Falaise de Coudraye, when she wired Paramount: *"Am Arriving With The Marquis Tomorrow Stop Please Arrange Ovation."*

And though not always elegant, purple invariably imparts a certain grandeur, even if occasionally a shoddy one. The ghostly old woman's "ancient, battered, outrageous hat with the awful plush flowers," with its jeweled hat pin, in Eudora Welty's story *The Purple Hat* becomes such a totem. "It is quite a hat, a great wide, deep hat such as has no fashion and never knew there was fashion and change. It serves her to come out winter and summer." And a purple knitted scarf—his "only frivolity"—can even enhance the look of such a Boeotian of Boomism as Sinclair Lewis's George F. Babbitt.

It can also have the flash of danger. The purple clothes certain black kids can often be seen insolently wearing today in Los Angeles—satin shirts, running suits, hats, and so forth—are in fact gang colors from the neighborhood of Grape Street in the area of downtown Watts, where the riots, which killed thirty-four people, started in 1965. Other gangs wear other colors, like the Bloods, who wear red, the color of Centennial High School, and the Crips, who call each other "cuz" and wear blue, which matches the color of their tattooed names, like "Thai Stick," "Baby Insane," and "Flacko." As to gangs, Bernardo and Chino's shirts, and even Anita's dresses, in the musical *West Side Story,* are purple, a color with connotations not only of Puerto Rican flash but which also in that film seem prefiguratively tragic.

Purple is also a sexy color. "Anna [Karenina] was not in lilac, the color Kitty was so sure she ought to have worn," writes Tolstoy in that great novel of his secretive sexual heroine in her stunning appearance—she wore low-necked black velvet and pearls—at the Korsunsky ball. What about the famous claret velvet ballgown Scarlett O'Hara wore in *Gone With the Wind* summing up her affluence as Mrs. Rhett Butler? On a lesser level, Gina Lollobrigida wears a highly sensual flowing imperial mauve gown in the film *Solomon and Sheba.* ("From de beginning of dime," she pronounces, "only queens have ruled Sheba. Dat is de law.") Jane Wyman is wearing purple velvet in her passionate kissing scene with Rock Hudson in *Magnificent Obsession,* and in *Giant,* per-

haps in her memory, he wears a purple tie to the wed-
ding, and I'm sure that's a violet suit. (So much more
attractive than the purple suits and pink ascots Burt
Reynolds seems to favor, which match in garishness his
Planet-of-the-Apes hairpiece.) In *Ziegfeld Follies* (1946)
Lucille Ball, taming a bevy of female "panthers" in the
"Bring On the Beautiful Girls" sequence, is all dolled-
up in a violet gown, with violet gems and violet feathers
and plumes. Al Capp's Daisy Mae Scraggs, Li'l Abner's
sweetheart, in color supplements often wore a blouse of
purple polka dots, and she was irresistible. (Did you
know that, according to research, men are supposedly
attracted to women wearing polka dots because dots
simulate the nipple?) Another Daisy, Daisy Buchanan
(Mia Farrow) in the film *The Great Gatsby,* wears a
matching violet dress, scarf, and hat when, after eight
years, she finally again meets Gatsby (Robert Redford),
who sports a purple silk shirt at Nick Carraway's cot-
tage. In the film *My Cousin Vinny,* sexy Mona Lisa Vito
(Marisa Tomei) sashays around in a saucy tight purple
dress—very Bronx—with spangles, an example for
which, perhaps, no better proof is necessary of British
high-fashion designer Katharine Hamnett's pronounce-
ment, "Women buy clothes essentially to get laid." It
was model Twiggy's favorite color in the early seventies;
in *Look* (May 4, 1971) we read, "Justin [de Villeneuve,
her erstwhile beau] had her Super Mini painted
aubergine ('just a posh name for purple,' she said) be-
cause that's her favorite color." World Champion Cow-
boy Casey Tibbs—he appeared on *Life*'s cover in October
1951—always wore a purple cowboy shirt and drove a

purple Cadillac. There is an enormous bronze statue of him riding the bucking bronc "Necktie" outside the Pro Rodeo Hall of Fame in Colorado Springs, Colorado. And singer Whitney Houston's jacket was also spangled in "The Concert for a New South Africa" given on November 12, 1994, as was the rest of her in-your-face purple outfit, slacks, and jersey, a getup conceptually close, if you ask me, to what poetaster Jenny Joseph must have had in mind in her inexplicably popular poem "Warning," the opening lines of which go:

> *When I am an old woman*
> *I shall wear purple*
> *With a big red hat which doesn't go*
> *And doesn't suit me*

She goes on to tell how, making up for the sobriety of her youth, she'll press alarm bells and run her stick along public railings and pick flowers from other people's gardens and learn to spit, and so forth, which, I am hard put to explain, many people—as a sort of declaration of independence—find cute. But what an aboriginal! It would be all I could do, I'm sorry, to keep from grabbing her fence stick or a large croquet mallet and whacking her over the head with it.

It is the unmistakable color in everything from the silk lining of good suits to Indian clothes in Guatemala to a fuchsia wool-and-cashmere Gianfranco Ferre shawl ($1,595 the copy). And what about Harriet Quimby? I doubt that a more beautiful woman ever lived. A pioneer pilot affectionately called the "Dresden doll"—the first woman in the United States to win a pilot's license and the first woman to fly the English Channel—she always sported, along with a pair of rakishly streamlined goggles, a hooded, plum-colored flying suit, which can be seen at the International Air and Space Museum in Centerville, Ohio. How sad her death—she crashed in Boston harbor on July 1, 1912, in an all-white seventy-horsepower Bleriot monoplane—but how elegantly she wore purple, unlike the *very purple* Minnesota Vikings football team or that of the University of Texas, whose pants, shirts, and helmets are of the most hideous purpureal grape imagineable, except perhaps for the ample oversufficiency of purple metal flake five-speed Schwinn bicycles ripping up and down the sidewalks of America. Hideola!

I was once allowed by the curator at the Martello Tower in Sandy Cove, Dublin, after striking up a friendship with her, one noon, when no one was about, to have the singular thrill of actually trying on James Joyce's purple waistcoat, the very one he significantly gave to Gabriel Conroy in the great and highly autobiographical story "The Dead": "His mother had worked for him as a birthday present a waistcoat of purple tabinet, with little foxes' heads upon it, lined with brown satin and having round mulberry buttons." I stood on the high iron steps outside the tower for a photograph, proudly invested. I have—and treasure—the photograph still.

Violet clothes, or added purple touches here and there, make vivid many modern paintings. May I mention some of my favorites? Picasso's *The Absinthe Drinker* (1901), a grim woman wrapped in her own strictured embrace and pondering air, wears full purple clothes, and even the seltzer bottle is purple. (Painters who are not colorists produce illumination, Delacroix reminds us, but not painting.) The girl in Henri Rousseau's *The Dream* (1910) reclines on a purple sofa. What about Pierre Bonnard's *Interior at Antibes* (1920), with its odd central figure shadowed before the viewer, in the haunting blue-violet dress? Elizabeth Griffiths Smith Hopper—Edward Hopper's *The Artist's Mother*—wears a purple dress. And then there is Cézanne's *Madame Cézanne,* which prompted John Updike in "Painted Wives" to observe,

> *Prim, passive, and wan, Madame Cézanne,*
> *Posed with her purple-ish clothes oddly on;*
> *Tipped slightly askew, and outlined in blue,*
> *She seems to be hearing, "Stop moving damn you!"*

Munch's original name *Black and Violet,* for the standing portrait of his sister Inger, now called *Portrait of the Artist's Sister,* is one of the most moving paintings ever done: violet background, violet touches to the dress, magnificently beautiful face, so lovely. The seated jitterbox in Francis Bacon's *Figure with Meat* (1954) looks almost electrified by the remorselessly kinetic purple he wears. What is Georges Seurat's *Side Show (La Parade)* (1888) but a pointillist study—he preferred the technical term *divisionism*—of the harmonies of purple, a shimmering and translucent screen?

What did purple mean to El Greco? The dazzling display of color in *The Burial of Count Orgaz* (1586) is somehow centered by the violet robe of the Madonna, who sits above all of that movement, the thrust of the soul, soaring up the canvas. But Pilate too wears purple in *Christ Before Pilate* (1567), attaining little dignity from it. Strange, chilly coloring—did El Greco imbibe it in Crete?—and the startlingly livid effects of his violet tones characterize much of his work. (Purple as a single color is a modern pigment. Artists generally use Cobalt Violet when a bright sole color is desired or combine Ultramarine Blue and Alizarin Red.) He seemed to love the way the color informed, not merely his artistic designs, but tragedy as human action, a uniquely aesthetic idea that calls to mind what Wallace Stevens advises the artist in "In a Bad Time":

> . . . *speak loftier lines.*
> *Cry out, "I am the purple muse." Make sure*
> *The audience beholds you, not your gown.*

It is a color in art that softens the silk clothes of Watteau's pilgrims and the wings of Fragonard's angels and the doublets of Caravaggio's young men. It rarely fails to dignify. I think of all the few select paintings mentioned here, my favorite is Titian's *Sacred and Profane Love* (1515), a picture, according to Henry James, that "glows with the inscrutable chemistry of the prince of colorists," which shows two beautiful women sitting on a low sculptured wall, one richly clad, the other with unbound hair, naked, radiant with sweetness and grace, "ungirdled," as James goes on to say, "by a great reverted mantle of Venetian purple." And in his light *Bac-*

chanal (c. 1518), with its drinking and dancing figures in full occlusive violet tunics and robes, Titian virtually defines by the use of dark grape-purple the nature of a wine-drinking gambol, reminding me of the Dionysiac Mystery Cult shown by way of purple robes, tunics, and drinking on the wall paintings at Pompeii (c. 50 B.C.). Incidentally, it was James Whistler's *Violet Note,* a nude sketch of his model Lyse Vazaeti, that Boston eccentric Isabella Stewart Gardner bought from the painter—his painting of her was called *Yellow Note*—and hung at Fenway Court, which created all the attendant gossip that *she* had been painted in the nude. And what about Dalí's portrait of himself and Lorca, *Still Life by Mauve Moonlight?*

Claude Monet loved purpureal blues. (How could a man with such a great love for beauty and for cooking have smoked cigarettes all his life?) His magnificent Clos Normand garden at Giverny was filled with mauve and white wisteria, delphiniums, rhododendrons, clematis (with its "purple stars," as Oscar Wilde called them), lilacs, azaleas, irises, lavenders, impatiens, lupins, valerias, wormwoods, astilbe, and santolians. What about the lilies in his fabled water garden? (Monet's profound horticultural passion prefigured, but never fails to remind me of, fashion editor John Fairchild's pronouncement, "I think that having a beautiful garden is more important than a beautiful house.") Unlike passionate gardener Edith Wharton, the lanes of whose mansion The Mount in Lenox, Massachusetts, were purple with Michaelmas daisies—she loved boundaries and enclosed spaces in gardens (even in rooms)—Monet disliked the look of formality, rejecting defined forms in favor of color, both in painting and in gardening. He once remarked, "I perhaps owe becoming a painter to flowers." Which calls to mind Marc Chagall's graceful compliment to the natural world, "Art is the unceasing effort to compete with the beauty of flowers—and never succeeding."

Nature is lavish with purple. A faint lavender sky with high blue above the clouds in early morning or late afternoon foretells good weather, according to Louis Rubin's *The Weather Wizard's Cloud Book*. The changing heavens can reflect either violet streaks or purple smears. "April evening spreads over everything, the purple blue left by a child who has used the whole paint box," insightfully writes F. Scott, the father of Scotty Fitzgerald in *The Crack Up*. Water often takes on a violet tone at dawn and dusk, and many red algae are purple or purplish black as well. Mountain ranges from afar seem forever bathed in violet light. Mt. McKinley in Alaska is the paradigm, which I once saw, holy, majestic, amethystine, and tranquil, rising in vaporous white mists north of Anchorage, a place where I remember wishing myself to be completely alone to ponder the beauty. And I have noted the same of Mt. Monadnock in New Hampshire. "Pyramids from a distance purple like mountains. Seem high and pointed, but flatten and depress you as you approach," Herman Melville notes in his *Journal of a Visit to Europe and the Levant* (1857), and then he adds, strangely, "It was in these pyramids that was conceived the idea of Jehovah. Terrible mixture of the cunning and awful. Moses learned in all the lore of the Egyptians." Emily Dickinson perceptibly writes,

> *The mountains grew unnoticed,*
> *Their purple figures rise*
> *Without attempt, exhaustion,*
> *Assistance, or applause.*

Edith Sitwell in "Switchback" writes of "horses fat as plums." In the air we have the violet-crowned hummingbird—so aggressive toward other birds—and the violet-green swallow, metallic green in its upper parts, but with such an iridescent violet on its rump and tail. Proust wonderfully calls pigeons the "lilacs of the feathered kingdom." And the purple martin is our largest swallow. As eloquently apostrophizes Amy Lowell in her poem "Purple Grackles,"

> *Tyrian-feathered freebooter*
> *Appropriating my delightful gutter with so extravagant*
> *   an ease,*
> *You are as cool a pirate as ever scuttled a ship*
> *And are you not scuttling my summer with every peck of*
> *   your sharp bill?*

Why do flying fish have such colorful wings? They vary from an almost translucent purple to a deep navy color, but what I find particularly baffling is why, when the wings are extended only during flight, they should show such differing colors. It is understandable if it was coloration used to blend in and avoid capture, but why such color for flight over crystal clear waters like the Coral Sea?

In his essay "Autumnal Tints" Thoreau writes passionately of purple grass *(Eragrostis pectinacea),* singly "thin and poor," but "high-colored" in patches with a "fine spreading panicle of purple flowers, a shallow, purplish mist trembling around [him]." He sings a paean to purple, celebrating the splendor of poke, with its purple fruit, purple wood-grass, and purple-spiked andropogons. He writes,

> Almost the very sands confess the ripening influence of the August sun, and methinks, together with the slender grasses waving over them, reflect a purple tinge. The impurpled sands! Such is the consequence of all this sunshine absorbed into the pores of plants and the earth. All sap or blood is now wine-colored. At last we have not only the purple sea, but the purple land.

All the lavenders, with the mauvelike of their tiny petals and often green-gray leaves, are shrubby perennials, and among their uses today are in sachets and in pillows to perfume linen. Dainty bundles of lavender and costmary *(Chrysanthemum balsamita)*—an herb that was used strictly for sniffing in old New England and that children preferred to cookies and called "Bible leaves," as they often served as bookmarks in prayerbooks and Bibles for devout churchgoers—were commonly made by colonial women "to lye upon the toppes of beds, presses, etc. for sweet scent and savour."

King Crimson maple leaves are purple, as are those of Japanese maples and the Copper Beech, a sort of bronze-purple. Many arborvitae, certain juniper species, and common cedars with anthocyanine showing through "bronze" for the winter, taking on a distinct touch of violet. And what of the purple trunks of the cryptomeria trees in Japan? The seed pods of a king palm? Joe-pye weed, with its pale purple flowers—used by the Iroquois as a remedy for kidney ailments—guarantees, if a young man will hold some in his mouth while talking to a young woman, success in conversation. Black currants paradoxically have wonderfully bold purple berries. Aren't these the treasured purples Alice Walker in *The Color Purple* tells us to savor? "I think it pisses God off," Shug tells Celie, in one of the less Ciceronian, if heart-felt, moments in that novel, "if you walk by the color purple in a field somewhere and don't notice it." Purple loosestrife, however, you cannot fail to notice. An aptly named perennial, years ago introduced as a flowering plant, now banned, purple loosestrife *(Lythrum salicaria)* has escaped from gardens and is overtaking everything in many areas in this country. It has a fierce reputation: witches are said to despise it, it is feared in Russia, snakes can't stand its odor, it drives away mosquitoes, it rids animals of flies, and it is a remedy for dysentery. A similar phenomenon on Cape Cod applies to purple mussels; transported by boats, they are now clogging many drainage pipes and waterways. They of course thrive on rocks. ("I think iridescent rocks stink," snaps Lolita to Humbert, who'd planned a naturalistic after-noon in *Lolita.*) The purple star of Jerusalem *(Tragopogon porrifolius)* has the distinction of closing its flower at high noon—vampirish!—for which it is also called "Jack-go-to-bed-at-noon." One of my favorite trees in all of nature is the purple-cone spruce, with its brilliant purplish red cones. And in San Diego I sampled the sour purple berries of the Eugenia tree, which even have a color-coordinated purple stone inside. As a boy, Red Sox slugger Ted Williams, who grew up in the North Park area of San Diego, used to practice his batting swing as he walked along by walloping these inch-size berries every time he saw one. Even deciduous trees in their bare winter starkness reveal, at least to Elizabeth Bishop in "Electrical Storm," a sort of color.

> *The Lent trees had shed all their petals:*
> *wet, stuck, purple, among the dead-eye pearls*

She also refers to the gloaming—that archaic word for twilight so popular with Victorians and lyricists of old sheet music—as "dark purple brown."

What a light show of purple perennials! Lilacs, primrose, gloxinia, the flowers of the myrtle, catnip, bugleweed, Ross phlox, velvet centaurea, dragonhead, dame's rocket *(Hesperis matronalis),* cranesbill, spike speedwell, hydrangea, larkspur, aster amellus, garden sage, the purple-leafed astilbe, aubretia (purple rockcress), monkshood, platycodon, lupine, iris, and there is the thistle. The showy garden flower catharanthus, popularly but incorrectly called vinca, is purple as often as it is pink. So is statice, a lovely purple flower. The penstemon, a low shrub with big flowers and a long season, actually grows out of cracks in limestone boulders. I have seen the hillsides of eastern Maine in June covered everywhere with purple lupins. Bougainvilleas, with bright purple flowers, climb the sides of stucco houses in the Southwest. Then there are lilies. Vergil, who was ever observant, mentions purple lilies in the *Aeneid* (*"Manibus date lilia plenis/Purpureos sparagam flores"* [VI. 885]), recalling for me Olive Custance's commemorial lines,

> *Lilies with violet-colored hearts that break*
> *In shining clusters round the silent dead*

But in the *Eclogues,* when he refers to a *Purpureo narcisso,* surely a narcissus with a purple calyx is meant.

And what is meant—what flower?—in sad Ophelia's last bawdy allusion?

> *. . . crowflowers, nettles, daisies, and long purples*
> *That liberal shepherds give a grosser name*
> *But our cold maids do dead men's fingers call them*

The answer is: "Bullspizzles."

Annuals, like prairie gentian, purple robe (or "cup flower"), campanula (Canterbury bells), gentian sage, the violet auchusa (Cape forget-me-not), heliotrope—Truman Capote once planned to write a novella-length profile of Babe Paley, to be called *Heliotrope,* after this purple-flowered plant she so much admired, but in fact he never began it—and Alpine wallflower, Asarnia Barclaiana show even wilder, more effusive purples. So do many wildflowers, like hepatica, dogtooth violet, asters (both New England and New York varieties), Tansy-leaf aster, bud-foot violet, passionflower, spiderwort, spring larkspur, sea lavender, Jacob's ladder, Venus's looking-glass, gray beardtongue, and even the deadly nightshade (*Atropa belladonna*). In Alexander Pope's satire *The Rape of the Lock,* haughty Belinda, egotistically preening at her dressing table, uses belladonna either to enlarge the pupils of her lovely eyes or to darken the surrounding skin: "And keener Lightnings quicken in her Eyes." But to my mind the best literary reference to this dramatic shrub is found in L. P. Hartley's splendid novel *The Go-Between* (1953):

> I knew that every part of it was poisonous. I knew too that it was beautiful, for did not my mother's botany book say so? I stood on the threshold, not daring to go in, staring at the button-bright berries and the dull, purplish, hairy, bell-shaped flowers reaching out towards me. I felt that the plant could poison me, even if I didn't touch it, and that if I didn't eat it, it would eat me, it looked so hungry.

Many passifloras—passion flowers—are so gorgeous that for many fastidious botanists, so taken with their exquisite beauty and complexity, they stand for perfection, and considering the rare *Passiflora caeruleo-racemosa,* with its spokelike petals radiating out in a mauve circle, one couldn't find anything more majestic even in the purpuraceous Imperial Crown of India, which I so admired in the Tower of London. There are purple zinnias, which are evoked in the strange lines of Louis Zokofsky's "Chloride of Lime and Charcoal,"

Zinnias you look so much like Gentiles
Born among butcher furniture

The violet, in Greek mythology, is the flower of Io and Ares. Violets are said to have grown from the blood of Attis, just as roses and anemones, according to legend, grew from the blood of Adonis. *Ionanthus* (Greek) means "with flowers like a violet." Most brides at weddings in Victorian times carried only violets. Yet with violets there are many associations with death. When St. Teresa of Avila died in 1582, the odor of violets is said to have emanated from her saintly body. Proust held in hand a bunch of violets as he lay on his pristine-white deathbed. It was also violets that in her "Directions for My Funeral" Boston's Isabella Stewart Gardner requested be placed on her coffin, helpfully adding "if in season," and she asked that a purple pall cover her coffin, the same one that she had used for her husband's funeral, because, as she explained at the time, "nothing black should shroud his airy spirit in its flight." We have mentioned Dorian Gray's need for Parma violets as plumage in his buttonhole. But decadent eccentric Des Esseintes in *A Rebours* also wears a bunch of Parma violets in the opening of his low-necked shirt. So does Proust's Odette. No purple, in my opinion, goes *deeper* than Parma violets, a solid, intense purple that never has that black look, that nasty, almost Woolworthian black stippling, although the purple columbine and pansies both show a very deep and intense purple, as does the purple alyssum and, one of my favorites, godetia.

Strangely, Thoreau in *Walden* at one point refers to "yellow violets," a minor miracle, I suppose, if you'll forgive the oxymoron. But violets are never orchids, not, in any case, for poet Arthur Symons, who may very well be making an oblique sexual confession of a sort (for *orchis* means the testes), when he writes—mystifyingly odd last line, is it not?—in his poem "Violet,"

> *The orchid mostly is the flower I love,*
> *And violets, the mere violets of the wood*
> *For all their sweetness, have not power to move*
> *The curiosity that rules my blood.*

Sweetness. But have they scent? Victorians constantly speak and write of the scent of violets. I have always wondered what they meant by that.

It is ironic to note that in what may be the loveliest collocation in all poetry, a litany, really, when Perdita at the sheep shearing in Shakespeare's *A Winter's Tale* (IV.iv.110–34) sighs for the flowers of spring to give her guests—and bewitches us with her enchanting words—in the significant passage that seems a literal riot of varied hues and beauty, as critic Caroline Spurgeon points out, *no single color is named!* "Violets dim," "lilies of all kinds," "the crown imperial," "pale primeroses," "gold oxlips," we hear the gorgeous chant. With the aid of perfect epithets, it is we ourselves who have to supply the misty purples, flaming yellows, heavenly blues, and so forth. And I love the lines from Winett De Rokha's "Waltz in Yungay Square,"

La Mujer de mármol, desnuda entre sus violetas
se ruboriza al contacto del aire

(The marble woman, naked among her violets,
blushes at the touch of air)

                                        (my translation)

African violets, did you know, are not *true* violets?
They are *Saintpaulias* belonging to the plant family Ges-
neriaceae, of which other notable members are gloxinia
and Cupid's Bower. The purplest African violets can be
found under names like Blue Boy, Norseman, Viking,
and Lady Geneva. Many African violets go through blue,
like Sailor Girl, Water Lily, and so forth, and approach
pink, like Orchid Beauty, Amazon Pink, and Du Pont
Lavender Pink. There is a curious symbiosis between
ants and violets. Ants harvest the violet seed and trundle
it along into their nests, mold grows on the seed coat,
the composted seed germinates and propagates more vi-
olets.

Another black-purple flower, like violets and dying
hydrangeas, is the anemone. D. H. Lawrence refers in
Flowery Tuscany to

> the big, sturdy, black-purple anemones, with
> black hearts. They are curious, those great, dark-
> violet anemones. You may pass them on a grey
> day, or at evening or early morning, and never see
> them. But as you come along in the full sunshine,
> they seem to be baying at you with all their
> throats, baying deep purple into the air.

My favorite purple poem relating to flowers is Robert Frost's sphinxish "The Quest of the Purple Fringed." There is a devotional, almost religious quest in the poem, a search that virtually forms a pilgrimage. Is it an allegory? On a chilly day in autumn, the narrator takes a long, meandering walk through high grasses, finds and then follows a path, and finally, under an alder tree, discovers the flower.

> *When the color flushed to the petals it must have been*
> *The far-sought flower.*
> *There stood the purple spires with no breath of air*

Then he *kneels.* He looks closely, counts the spires, rises, and silently heads home—there is a total and almost supernatural quiet in this poem—feeling now, at long last, that fall can come, for "summer was done," after having put out, as it were, its last, most magnificent bloom.

A strange ambivalence resides in purple. It is red withdrawn from humanity by blue, "but the red," writes Kandinsky, "must be cold, for the spiritual need does not allow of a mixture of warm red with cold blue." Purple is therefore a cooled red and consequently rather sad and ailing, a frail and, when pale, even hobbling hue, that can meekly requisition help at the curb or hide itself from the glare of day with a diffidence born of the self-conscious or the sacrificial.

There also prevails in noble purple something that asks one to kneel, that exacts obeisance, that communicates the power of its piety and penance. "I tremble with pleasure when I think that on the very day of my leaving prison both the laburnum and the lilac will be blooming in the gardens," writes Oscar Wilde, "and that I shall see the wind stir into restless beauty the swaying gold of the one, and make the other toss the pale purple of its plumes, so that all the air shall be Arabia for me." It evokes Arabia, like myrrh and incense, caravans swaying, houris dancing under moonlight, and yet for all its grace and mystery, all its tenderness, it also stands for the imperium, the authority, the rule, the austerity of law, the weighty robes draped across an emperor's arm as he stands bold before the forum. Purple is frailty and force, both. Neither should come as a surprise. After all, meekness is also guaranteed its inheritance, is it not? And that is something we should never forget. Real power never impairs beauty but often bestows it. Gentleness empowers in the way that submission, in a sense, is only an aspect of strength.

Green

GREEN IS POWER, nature's fuse, the color of more force and guises than are countable, a messenger announcing itself, paradoxically, as the hue of both renewal and reproduction or infirmity and illness. It is at once the preternaturally ambiguous color of life and death, the vernal sign of vitality, and the livid tinge of corruption, a "dialectical lyric" (to borrow a term from Kierkegaard), responding with the kind of answers that perhaps depend less on itself than on the questions we ask of it. Many people still insist that green is a primary color. Why not? M. Voltaire has a character from *Micromegas,* a visiting inhabitant from Sirius, assert that on that planet, they have thirty-nine primary colors! The color green is compounded of blue and yellow, heaven connecting with earth, a color combining the cold blue light of intellect—it slows down the pulse—with the deep emotional warmth of the yellow sun to produce the wisdom of equality, hope, and resurrection. As the color of Venus and Mercury, devoted lovers, green is peace, vegetation, gladness, and rebirth. It is associated with the number five and is the fairy color, the primal wash, the heraldic tint of envy, of nausea and of hope, of solid gems and eerie mists, of sea cabbage, eelgrass, salt thatch, subaqueous plants, algae, and sea lettuce bearding the rocky shore. "Green derives from blue and surpasses it," says an old Chinese proverb, referring to the student who, learning from a teacher, grows to surpass him. Did you know that "greenth" is a legitimate word, although rare, meaning verdure? To "green" is even a verb, in Scotland, meaning to yearn. So many hues and shades and tints of green exist in the natural world, so multifarious are its guises, it is impossible ever fully to know them. It is in its numinous energies as infederated as Burma and as various and unpredictable as nature herself. It is ironic, furthermore, that the color green cannot even claim primacy in nature, at least according to Robert Frost in his poem "Nothing Gold Can Stay." "Nature's first green is gold," he writes, "The hardest to hold." (Shakespeare always thought green and gold went together.)

In a very real sense, green as a color is almost a substance. It is rank with smells, cushion-soft, fruit-pulpishly irrepressible, spreading, ubiquitous, and uneconomical, the way wasted space equals prestige in Tokyo, a color swirling and madly voluptuous in its abundance. It seems to flow up your arm, where, instantly, you feel it is the one color truly drawn from life—*dal vero,* "from the true."

It is the color of hope, aspiration, and struggle, in the psychology of spirituality and thought. Color is Zoroastrian, however, and ambivalent its gods. "Green must always have a large following among artists and art lovers," Richard Le Gallienne writes in "The Boom in Yellow," but then without hesitation adds, "There is something not quite good, something sinister about it—at least its more complex forms." As a color, it is both the Lady of the Strachy *and* the yeoman of the wardrobe. It symbolizes nobility. It also signifies callow, unsophisticated, bad, ill prepared, inexact, unskilled, ignorant, amateur, unripe, rude, bitter, incomplete, and uninformed—and as an adjective of notable reservation unfailingly describes moist cement, immature liquor, coarse salt, unripe cheese, tart wine, virgin lumber, hot manure, unsalted fish, new meat, wet sap, raw hides, unburnable wood, infirm pottery, uncured pelts, just-quarried stone, sour grapes, young coffee, bad beef, weak ginger, and, to the French, even a sharp and thoughtless comment *(une verte réponse).*

There is in green the force of bravado and the seeds of urgent, young rebellion. ("Natural rebellion, done i' th' [grass] blade of youth," says the Countess of Rosillion, defending the excesses of her son Bertram in *All's Well That Ends Well.)* In the seventeenth and eighteenth centuries, sea green, rather than stark red, was the color of revolutionary zeal. Cromwell's troops during the English civil war wore bright green ribbons. The badge of opposition to Popishly-affected King Charles II was a Green Ribbon, most proudly worn by his nemesis, "the little man with three names," Anthony Ashley Cooper,

Earl of Shaftsbury, a virulent persecutor of Roman Cath-
olics. It was Napoleon's favorite color. Thomas Carlyle
in *The French Revolution* describes the radical Robes-
pierre as a "sea-green incorruptible." Hungarian Mau-
rice Jókai's *The Green Book* (1879), a novel of Russian
life, involves the doings of a band of anticzarist conspira-
tors, whose activities are recorded in the large green
revolutionary volume to which the title of the book re-
fers. (The czar in the novel actually dies at the hands of
the Man with the Green Eyes.) The hieroglyphs found in
the sacred pyramid of Pepi I at Saqqara are aquamarine.
Green is associated with vigor and activity and freshness.
Charles Dickens came up with the "bold idea" of pub-
lishing the monthly installments of his novels with
green covers, saying, "This will give [them] the interest
and precedence of a fresh weekly portion during the
month." Greenpeace saves whales. The "green card" ten-
ders freedom for various visitors to live in the United
States. It is a color also associated somewhat with im-
moderation and even recklessness. Is that why Amando
Zegri in *The Golden Book* wrote, "Joy is a fruit Ameri-
cans eat green"? That green is invariably connected to
youth and life is incontestable. Could that be the reason
why the fictitious town of the old *Our Gang* series (later
the *Little Rascals)* was named Greenpoint? Youth is
hope. Youth is new. Youth is green, in every sense of the
term.

Does green always denote youth? Curiously, the Ro-
mans referred to those persons who, having passed the
age of forty-five but not having reached sixty, as *viridus,*
having "green old age." We can find in Vergil's *Aeneid*

VI: *"Jam senior, sed cruda deo viridisque senectus,"* which is what Catullus probably means in his poem to Camerius when he uses the expression *"seni recocto."* The Greeks said ὠμόν γέρας. At the age of sixty, Queen Elizabeth I, rendering Boethius, spoke of "happy griny youth." Young. Old. Green is equally the color of flourishing midlife and the competence of vigorous health. How explain it? We choose our own hats. It is always summer somewhere. And didn't Keats tell us that man's life was all allegory?

A green crystal paperweight, given to him by the workers of a glass factory in Bryansk—this is my favorite "hope" anecdote—sat on novelist Leo Tolstoy's writing desk. It was engraved with this message: "Let the Pharisees and the Holy Fathers excommunicate you as they wish; the Russian people will always hold you dear." No vast sepulchre, Tolstoy's grave, by the way, is only a grassy mound in a simple clearing in the deep green of the surrounding woods. It was the spot where he wanted to be buried, near a ravine where he and his brothers, when they were youngsters, believed that a green stick had been buried on which was written the secret of happiness for all human beings. There is no cross and no marker on the spot. There is only serenity. The wind is still. Birds sing.

What is the essence of green? It means life. It means go, grow, grass, class, the elite, the incomplete, it incorporates mold and memory, naïveté, corruption, production, and the hope, always, of new beginnings. An Anglo-Saxon word (ME *grene,* from OE *grēne),* it is a color that represents in some of its more obvious simplicities youth, prosperity, tranquillity, good health, freshness, sympathy, adaptability, and immortality. A fluid color, it goes from sea green hues to coppery verdigris to bright emerald green to deep olive green, is kinetic, fleet, never in one place, and is almost maddeningly difficult to duplicate by the use of materials other than those fully identical to the ones that composed the original paint. The little functionary Bitzer, in Charles Dickens's novel *Hard Times,* might technically have defined the color in his factual, utilitarian way: "Any color normally seen when the portion of the physical spectrum of wave length 495 to 515 Mμ, most characteristically 505.5 Mμ, is employed as a stimulus." Any real enterprise of denomination intended to list this color of protean uncanniness, never mind clarify or classify, can only be frustrated, for in the way it skips from one alias to another, challenging the stability of all proper names, it reminds me of Rimbaud's *"Je est un autre"* ("I is another"). It can turn faster than the plot of *The Big Sleep* and has more changes than the channels of the Mississippi, a river Mark Twain once described as having "shortened itself thirty miles in a single jump!" We can only appropriate the color's aberrations as we do Rimbaud's idiom, recalling that the word *color* itself not only comes to us from ancient Rome with its original sense practically intact, meaning "complexion" or "hue"—both Vergil and Horace, by the way, use it to signify "a beautiful complexion"—but also that another Latin meaning of the word is "artful concealment of a fault"; here some scholars relate the word to the Latin verb *celare,* to conceal. What particularizes, arguably, limits. Who was it who said, "Too bad for the wood that happens to be a violin"? The fluency of green, however, that creates its enigma is also its first splendor.

A thousand variations of the color exist—remember the Ames Brothers' song "49 Shades of Green"?—and so entirely sensitive and multifarious is the color, it is almost impossible to mix the same green twice. There are dead greens and red greens and striving greens and driving greens. It fades and fertilizes, shines and realigns, stands and falls. In Virginia Woolf's novel *Orlando,* one may recall how confused the young poet becomes when trying to describe nature ("Green in nature is one thing, green in literature another"), finding to his dismay that the shade of green in a laurel bush outside cannot fit the scope of his poem. There are hundreds of shades of green in the chaparral growing in the Southwest and California. I'm always reminded of that, for some reason, looking at Botticelli's painting *Primavera,* or even Henri Rousseau's jungly *Joyeux Farceurs* and its mass of carefully painted leaves of varying shades. How much to have to know to separate one from another! "I once met a spice importer," said Mimi Sheraton, "who could tell just by looking at a bay leaf whether it'd been grown on the sunny side of a hill in Turkey or on the shady side of a hill in California, and which year's crop it was from." Speaking of shades of green, Cape Cod marsh grass can now be found only in remote and inaccessible areas as the delicate celandine green it was when the Pilgrims saw it four hundred years ago, as its color has been altered by the fluxes, effluents, and seepage of human habitation down the centuries. Army green, from helmets to trucks, is more or less that dogged, predictable *thud* green, like U.S. postal relay boxes and stairwell walls and the kind of railings commonly used in old schools. A dead television screen is prosopographically green, like the very *word* television, which T. S. Eliot in 1942 declared was ugly—the upshot of "ill-breeding," he said, disgusted by the lame and misbegotten usage of yoking Latin and Greek roots together. But even early TV sets, when turned on, were a kind of carsick green, like the Zenith Flash-Matic remote control or the relatively expensive CT-100 Compatible. And I have always thought that pressure-treated lumber, hard and verdescent and gill-ill, has a sort of moronic look to it, a dumb grainlessness, like the faces of actors and sports broadcasters and professional athletes. No one has ever been able adequately to photograph the particular green of van Gogh's *Self-Portrait.* Degas referred to "poisonous emerald green," a raw, garish color by which he no doubt meant Paris green. Joyce unambiguously refers in his novel *Ulysses* to the "snotgreen sea," while Galway Kinnell in "The Avenue Bearing the Initial of Christ into the New World" refers to a sea "the green of churchsteeple copper." Little Black Sambo's umbrella is "candy green." A fading sun in Hardy's *The Mayor of Casterbridge* turns Jopp's coat to "scarecrow green." And shouldn't a tip of the hat be given here to Abbott Thayer (b. 1849), the man who invented camouflage, that combination of intentionally garbled neoterrain, mostly green but with much brown and motley yellow, used for military uniforms, helmets, tents, and so forth, to disguise soldiers in combat?

Colors can be patented. There are trademark colors. But with green, what glittering forfex could ever be found to snip, with a view to discrete exactitude, one precise shade from another? And how can one ever be certain it will stand still?

There is melon, spearmint green, pea green, which is green as a gremlin, absinthe, which has a sort of arsenic hue—a color I always associate with sycamore trees—and chintz green, a sort of neon. Sagebrush is gray-green. Sap green is also a neutralized or "grayed" green. And sage green is grayish. (To expel ants—a Victorian household hint—a small quantity of green sage placed in a closet will cause them to disappear.) Darryl Zanuck, founder and production head of 20th Century-Fox, was famous for the "Zanuck green" color (a phrase actually used in Hollywood) of his limousine, his office, and the Fox pool and steam room. I have a friend who boasts that his Mercury Tracer is "jewel green." Green is a color that in the depths of its chromal motion somehow always manages to whistle up another, gray or blue, yellow or lavender, and in that regard always reminds me of Simon's insightful remark to Victoria in Noël Coward's *Shadow Play,* "Everything smells like something else." I enjoy many of the Bruning names for green paint, such as Nile Mist, Washed Needles, Scuba Sea, Arboretum, Misty Rain, Leaflet, and Amenity, along with several Pratt and Lambert paint colors, like Parcae, Aeroe, Cozumel, Nephrite, Bezique, Leek, Icy Morn, Tea Leaf, Rainy Day, Fairway Green, and Hedgrow Mist, that never fail to summon in simple but evocative words the multiplicity of polynominal green's many tints and hues. In his poetry, Vergil uses *viridis* (natural green) and *glaucus* (bluish gray–green) and *pallens* (pale green, even wan).

Wetness, or at least moisture, poetically invigorates green, or so the paint colors above seem to imply, reminding me of the non sequitur that was William Blake's postscript in his theological letter, dated November 22, 1802, to Thomas Butts—"A Piece of Sea Weed serves for a Barometer. It gets wet and dry as the weather gets so."

Verdigris is greenish yellow in hue, a sort of seaweedish color, like artemisian green or pistache. *(Vert-de-gris* was an old nickname in French slang for a German soldier, on account of his uniform.) Celadon, or celandine, is also a yellow-green, sort of like Kilkenny or Chartreuse, an opaque yellow-green, like virgin olive oil. Ondine is another variation of yellow-green. Robert Lacey in his biography *Grace* [Kelly], refers to "the yellowy-green of Warner Color," as specifically found in the eerily crepuscular movie *Dial M for Murder.* And Wordsworth found western skies to be a yellow-green. Green naphtha is darkish green. There is green ebony, a melanoxylon. Verdantique, or ophicalcite, is a green mottled or veined—we might say stippled—serpentine marble, which was often used for indoor decoration by the ancient Romans. Chrysoprase is apple green, and agrostine, like grass. Olive has its own khakilike drabness as a paint. But how lilting, how beautiful, how flowing the fickling leaves of olive trees! "She laughs like an olive tree," we read in Scripture. There *is* an oceanic look to olive trees, an undulant rippling when the wind blows, silver, green, silver, green. If you could put laughter into flora, it would be exactly that, an image of flowing beauty, not unlike the equally lovely image found in the *Song of Songs* (4:1): "Your hair is like a flock of goats moving down the slopes of Gilead." Nature, in Milton's ode "On the Morning of Christ's Nativity," sends Peace, personified, "crown'd with Olive green," who, waving a myrtle wand, brings tranquillity to the world at Christ's birth. ("O music, the color of olives," writes Thomas Merton in his poem "In Memory of the Spanish Poet, Federigo Garcia Lorca.") Emeraude perfume is a sort of olive-oil green, which I have also heard whimsically described as floradora. In his poem "Sera," Giuseppe Ungaretti writes,

> *Appiè dei passi della sera*
> *Va un' acqua chiara*
> *Color dell' uliva . . .*
> *E giunge al breve fuoco smemorato*

> (At the close of evening
> the clean water
> becomes olive-colored . . .
> and touches the brief forgetful fire)
>   (my translation)

In his poem "Homunculus et La Belle Etoile," Wallace Stevens refers to a "biscay green" that "charms philosophers" and provides the essential light for self-realization and does away with abstract thought. Isn't there a tinge of green in the bronze of ginger ale? In many putties? In brass? James Joyce fussily selected a special color of green for the cover of his *Pomes Penyeach,* specifically the shade of the Irish Calville apple, which nevertheless faded badly over the years, not unlike the way the unique Greek blue did, which was the color he had chosen for the cover of his controversial novel *Ulysses* in 1922. And Granny Smith apple green—isn't it unlike any other green on earth, with the melancholy exception of those ugly, sour-shiny cardboard leprechaun hats sold at Woolworth's on St. Patrick's Day—*and* that green vertical mysteriously running down the somber face of potato-headed Mme. Matisse in her husband's 1905 canvas *The Green Line?*

Doesn't Boy Scout brown have a hint of queachy green? What about the miniscule beads of green in oak-grain found in old benches, pews, and handsomely carved misericords? Glaucous is a greenish blue hue. The dark, overcast sky and thick, wintry green ice ponds in Pieter Brueghel's *Hunters in the Snow* perfectly define the word *glaucous.* (The proper name of the pussy willow is glaucous willow.) There is "spinach green," which shows a distinct undertone of bluishness. Surgeons always wore white until about 1914, when it was seen not only that blood against a white uniform was repulsive but that high-intensity light also made the glare from white uniforms painful. And so spinach green was used. At the end of World War II, however, lighting had changed in most hospital operating rooms, whereupon surgeons switched to a color called "misty green." Since the early 1960s, "seal blue," a kind of Confederate gray-green, has been generally favored. Why? According to the Career

Apparel Institute of New York, "seal blue simply shows up better on the TV monitors used to demonstrate surgical techniques to medical students." And remember oxymoronic "lavender green, dilly dilly" from the 1946 Walt Disney film *So Dear to My Heart,* my favorite childhood movie? (And supposedly Disney's.) Upon first seeing the little girl in it—an inenubilable little beauty named Luana Patten—I fell in love for the first time in my life. Complete eudaemonia! I felt a thrill in my helium-filled heart that set in me an ongoing pattern of love and appreciation for women, often movie stars like Eleanor Powell and Claudia Cardinale, and especially Louise Brooks, the goddess, ever since. But do you believe in cognitive distortion? I know a writer who has criticized me in print as a woman hater, an absurd calumny I can just about barely bring myself to identify in order to refute. The sad fact of the matter is, he was consistently unfaithful to his wife for almost thirty years (I believe it was his own infidelities that allowed him to stay married, in fact) but then with revalorizing arrogance had the cruelty to write about *her* until she could take it no longer and divorced him. Have you ever noticed that we tend to condemn in others the very fault we ourselves often have? ("The reversal," Gore Vidal called it; he also said somewhere that lying was the most notable American trait.) It is my judgment that, feeling, intolerably, that the many women who have loved me in my life have somehow, not only in the grotesque compote of his own envious grief and pluming self-regard but also by a fatal symmetry all of his own making, forcibly deprived him of like attention—along with the tendency to plot is the corollary to believe oneself plotted against—he hatefully repeats libels about me in his books that his own femicidal compulsions belie. It is the legacy of those driven by pusillanimity and the brainless apostatism referred to in 1 Timothy 6:3–5 that drives such people. And ruins them. And often their work. "A person whose features are too marked," observes Feodor Chaliapin, "is at a disadvantage as an author."

As colors, blue and green have almost always danced a graceful and harmonious pas de deux. "Blue!" writes Richard La Gallienne, "Gentle cousin of the forest green/Married to green in all the sweetest flowers." A close spectral relationship between the two can be found in everything from lichens to Lalique, from turtles to turquoise, from hills to the hues of shampoo. Even the McGraw-Hill building at 330 West Forty-second Street, built in 1931, is a startling blue-green color. A peacock, when spreading its feathers, displays a tableau of green-and-blue eyes, each with an iridescent blue iris, green rim, and brown sclera. "Bluegreen Juneau," notes Thomas Merton, observing the mountains as he flew over Alaska in 1968, just prior to his fateful trip to the Far East. Lawrence Durrell in his novel *Justine* describes champagne bottles as "gleaming bluish-green like aged carp." As to cats, not carps, a white Persian with one blue eye and one green can hear, as Darwin discovered; a white Persian with two blue eyes is deaf. Speaking of infirmities, the blind writer Jorge Luis Borges once remarked, "I can still make out certain colors. I can still see blue and green." A color he could *not* see, oddly

enough, was black, the color of night. "I, who was ac-
customed to sleeping in total blackness, was bothered
for a long time at having to sleep in this world of mist,
in the greenish or blueish mist, vaguely luminous,
which is the world of the blind." Both the Blue Nile
and the White Nile are in fact green. In the song "Blue
in Green," Miles Davis with his trumpet brings out the
beauty of the two colors. Mescal—*aquardiente*—is ex-
tracted from the agave plant, also known as *mezcal azul*
("blue mescal") or blue maguey plant, because of its
blue-green metallic leaves. My favorite blue-green can
be seen in the eight slender vases, called *hes,* found in
King Tutankhamen's tomb, that were made of faience
and consisted of a core of powdered quartz heated until
it fused into a compact mass and then coated with glass.
The bluish green colors were obtained by copper com-
pounds, which is of course the reason (high copper con-
tent) water is usually blue-green. (Tut's royal scepter was
also part faience.) Although Patrick Kavanagh in his
poem "Canal Bank Walk" hadn't Tut in mind, I fondly
think of the young king when reading,

For this soul needs to be honored with a new dress woven
From green and blue things and arguments that cannot be proven

It is arguable that ancient artisans, more so than
moderns, were more at home with the dyadic combina-
tion of blue and green, which in some instances clash.
Leon Bakst's designs for *Scheherazade* in 1910, the main
scheme of which was, according to Richard Buckle, "an

unheard-of violence of peacock-green and blue," suppos-
edly "gave the jeweller Cartier the idea of setting sap-
phires and emeralds together for the first time since the
Moghul Emperors." Old Cape Codders are perhaps less
flexible and more hidebound. The front shutters of Cape
Cod houses were, and still are, almost always tradition-
ally painted green, especially when the house is white.
Many years ago, however, a self-reliant woman, with
paint left over from another job, painted her blinds blue.
Her neighbors were aghast. "The House with Blue
Blinds" in Barnstable still stands. (When the old woman
died, she left the house to relatives with the strict pro-
viso (old typical New England radicalism) that the
blinds always be kept the same color.)

Sakhrat, in Muslim mythology, is a sacred emerald, a
single grain of which, according to legend, grants mirac-
ulous powers to the possessor, and yet the reflection of
the stone colors the sky blue. Upon it rests Mt. Cat, the
fabulous mountain that encircles the earth and functions
as the home for giants and fairies. (Remember, an emer-
ald is the green, and an aquamarine the blue, variety of
beryl, just as a ruby is the red, and a sapphire the blue,
variety of corundum.) As to fairies, remember the riddle
in *The Hobbit* that Bilbo solves:

> *An eye in a blue face*
> *Saw an eye in a green face.*
> *"That eye is like to this eye,"*
> *Said the first eye,*
> *"But in low place*
> *Not in high place."*

The answer is: sun on daisies.

Isn't there a skein of blue in bay-leaf green? And in rosemary, in caraway-seed green, and in the trunks of trees, which often have a lot of purple-green? Arguably, even in most green paints used on canvas? (Color in painting is about light, remember, not necessarily the color of the object.) The blue-green deposit on older, wave-dashed rocks at the water's edge, caused by algae, is commonly called "green paint" by mariners. And rock tripe is a greenish blue crust that grows on sea boulders and ledges. "When boiled it has a sickish and offensive smell," writes Kenneth Roberts in *Northwest Passage,* "like stale paste, but supposedly it is nourishing." No, there is between the colors blue and green a basic symbiotic relationship everywhere, from spinach to grass to the Cape Cod beach weed called "poverty grass" to the blue-green packets of Kool cigarettes. As to the cooperating sky and sea, John Updike's "Shipbored" gives us an essential object lesson:

> *That line is the horizon line.*
> *The blue above it is divine.*
> *The blue below it is marine.*
> *Sometimes the blue below is green.*

A green ultramarine, it should be noted, is produced by grinding the sky blue stone lapis and then removing the gray rock that was mixed with it. It is, somewhat ironically, don't forget, the *green* of the lilac, not the blue or purple, that Walt Whitman celebrates of the flower in his poem "When Lilacs Last in the Dooryard Bloom'd":

> *In the dooryard fronting an old farm-house near the*
>   *white-wash'd palings,*
> *Stands the lilac-bush tall-growing with heart-shaped leaves*
>   *of rich green*

I have personally never seen nature such a rich, basic declarative green as on the island of Puerto Rico ("All youthfully green, and none [speaking of trees] without some fruit or other," writes George, Earl of Cumberland of Puerto Rico in *Purchas His Pilgrimes* in 1625). Ireland is positively pallid next to the lush, verdant hills of Caguas, Humaçao, and the Cordillera Central. The sodden turf of Scotland, Skye, the Orkneys are an intense green. So are the lush hills and vegetable green jungle forests of Rwanda. I have never forgotten, as who could, the dark green of the cypresses in the south of France. Boston's Fenway Park, home of the Boston Red Sox and site of the Green Monster—the imposing thirty-seven-foot left-field wall—is a sort of cordially soft machine green, easy on the eyes, especially surrounding the smooth green grass, whereas the official baize of gambling and gaming tables is, at least to my mind, a defiant, almost too electric green. Dickens in *Bleak House* calls billiard players "Gentlemen of the Green Cloth Road." Elizabeth Bishop eerily refers to a "drowned green." (When I was a lifeguard in my teens in Medford, I once pulled a dead, dripping boy out of the water at Wright's Pond—he had drowned, swimming alone, the previous night—who was precisely that color, a sort of reseda.) What exactly is the shade "boat green"? Bulph, a pilot in Dickens's novel *Nicholas Nickleby,* sports a "boat green" door on his house, where the window frames are of the same color. (He also commemoratively keeps on his parlor mantel, along with other maritime and natural curiosities, the little finger of a drowned man!) But, as a matter of fact, isn't green, as in chlorine, the mortal color of drowning?

It is the color of parrots, S & H Green Stamps, lotus leaves, young bamboo, sea light, copper patina, wine bottles, Wellington boots (worn by women, along with Barbours, on English country weekends), iguanas, visors, pine soap, computer screens, moss, terrariums, stand-bottles in barber shops, swamps, mint, peridots and emeralds (good emeralds are clear, dark green), algae, most lawn mowers, John Deere tractors, eye shades, spearmint leaves, gardening gloves, army fatigues, pickles, the tights and doublets of Santa's elves, windshield tints, soda bottles, antifreeze and coolant, air fresheners and deodorants, tincture of evergreen, Comet cleanser (which artist Andy Warhol especially favored in preparation for his "toilet art"), chlorophyll, almost all paper currency, particularly Civil War money, peppercorns, mint juleps, June bugs, bankers' lamps—accountants, in slang, are called "green shades"—mouthwash, sea urchins' roe, Clorets, tongue fur, and the Statue of Liberty. "Greenbacks" were first issued in 1862 as a war revenue measure. "Greenies," new cigarettes made from unaged tobacco, is also slang for pep pills. "Vietnam Green," even more so than Panama red, New York white, and famous Acapulco gold, is—at least according to *The Anarchist's Handbook*—the best marijuana to be had on the American market. "Green lion" in alchemy is a universal mineral dissolvent. Green, like red, its complementary color, has always been a demotic favorite. It is commodious. It colors persons, things, even places. "Places are persons," writes Proust in *Jean Santeuil,* and to that sensitive novelist names conveniently and commodiously revealed colors that also enriched them. "The name of the Prince of Faffenheim-Munsterburg-Weininger kept in the freedom with which its first syllables were, as one says in music, attacked," he writes, "and . . . projected, like greenish branches." The state of limbo I have always more or less thought of vaguely as terrarium green. Much of Bosch's musical hell, *The Garden of Delights,* is sour green. Aren't certain times of the day or seasons green as well? I am thinking of the wet, cold, dank green evenings of an English September. And have you noticed that digital numbers are almost always green? Nothing is predictable. If Cecil Frances Alexander is correct in his poem of 1870, "There Is a Green Hill," even the holy hill of Calvary was green.

> *There is a green hill far away,*
> *Without a city wall,*
> *Where the dear Lord was crucified*
> *Who died to save us all.*

Liverworts and lichen are green, and not only shamrocks and the Emerald Isle and St. Patrick but, sadly, the chlor within the choler (for isn't bile a greenish viscid fluid?) that often informs that restless people's well-known penchant for anger, grudge holding, injustice collecting, and legendary incapacity to forgive. "I am troubled, I'm dissatisfied, I'm Irish," writes Marianne Moore in "Spenser's Ireland." Or as Kipling puts it in *Something of Myself* (1937), "The Irish, whose other creed is Hate." Moore's poem celebrating Isaac Oliver's miniature on ivory of Sir Philip Sidney ("leaning in his striped jacket against a lime"), moved, as she was, when she saw "that French brocade/blaze green as though some lizard in the shade/became exact," is surely one of the great "green" poems in English. The first attempt at a Technicolor movie, *The Toll of the Sea,* which was screened at the Rialto in New York City, managed to show only *one* color: the green of the ocean—a virescent hue that, by some chromatic slipup or other in that film, unfortunately, also tinted the passengers' faces on board ship. Technicolor, however, scored its first major success in 1926 with *The Black Pirate,* starring Douglas Fairbanks, a film that used the color process throughout but with a palette that showed a strong propensity for blue or green and orange, "while the flesh tones," according to critic Arthur Knight in *The Liveliest Art,* "altered unpredictably from deep ochre to shrimp-pink." There is no green lipstick.

Well, there is and there isn't: green is one of those off-register lipsticks, odd to find in a tube but sold at cosmetic counters nevertheless, which although of a green color—a shade like Lava soap, according to my friend Carol Gardner, who seems to know and have read everything—changes color on one's lips to pink or red or whatever.

Vladimir Nabokov, a novelist with astute chromo-esthetic gifts, saw the color green in several letters—he described the Russian letter Л as "gouache" green, while for him the Latin letter *f* was "alder-leaf" green, *p* an "unripe apple" green, a brighter shade, and *t* pistachio green. And in *Voyelles* (1871), his sonnet on the subject of *audition colorée,* Rimbaud asserts that the letter *u* was green, writing,

> *U cycles viridian seas divinely shuddering*
> *Peace in creature-sown pasture, and peace*
> *In sorrows alchemy sows intellectual raptures.*

When he was a boy growing up in Russia, young Nabokov's governess showed him the art of selecting autumn maple leaves and imaginatively arranging them, as he later enjoyed recalling, into "an almost complete spectrum (minus the blue, a big disappointment!), green shading into lemon, lemon into orange, and so on through the reds and purples." It is amazing the way the color appears and where. A young instructor in a green jacket in *Pale Fire* is wonderfully called Gerald Emerald, pseudonymously, by Kinbote.

Star Trek hero Mr. Spock's blood—T-negative Vulcan—is green, due to its copper base. So is the blood of the Thing in the 1951 movie. And when the protean hostile entity in the film *Alien* is cut, lethal in its arachnoidally tenacious web-clutch over actor John Hurt's face, the blood, actually acid, is an obscene milky-green celadon. And what about the green blood that transmogrifies into fire and horripilantly reifies wet flesh-eating ghouls in the movie *Tales from the Crypt: Demon Knight*? "You're a green-blooded all-American boy,"

Jimmy Stewart humorfully tells his son in the comedy *Dear Brigitte.* "Fast blood in the ascending aorta shows yellow, then red, brown, blue, pale blue, and green," writes Paul West, speaking of color Doppler echocardiography, which targets blood cells and gives a colored image depending on the speed and direction of the blood's flow. As reflected ultrasound signals shift frequency, their color changes. Edith Sitwell in "Anne Boleyn's Song" writes,

> *After the terrible rain, the Annunciation—*
> *The bird-blood in the veins that has changed to emeralds*
> *Answered the bird-call*

Green eyes, in life and literature—they haunted Bob Eberle and Helen O'Connell in the 1940s song of that name—somehow bode ill. Rasputin, the mad monk, had "green viper eyes," according to Prince Felix Yusupov, his killer. So did Ichabod Crane, Bazarov in *Fathers and Sons,* and the weird domineering feminist Olive Chancellor in Henry James's *The Bostonians.* The immoral Becky Sharpe of Thackeray's *Vanity Fair* has green eyes. As does the beauty Aziyadé, who so tempted Pierre Loti, who passionately wrote, "They were green—that seagreen of which poets of the Orient once sang." Mr. Squeers, the nasty schoolmaster in *Nicholas Nickleby,* has only one good eye—"the popular prejudice runs in favor of two," adds Dickens—"of a greenish gray, in shape resembling the fan-light of a street door." (Chaucer's prioress mentions eyes "greye as glas," a color that today would be called blue.) Even worse, the mage in Bulwer-

Lytton's *The Haunted and the Haunters,* who reveals a serpentlike "flatness of frontal," has a "long, large terrible eye, glittering and green as the emerald." Mathilde Carre, a Nazi Frenchwoman known as "The Cat," the most notorious female spy of World War II—"a brain without a heart," as she was described—had "green feline eyes." Peggy Guggenheim described Samuel Beckett, with whom she had a brief affair, as having "enormous green eyes that never looked at you." Detective Hercule Poirot's eyes appeared green when he was excited. I have always been convinced that green eyes were more notoriously libidinous than any other color. We can almost intuit the green in Gene Tierney's eyes in Otto Preminger's 1944 black-and-white film *Laura,* finding in them the most beguiling source of her mystery. A female doctor in Yevgeny Yevtushenko's *Wild Berries* has "malachite eyes" that are unsettling. Doesn't Kathy Ireland, the oddly vacant-eyed *Sports Illustrated* swimsuit model, have a sensual but slightly unearthly look? But isn't there something about green eyes that seems already half insane? The fat red-coated coachman in Disney's *Pinocchio* who squires boys to Pleasure Island has loonybin green eyes. Comedian Jerry Lewis's goose-green eyes are scary, vulgar, insincere, cruel, and soulless all at once. And the pervert in James Joyce's short story "An Encounter," a "shabbily dressed stranger" in a suit of greenish black who speaks to the young protagonist of whipping and chastisement, is even worse. The boy's unnerving remark, "I met the gaze of a pair of bottle-green eyes peering at me from under a twitching forehead"—I envision the opaque, glazed green of a Na-

poleon brandy bottle—almost echo the lines of Baude-
laire in his poem "Poison,"

> *. . . le poison qui découle*
> *De tes yeux, de tes yeux verts*

I recall lines from "Il Bove," by Giosue Carducci
(1835–1907), which, though memorializing the green
eyes of an ox, contain the passion of a love poem:

> *E del grave occhio glauco entro l'austera*
> *Dolcezza si rispecchia ampio e quieto*
> *Il divino del pian silenzio verde*

> (In the grave sweetness of thy tranquil eyes
> of emerald brood, and still reflected dwells,
> all the divine green silence of the plain)
> (tr. Frank Sewell)

And one can only wonder whether the poor feline's
coat with its fatally wet fur in Thomas Gray's "Ode on
the Death of a Favorite Cat, Drowned in a Tub of Gold
Fishes"

> *Her coat, that with the tortoise vies*
> *Her ears of jet, and emerald eyes*

recalls the tortoise, grimly, in its stiffness and whether
those eyes are natural or merely staring hopelessly into
its ghastly and terminal experience.

When forcefully alive, however, the eyes of many

animals, including some spiders, have a mirrorlike layer behind the sensitive cells in order to operate at low intensities of light. Any energy the retina fails to absorb is reflected through its cells once again, a second chance to capture energy. Thus at night we have "eyeshine," which in the case of the bullfrog glows an opalescent green, although, curiously, a raccoon's eyes are bright yellow, a bear's orange, and an alligator's or caiman's ruby red, giving legitimacy to the old pineywood nickname for that creature, "Ol' Fire Eyes." And a cat's? Cats, with tapeta flashing behind their retina, with more rods than cones for exquisite night vision, seem to cover the spectrum. Baudelaire in his poem *"Le Chat"* wrote,

> *Je vois avec étonnement*
> *Le feu de ses prunelles pâles*
> *Chairs fanaux, vivantes opales,*
> *Qui me contemplent fixement*

> (I see with amazement
> The fire of its pale pupils,
> Clear beacons, living opals,
> Looking at me fixedly)
> (tr. William Aggeler)

Nevertheless, Ted Williams, the greatest hitter in baseball—and whose perfect eyesight was legendary—has green eyes. "His green eyes glinted—someone once called them 'Lindbergh eyes,' " writes Edwin Pope in his biography of the great Boston Red Sox slugger, who in fact had also been a flying ace (decorated) in both World War II and Korea.

Aligned to eyes is the odd detail of green as shade and shadow, worn, like automotive window tints, by the crippled and covert. Tiny, shrunken, bent ninety-year-old Miss Juliana Bordereau, a spinster in Henry James's *The Aspern Papers,* wears a "horrible green [eye] shade," almost as grotesque as a Venetian carnival mask, "so that from underneath it," or so believes the scoundrel of the tale, "she might scrutinize me without being scrutinized herself." And Edgar Allan Poe's detective, Arsene Dupin, characteristically wore green spectacles to cover his eye movements.

"No one has yet seen the green wrinkles on my brow," writes the narrator of Lautréamont's *Chants de Maldoror.* A woman in Naguib Mafouz's *The Thief and the Dogs* has a green tattoo on her chin. What about green urine? This striking feature is nearly always the result of having ingested methylene blue by way of sweets or medicine. Stephen Daedalus had green teeth. So did Johnny Rotten, the Sex Pistols' singer, the honor-ific of whose surname came to him that way. "We used to talk about his green teeth," said Mary Rotolo of un-hygienic, young, bohemian Bob Dylan, who in the early sixties dated her daughter Suze. It was Sappho who, with her plaintive, lovelorn words, "I shudder, I am paler than grass," first gave shape to the Western con-cept of romantic love. There are bizarre green-skinned people on Pluto (not the planet) in the anonymous *Voy-age au centre de la terre* (1821), not unlike the "flabby green Plutonians" in Allen Ginsberg's "Poem Rocket."

"Green men, leaf tips moving in the breeze," William Burroughs writes in *Painting and Guns,* adding, not surprisingly, "I don't have to go to outer space for aliens. They are all around me." The Incredible Hulk, a metamorphosed Dr. Bruce Banner, altered by massive doses of radium, turns bilious green in his fury, a giant green id, inturgescent, howling in the hell of hulkitude! But of how many ghouls and giants, dragons and draculae, is this *not* the color? Jelly monsters in comic books, contorted and grunting with talons and oversize incisors, are green and almost always drool green saliva. The quidnuncish creatures of cartoonist Gahan Wilson, who claims that in matters of color Paul Klee most influenced him, are almost always sickly green. Smangle, a prisoner of the Fleet in the *Pickwick Papers,* with his long dark hair, has a weirdly olive complexion. "Her complexion was a rich and mantling olive," writes Melville of the beautiful native girl Fayaway, whom he met in the Pacific islands, "and when watching the glow upon her cheeks"—which crown her like a pimiento!—"I could almost swear that beneath the transparent medium there lurked the blushes of a faint vermilion." Her "light olive" skin, tantalizingly, composed her *dress,* as the voluptuous girl, notes Melville, "for the most part clung to the primitive and summer garb of Eden. But how becoming the costume!" Needless to say, Melville had more than "a peep at Polynesian life," which is the wryly understated subtitle of his novel *Typee.* As a young man, T. S. Eliot was said, eccentrically, to have used green powder on his face—"pale but distinctly green," said the Sitwells, "the colour of forced lily-of-the-valley."

As to green hair, it is found not only in Punk Moderne with people like Siouxsie Sioux, Wendy O. Williams of the Plasmatics, and seminal punk icon Sue Catwoman, who wore her short, dyed shag on a partly bared scalp with spikes. According to legend, the girls of Tupia in Melville's *Mardi* (1849) do not embrace their lovers but hold them—what could be more erotic?—with their "vegetable hair." When they are very young, their hair begins to flower, and although once it is in full bloom, they die, on their lovely tombs their hair of grass continues to grow and flower forever. A young man about three feet high with skin lustrous as pearl who sings of old prophecies in Alan Garner's *The Weirdstone of Brisingamen* (1960) has hair rippling to his waist in green sea waves. Young Peter (Dean Stockwell) in Joseph Losey's 1948 film *The Boy with Green Hair* suffers this anomaly when he hears that his parents were killed in an air raid, and we are shown the effects of it, not always charitable, in the community in which he lives. I have noticed the hair of many blonds in a certain determined light turns pale golden green, almost the shade of sea foam that is supernatural in beauty. Oscar Wilde described the artist Aubrey Beardsley as having "a face like a silver hatchet, with grass-green hair." Amy Freeborn, one of the ARRIA group who "defy men" in Ruth Rendell's mystery *An Unkindness of Ravens,* has green hair (her sister Eve, purple). Sidney Trampelvis dyes his hair green—laughably—to escape identification as he crosses to Dover on the dust packet in Lawrence Durrell's *Stiff Upper Lip* (1959). Ramazzini in his classic eighteenth-century work on industrial diseases, as cited by M. Dorothy George in *London Life in the 18th Century,* describes how coppersmiths "were affected by particles of copper which entered their lungs and stained their hair and beards green." And then of course who can forget those memorably lilting lines from Gilbert and Sullivan's *The Mikado,*

> *The lady who dyes a chemical yellow*
> *Or stains her grey hair green,*
> *Is taken to Dover*
> *And painted all over*
> *A horrible ultramarine*

(II.358–59)

A. P. Herbert's comic alternative lines for the politically uncorrect, pre-1948 theatergoer goes, "Is blacked like a nigger/With permanent walnut juice." No, as Mrs. Dane says to Joseph Day in Julien Green's novel *Moïra* (1951), "Green is the right color for hair." On Broadway, starring in *South Pacific,* Mary Martin, incidentally, used Christmas green Prell shampoo for suds—the enormous bar of soap nearby was only a prop—when she sang, "I'm Gonna Wash That Man Right Outta My Hair." And, of course, Oswald Cobblepot, better known as The Joker, the fiercest of Batman's archenemies, has green hair.

Havelock Ellis said that green is the most popular color with poets. It was certainly the case with the Romantics. The rustic "green worlds" of Shakespeare's comedies are always sportive sites for enchantment. We see in *Romeo and Juliet,* his greenest play, a play of youth—and of unnatural haste and rashness, the foibles of youth—the green, quick, fair eye of Paris described by the nurse and, in contrast, Juliet in agony thinking of "bloody Tybalt, yet but green in earth." There is the sick green "vestal livery" of the moon, Capulet's description of Juliet's pale face, "You green-sickness carrion!" and the single touch of clear color, "green earthen pots," that stands out against the dark, misty, disorderly background of the vividly painted apothecary's shop. Green for Andrew Marvell is the color of natural harmony, always divorced from "the busy company of men." Wordsworth found nature's green pantheistically holy and comforting ("One impulse from a vernal wood"). Whereas for Dylan Thomas, the color embodies spontaneous, primitive feelings, a "force that through the green fuse drives the flower," acts unhampered by the strictures of the rational mind. Poet Wallace Stevens tended to see green as reality, the ramparts of fact, a place of objectivity—the actual, factual, satisfactual world, as lime green as pity, as lean as a bean, as green as Lima, the city founded by Pizarro. (Blue Stevens identifies more or less with the imagination, the lunar, the dreamy, the subjective, the transforming self.) Like Penelope in his poem "The World as Meditation," he realizes that there resides a "barbarous strength within" that survives and endures, a vitality that has a snarl, a spirit, growth, and it is distinctly associated with the color green. He points out that

> *a green plant glares, as you look*
> *At the legend of the maroon and olive forest,*
> *Glares, outside of the legend, with the barbarous green*
> *Of the harsh reality of which it is a part.*

Green is for Stevens "the strictest reality," objectivity to a degree, what he calls "things as they are." What is "harsh" and "barbarous" is in fact "real." It is part of "the fluent mundo," in his terminology, a symbol of the blessed state before "the false engagements of the mind" have divorced us from green and "those for whom green speaks." He refers in his poem "Aunts at the Waldorf" with pistol-shot accuracy, to "that alien, point-blank, green and actual Guatemala."

But green can be subjective as well. Oswald Spengler understood green, like blue, to be an unsubstantial, "essentially atmospheric color." He loved the "full gorgeous and familiar green that Raphael and Dürer sometimes used for draperies," in contrast to the "indefinite blue-green" of earlier historical landscapes and skies in paintings. And just as Proust tended to see shadows in terms of colored tones, so at times he also often viewed sunlight, not conventionally as white or yellow or orange, but the impressionistic way it happened to appear at specific times and places, as for example in *Albertine disparue,* when seen through an open window, above the shimmering Venetian waters of the canal, as weirdly greenish: *"le soleil verdâtre."* What about a green sun? Nabokov—or Humbert—knew his Proust. Remember the poem in *Lolita*?

My Dolly, my folly! Her eyes were vair,
And never closed when I kissed her.
Know an old perfume called Soleil Vert?
Are you from Paris, mister?

What isn't—or can't be—green? The Seminoles and
Creeks eat green corn. Their annual purification is called
the Green Corn Dance. And of course there's Emlyn
Williams's *The Corn Is Green,* a tale about a schoolteacher
and the children of Welsh miners. (Green corn is actu-
ally field corn, sown in May, harvested for feed in Au-
gust but picked in July for eating, before the outer husk
turns yellow and the inner grains turn hard.) In
"Cornkind" Frank O'Hara refers to "a green Bette Da-
vis" sitting under corn, reading a volume of William
Morris. Green sand is mentioned in Tancrède Vallerey's
L'Ile au sable vert (1930). Neruda wrote of "green
wounds" *(jade entreabrió).* And Federico García Lorca in
Romance Sonambulo spoke of the "green wind." Emily
Dickinson speaks of "a green chill upon the heart." Am-
brose Philips in "To the Earl of Dorset" in *The Tatler*
(1709) alludes to the "Alps of green ice" in Denmark.
"The green roses drifted up from the table/In smoke,"
writes Wallace Stevens in his poem "Attempt to Dis-
cover Life," where two cadaverous creatures are seeking
the meaning of life in a café in San Miguel de Los Baños,
while Stevens in the meantime creates a new color for a
rose, the existential possibility of which Stephen Daeda-
lus in an entirely different time and space separately
conjures up for himself in Joyce's *A Portrait of the Artist*

as a Young Man: "But you could not have a green rose. But perhaps somewhere in the world you could." Indeed, you could—in the world of the imagination, in the world of dreams, in the world of *art!* There is a velvet grass called "Yorkshire fog." And Anne Sexton mentions green rain in "Man and Wife": "Now there is green rain for everyone/as common as eyewash." A green moon is a sci-fi staple. Vacationers to Key West, Florida, frequently report seeing an occasional green flash—atmospheric refraction, no doubt—at the moment the sun sets on the horizon. And George Meredith in his "Hymn to Colour" (stanza 10) gives us a green *sky:*

> *Of thee to say behold, has said adieu.*
> *But love remembers how the sky was green,*
> *And how the grasses glimmered lightest blue;*
> *How saint-like grey took fervour: how the screen*
> *Of cloud grew violet; how thy moment came*
>   *Between a blush and flame.*

But Lord Byron wasn't convinced, according to Edward Trelawney, his friend and contemporary. " 'Who ever,' asked Byron, 'saw a green sky?' Shelley was silent, knowing that if he replied, Byron would give vent to his spleen. So I said," writes Trelawney in *The Last Days of Shelley and Byron,* " 'The sky in England is oftener green than blue.' 'Black, you mean,' rejoined Byron." "The hills in the west were carved into peaks, and were painted the most profound blue," writes Stephen Crane in his short story "Horses-One Dash," describing the scenery of Mexico. "Above them, the sky was of that

marvelous tone of green—like still sunshot water—
which people denounce in pictures." Aesthetic pedant-
ries, needless to say, never end. " 'The sky is *not* blue,'
answered the young man in a strange voice, 'it is *vert de
paon,'* " we read in Ronald Firbank's story "A Tragedy in
Green," where he also calls our attention to a "gold and
peacock-green cloud, like an Eastern prayer carpet." And
remember Connie Chatterley in D. H. Lawrence's *Lady
Chatterley's Lover,* stripping off her clothing and running
outside into the heavy rain? Lawrence writes, "She was
ivory-coloured in the greenish light."

The sky often reflects a baleful greenish light just as
the sun goes down, a color sort of like plumbago or ice-
plant, unless the clouds are touched with a fleeting bril-
liance. As a matter of fact, nature photographer Ansel
Adams for years at parties in the Sierras habitually di-
rected everyone's attention out the window to watch for
the green flash as the sun dropped below the horizon.
(He usually followed this up, anticlimactically one sus-
pects, with his famous foghorn imitation, done with
cow-hoots and a revolving head, along with the recita-
tion—his habit—of silly limericks.)

But why does the sky sometimes turn green before
a tornado? There are several theories. Most scientists
agree, however, that the eerie and portentous green hue
it assumes at such times, not unlike that of the almost
prelapsarian moss-green light of a terrarium or sea cave,
is the result of the scarlet light of the setting sun—
thunderstorms are most frequent in early evening—cou-
pled with the water-heavy, dark blue clouds of an im-
pending storm. "You are not adding two colors together,

like a paintbox," observes Colin Marquis, meteorologist at Penn State University, "but removing part of the visible spectrum of light, which ranges from the shortest wavelengths, blue, to the longest, red. This could theoretically produce a peak of the spectrum in the green wavelengths."

Nature is green. It is abundance. It is growth, vegetation, fertility of the fields. When green is prominent in a rainbow, according to legend, it signifies abundance. (Yellow predominant means death; red, war.) Green changing to gold is the young corn god, the green lion, or the green man, before turning into the gold of the ripe corn. BE GREEN, reads the bumper sticker, HELP THE EARTH LIVE. Green is more than any other color autochthonous: born of the land itself. It is not only democratic, ubiquitous, kinetic, available, and common, it is the one color, hue of leaf and tree, moor and mountain, stem and stalk, diatom and daisy, bole and branch, that of all the others is easiest on the eyes. It has *Blendschutz,* antidazzle—*antiéblouissant*—and so has earned the color contract for the greater bulk of natural and vegetable life on this vast globe, the same way earth-moving machines are yellow and the computer world has settled on putty, and yet it is a monotonous business, a flat and continuously ongoing spatial coincidence of miles and miles of grass, grass, grass, trees, trees, trees, ad infinitum, a tableland of a single textile, an endless and euthymic monochrome we are stuck with, whether it is mollifying or a relentless morosus, dull to the eyes or wondrous, and as old as time. ("Haute couture cannot be modernized," says Yves Saint Laurent perspicaciously.) Greenbelt stretches of country are restful. Green is the soothing color, from vast plantscapes to road signs to densest jungles to greens worn by hospital employees (and hospital walls) to hills of rolling meadows. ("A meadow is the transition between forest and city," says Guy Davenport.) And it is a comforting color. I have always made a lot of the fact that in John 6:9, when Jesus performed the miracle of the loaves (five barley loaves) and fishes (only two), the site or location as form served the function of the Messiah's work: "Jesus said, 'Make the people sit down.' *Now there was much grass in the place;* so the men sat down, in number about five thousand" (italics mine). And they all ate well. (Palestine was more verdant in Jesus' day than it is now. And Isaiah spoke of thick cedar forests on Mt. Lebanon in Syria, which is now stripped [Isaiah 37:24]. Is it therefore likely that Jesus *might* have seen a fox?) Fields of grain are green, so are rivers, and, interchangeably, sometimes both are. "When green as a river was the barley/Green as a river the rye," writes Edith Sitwell in her poem "The Soldier's Song." But is the color unobtrusive? Yet in an opulent way? Can it be both? Is that an underlying and protean paradox of the color green? "I don't like diamonds," writes Marianne Moore in her poem "Voracities and Verities,"

> *the emerald's "grass-lamp glow" is better*
> *and unobtrusiveness is dazzling*
> *upon occasion*

It is the rich, vital, energizing color in nature of vines, tendrils, nettles, stalks, plants, shoots, and reeds, the world of elemental nature, of valley and vale, moss and meadow, sedge and spruce, in short, the leafy "green mansions" of W. H. Hudson and his famous romance (1916). No color in nature can approach its final hue without passing through its shadow. It has even the scent, green does, of deep-down freshness, coloring air itself and making it green-grass fragrant. Stephen King in one of his rare poems, "Brooklyn August," refers to "the green smell of just-mown infield grass" on a baseball diamond. Vert was an old New England word for forest vegetation used as food by deer. (Thoreau writes in *Walden,* "But I was interested in the preservation of the venison and the vert more than the hunters or woodchoppers, and as much as though I had been the Lord Warden himself.") To have a "green thumb" is as important in gardening as is having a "green hunch" in the field of archaeology, the instinctive feeling for terrain, to know where to sink a spade. Green tiles in mosaics, as, say, on the mosques in Samarkand, always stand for nature (the blue ones stand for heaven). Green is the color of the Ming Dynasty. And what about the Sung potters? Sung was the classic period of Chinese porcelain—the oldest extant wares and still, far and away, the best. The great factories of Ching-te-chen, founded in the sixth century near rich deposits of minerals used for making and coloring earthenware, gave us those jade green pieces known as celadon, a seventeenth-century French term applied to them from the name of the hero of d'Urfé's novel *l'Astrée,* who was always dressed in green. Specimens of celadon were sent to Lorenzo de' Medici by the sultan of Egypt in 1487, and the Persians and the Turks valued it not only for its beauty but also, curiously, as a detector of poisons—vessels would change color, they believed, when poisonous substances were placed in them. The Chinese assign to the five elements (fire, earth, wood, metal, water) directions, seasons, internal organs, and colors. For them, wood is correlated with east, spring, the liver, and green—earth, midautumn, west, and the spleen are orange—a sort of philosophy that addresses nature as a kind of ontological pavane.

Wasn't the English scientist Thomas Young correct when, presenting his famous paper to the Royal Society in 1802, he said that color is sensation and the matching of color a psychological process? "Colors, like features, follow the changes of the emotions," said Picasso. The dying swan song light of autumn never fails to speak to me of death, as ominous as the sheet of off-white behind the ink characters you read even on this page. There is always a background. Horseman, pass by.

Just for the record, did you know that the Rodgers and Hammerstein hit musical *Oklahoma!* was based on the play *Green Grow the Lilacs*? Richard Wagner thought all woodwinds, along with the French horn, sounded green. And Alexey Scriabin judged the key of A green. Was not Walter Pater correct when he suggested that all objects aspire to become music, which to him was pure form? An invention called an optophone, found on the island of Helikonda in Alexander Moszkowski's *Die Inseln der Weisheit* (1922), bringing Pater's dream alive, transmutes any object into its musical equivalent.

Rest for the eyes is just as important in the quotidian world. We are often only as calm as surrounding colors allow us to be, creating either strain or serenity. Sarah Rossbach and Lin Yun write in their book *Living Color,*

> Highways should ideally have shoulders and dividers with abundant greenery and flowers to keep drivers' minds stimulated and awake and to generally inspire. The best color for road paving is green, symbolizing a hopeful course, full of life force.
>
> In the city, surface color should complement the color of the buildings. Here the Five-Element Creative Color Cycle Scheme should be used. For example, if the buildings are mostly red brick, green paving is best because wood (green) feeds fire (red). Conversely, if a factory is black, a tan or white road is best, because metal (white) creates water (black).

Highway signs are green, and median strips are green grass. There are even special blends of grass for professional baseball parks. Bermuda grass is used on the West Coast, bluegrass on the East Coast, and in the Midwest, a Bermuda hybrid called "Tifgreen," which, also used in Dodger Stadium in Los Angeles, withstands heat during the hot months and doesn't require much watering. In 1937, the Cincinnati Reds artificially colored its baseball diamond and today actually dye sunburned grass green with a product that was recommended by the U.S. Greens Association.

What about the climbing green vines on the outfield walls of what Ernie Banks commonly referred to as "the beautiful confines of Wrigley Field"? It was the belief of the Wrigley family that greenery, no matter how sparse, gave the field a bucolic look, leaving people with the impression that they were on some kind of picnic or a trip to the country. As owner Phil Wrigley once put it, following his own logic, "We're aiming at people not interested in baseball."

As to green's soothing tone, the theatrical "green room," a common waiting room beyond the stage for actors, was painted that color for that reason—to relieve eyes affected by the glare of the stage lights. The first reference to such a room occurs in Thomas Shadwell's *A True Widow* (1678). In Colley Cibber's *Love Makes a Man* (1700), Clodio says, "I do know London pretty well . . . ay, and the Green Room, and all the Girls and Women-actresses there." It was also known as the Scene Room, and the theory has been advanced that the word *green* was in fact a corruption of *scene*. Incidentally, in Restoration theater, Green-coat Men were footmen in green livery who shifted scenery—in full view, it might be added. And green boxes, now obsolete, used to be the top-most boxes in such theaters. Henry James wrote in his Green Room at Lamb House, a little square room, with two windows, upstairs.

What green room doesn't try to evoke a bower of bliss, call up nature's green hills, mime the verdant glade? It is, half the time, almost a state of mind. "The forest of the Amazon is not merely trees and shrubs. It is not land. It is another element," writes H. M. Tomlinson in *The Sea and the Jungle* (1912). "Its green apparition is persistent as the sky is and the ocean . . . a complexity of green surges." John Betjeman's lines in "A Subaltern's Love-Song" evoke, if not Amazonian forest, the very scent of green vegetation:

> *Into nine o'clock Camberley, heavy with bells*
> *And mushroomy, pine-woody, evergreen smells.*

Aren't trees, almost by definition, the thing children first think of as green? I never fail to see in my mind, for some reason, whenever I come across a kid's generic stick drawing of a tree, the California pepper tree, with its symmetrical shape, tidy precise leaves, and green "bubbles" of fruit. The Christmas tree, evergreen, is the tree of rebirth and immortality, the tree of paradise, of lights and gifts. It is the part of the winter solstice, a new year, fresh beginnings, a hopeful green like the stout green needles of the ponderosa or myrtle indicating joy and peace and constant renewal. J. R. Ackerley observes in *Hindoo Holiday:* "When I was riding in the jungle this morning I saw a tree in the near distance more beautiful, I thought, than any other tree I had seen. Its feathery foliage was so light that it seemed to me like a soft cloud drifting a little in the breeze. It was a mango tree." Saul Steinberg in Africa thought baobabs more impressive than elephants (but then the cartoonist also thought one of the most attractive things about the Smithsonian was its stationery!). The creosote bush, a desert shrub that will grow continuously for twelve thousand years, is the oldest living organism. "It spreads out from its center," writes Albert Goldbarth in *Great Topics of the World,* "the stems on the inside dying, the stems on the outside ever pioneering—this can eventually make a green ring up to twenty-five feet in diameter, on the sands." Locust wood, when freshly cut, is green and hard as a boulder, even more lasting, durable, and intrepid than that forest-green preservative product Cuprinol, a creosote it does not *need* in order to endure thirty years or more in the ground. Isn't it strangely paradoxical, by the way, that the larch is an evergreen that is *deciduous?* So are the bald cypress and the metasequoia. I think it would be difficult to find in the poetry of any country a more splendid line about trees than Edith Sitwell's simple sentence in "The Bean,"

> *Water-green is the flowing pollard*
> *In Drowsytown*

And, by the way, Skylark, have you seen a valley green with spring?

Spread over the earth, all over the world in a brisk fraternity of timing, a force of green with strong odors, hot indolence, and sensual allurement, with animal strength and rude, struggling, imperial pride, in a loud, quacking, primavernal racket, explode milkstalks and mosses, waterlily pads, stands of pines, ferns, groves and gardens, snapweed, loment, bounding oak leaves, lunchred rhubarb, quillwort, sawwort, ramps, goosegog, round and lucent green and hairy, snap beans climbing sticks, foxtail, ferns, saplings, velocity cabbages, ribbony shoots and tendrils, immaculate grapes, cacti, mimosas, tupelo gums, cypresses, peas and pods and prickly pear, the limelit flukes of wagging catalpa, evergreens, baldachins of beeches, japonica, escarole, dripping smilax, weeping willows, the gilded shafts of saxifrage, chinaberry, fruit vines, honeysuckle, and sharp soap-colored yucca! Even green algae burgeons! Rock weed, soft kelps, marine thallus! Manatee grass, sea lettuce, and juiceful multicolored seaweed! Listen! Catch the spasmatomantic music of Frederick Delius's "On Hearing the First Cuckoo in Spring"! Ragweed, witchgrass, wild fringecups, giant eryngo, lime mallow, batterdock, small teasel, butterbur, common comfrey, sorrel, and large-flowered self-heal! Green music! Chthonic viols and violins! Shoots! Squeaks! Whip-flicking cracks! The snap of succulents! Bog rhubarb, birthwort, weeping forsythia, feverfew, skunk cabbage, larkspur, scabious, and running vincetoxicum. This is rebirth and revitalization. It is spring! Time for renewal! All things are bursting forth, shooting up, coming alive!

But there is more. In the dinlike, convulsive, and clattering noises of spring is perhaps also recalled Stravinsky's elemental *Le Sacre de printemps,* "a biological ballet," according to Jacques Rivière, editor of *La Nouvelle Revue Française,* who, acknowledging in 1913 that Stravinsky wanted to portray the surge of spring, also insightfully observed that the work was "not the usual spring sung by poets, with its breezes, its bird-song, its pale skies and tender greens [but rather] the harsh struggle of growth, the panic terror from the rising of the sap, the fearful regrouping of the cells. Spring seen from inside, with its violence, its spasms and its fissions. We seem to be watching a drama through a microscope." Alma in Tennessee Williams's *Summer and Smoke* literally finds the meaning of life in "how everything reaches up, how everything seems to be straining for something out of the reach of stone—or human—fingers. . . . To me—well, that is the secret, the principle back of existence—the everlasting struggle and aspiration. . . ."

Spring means regreening. The classic *reverdie*, "greening again" after winter—the medieval French celebrated spring in fact with a type of dance called a "reverdie"—is found of course in the opening lines of Chaucer's "General Prologue" to *The Canterbury Tales*, where the color green is, curiously, never once mentioned:

> *Whan that Aprille with his shoures soote*
> *The droghte of March hath perced to the roote,*
> *And bathed every veyne in swich licour*
> *Of which vertu engendred is the flour. . . .*

This lovely poem can be traced to certain other, pre-Chaucerian—and perhaps influential—reverdies, such as several places in Vergil's *Georgics,* Boccaccio's "Filocolo," and Petrarch's Sonnet IX, *In vita di Madonna Laura.*

We have other, smaller examples of a sort in Shakespeare's *Love's Labour's Lost,* where all of the characters of the comedy stand silently to hear the dialogue in a little song of praise to the owl and cuckoo ("When daisies pied, and violets blue/And lady-smocks all silver-white" [V.ii.894]), as well as in Autolycus's first song in *The Winter's Tale* ("When daffodils begin to peer . . ." [IV.iii.1–4]). In her novel *Summer,* which takes place during July and August, Edith Wharton's prose, celebrating things that grow, equals any of literature's great reverdies.

> All this bubbling sap and slipping of sheaths and bursting of calyxes was carried to her [young Charity Royall] on mingled currents of fragrance. Every leaf and blade seemed to contribute its exhalation to the pervading sweetness in which the pungency of pine-sap prevailed over the spice of thyme and the subtle perfume of fern, and all were merged in a moist earth-smell that was like the breath of some huge sun-warmed animal.

"Ver jam appetebat"—"Spring is now at hand"—writes Livy in his *History,* at the opening of book 20, as Hannibal, after a long winter, prepares at long last to pass over the Apennines. So brief, so optimistic, unlike the underlying tone of Anne Sexton's "Suicide Note," where suspicion seems sadly, paradoxically, aligned to fecundity: "June again . . . so concrete with its green/breasts and bellies." As a book, *Walden,* Thoreau's masterpiece, is in fact a reverdie in its entirety, with renewing and reawakening images throughout of rebirth, of dawn, of morning, of spring, of the new, full life that is ahead, the continuing hope of the permanence of life. Leonie Adams in her poem "April Mortality," as in the opening of T. S. Eliot's cento *The Waste Land,* makes use of the reverdie tradition by contrasting the green of spring with the sense of alienation that the poet feels:

Be bitter still, remember how
Four petals, when a little breath
Of wind made stir the pear-tree bough
Blew directly down to death

A paradox is at work. Leaves are green because they absorb the color of visible light but transmit green because it is the color they do not use. In other words, leaves transmit green to get *rid* of it. In a sense, nature rejects in green what we generally insist on thinking defines it. The fact of the matter is that plants do not use the color green. They are bathed in their own waste, as in a sense a menstruating woman is in her blood. "Women are perpetual invalids," writes Joanna Scott in her novel *Arrogance*. "They are lakes." And so is nature fecund as well, perpetually processing green. Sylvia Plath in a pregnancy test, after three years of marriage, yearned for the green of fertility. "And, taking out the little stick with cotton on the end from my cervix, [the doctor] held it up to his assistant nurse: 'Black as black,' " she wrote in a letter of June 20, 1959. "If I had ovulated it would be green. . . . Green, the color of life and eggs and sugar fluid."

In a sense, green and wetness are in the natural flow of things almost synonymous, the word *hydrochloric,* at least poetically, almost redundant. The Greek word *hugros* (ὑγρός) denotes wet and moist—as opposed to *xeros* (χέρος), meaning dry—but when said of wood, it connotes "sappy," "green." As Jesus says when he is about to be crucified, "For if they do this when the wood is green, what will happen when it is dry?" Jesus is saying that if by the fire of their wrath they treat him this way, guiltless, fruitful, and holy, what will then happen to the perpetrators who are like dry wood when they are exposed to the fire of divine wrath?

A green sea is a combination of the natural blue color with yellow substances in the ocean—suspended debris, humic acids, and living organisms, for the visible green color of the sea often represents it in algal bloom, attracting crustaceans. (Below a depth of two hundred fifty feet in the ocean, green plants cannot exist.) Green absorbs red light, although shafts of sunlight penetrating depths of water are, oddly, eerily, not light green or green-gold, but a sinister blood red. Red water, usually in coastal areas, is created by an abundance of algae and plankton near the surface of the water. To show any blueness, water must be on the order of at least ten feet deep or deeper. When sunlight hits the water, red and infrared light absorb rapidly and blue the least easily. Unnatural green water, by which pools from Hollywood to the Hamptons are kept bright, is another matter, and poet Charles Olson owlishly disapproves: "green dye to make the pool corrupt . . . gum from Araby to make it smell right." Are you aware of the strange fact that a deep ocean-green line, ten miles wide, stretches for hundreds and hundreds of miles across the blue Pacific? Sailors down through the years have remarked on it. It is so large that astronauts on the space shuttle *Atlantis* were able to photograph it from miles up. Sample analysis proves the line to be a particularly dense concentration of phytoplankton that thrives along the boundary where the north equatorial countercurrent meets the colder south equatorial current. The microorganisms in it feed in the richer, cooler, sinking waters of the latter and then rise to the surface to create the green line.

No animals have green fur. A zebra cannot hide from a lion. And so is life unfair? To a cat, which sees in black-and-white stripes, *everything*'s a zebra. Green represents camouflage to no large animal. Sloths in the Amazon seem to have green fur only because of the algae in it that they accumulate from swimming—and that they in fact eat. Could it be said, paradoxically, that green, except by default, isn't important to nature? Not at all. Many insects owe their lives to the color. Remember, a frog looks green only to the birds above; protectively, he's white to fish below. The guanophores reflect three colors: blue, green, and violet. When these color rays pass through the lipophores, just under the epidermis, the blue and violet rays are absorbed and only the green rays escape. The frog appears green, because the chromatophores have absorbed all of the light rays except green. Curiously, Mother Nature in her soul is weirdly achlorobleptic, leaving us in abundance what she herself somehow cannot see to use. Lobsters are, in their natural state, green (not red), like canaries (not yellow). And the tiny grasshopper ("Poor verdant fool!" apostrophizes Richard Lovelace, addressing it, "thy joys/Large and as lasting as thy perch of grass"). And mallard ducks (male), with their green iridescent necks. Who else can we number in nature's green chorus? Salamanders, caterpillars, iguanas, newts, beetles, turtles, snakes, leaf-green katydids, green lynx spiders, aphids, preying mantises, treehoppers, luna moths, and that American horsefly known as the greenhead, which has the painful stinging bite of a needle but is also a sloth-slow cunctator and dumb enough easily to swat dead. Toulouse-Lautrec considered green parrots, which he compulsively drew as a boy, to be the symbol of evil.

"Green has always been my favorite color," novelist and video watchdog Tim Lucas once told me. "It was imprinted on me by the lollipops in *Henry in Lollipop Land* and an inflatable green brontosaurus sold as a promotional item by Sinclair gas stations in the late 1950s. As a toddler, I loved to sit behind its neck. I look back on this beloved, seemingly unattainable artifact as my Rosebud."

Green is the color for first-aid equipment, gas masks, stretchers, rescue stations and their locations, and indeed for safety itself. It is the traditional color on maps for escape routes and refuges, as well as the signal color in auto racing to start, the indication for average surf, the color for safe materials in piping, and indicates, nautically, water in a liquid state. (Speaking of automobiles, isn't the most famous of all green cars, at least to *I Love Lucy* fans, the green 1955 Pontiac convertible the Ricardos and the Mertzes used to drive to California?) Green ivory is a type of fine African ivory, also known as "pangani." Along with hope goes healing—remember, "green soap," made chiefly from vegetable oils, is used in the treatment of skin disorders—and the doctoral hood for medicine is green, as it is for optometry (sea green), pharmacology (olive), podiatry (nile green), and osteopathy (dark green). Green is honor. What French writer of note is not at some time or other stricken with

what is derisively called the "green fear," the irrepress-
ible urge to don the green-trimmed uniform of the
Académie Française and take his place among the Forty
Grand Immortals? (Voltaire had to try three times be-
fore he made it, and Balzac never got in.) Saul Bellow's
Von Humboldt Fleisher, "poet, thinker, problem
drinker, pill taker, man of genius, manic-depressive, in-
tricate schemer," who dies not only poor but badly, for-
gotten if not discredited, is a chevalier of the Légion
d'Honneur with a beribboned medal to prove it ("never
mind the punk green ribbon"), but the honor is of a
higher, more authentic order if the ribbon is *red*. Green
is wonderfully now innocent, and at other times almost
perversely corrupt, tainted with a dark and unedifying
aura. Perhaps nothing more concisely shows this than
Baudelaire's unforgettable lines,

> *Il est des parfums frais comme des chairs d'enfants*
> *Doux comme les hautbois, verts comme les prairies,*
> *Et d'autres, corrompus, riches et triomphants*

> (There are perfumes cool as children's flesh,
> Sweet as oboes, green as prairies,
> And others, corrupted, rich and triumphant)
> (my translation)

There is a strong sexual quotient to the color green.
Is that strange? Does it seem too natural, too obvious,
too uncomplicatedly healthy to stand as a color for the
libido? Is the libido darker and unappetizingly subterra-
nean and more covert? To have, get, or give one's greens,

used for both sexes, is generally a slang phrase for heterosexual intercourse, meaning to enjoy, procure, or confer sexual favors. The phrase "to get a green gown," used a century or more ago, meant the same thing. A "green boy," for homosexuals, is a pretty boy, a pogue, candy pants, a young brat. A "green queen" is a gay man who thrills to the danger of having sex in a park or other public areas—an "Erle Stanley Gardner" {sic} or a "park-mouth" are synonyms—and a "greenhouse" is a public toilet or trading post used for gay commerce. A "green discharge" is a dishonorable discharge from the navy (a "blue discharge" from the army) for being caught in flagrante delicto with another man, or a "Tiny Tuna" (sailor). "One man's dick had the quaint/malleability of Gumby," writes Wayne Koestenbaum in his poem "Erotic Collectibles." And Mordaunt Sharp's 1930 play *The Green Bay Tree* was a highly controversial drama of homosexual life. "By the 1950s green had supplanted red as the gay shade," notes Nan Richardson in the introduction to her book *Drag,* but I suspect it goes back further than that. The expression for "dirty old man" in Spanish, *viejo verde,* for example, shows that green in that language has, and no doubt has had for some time, the same connotations as does the word *blue* in English. Green is definitely associated with the planet Venus, according to Wallis Budge in *Amulets and Talismans.* The green light in *The Great Gatsby,* the "orgiastic future," symbolizes Jay Gatsby's continuing ideal for Daisy and his dream and the ongoing hope to win her over. At one point he even gives her a jade ring to match that light. I have always thought it passingly flatterful that a woman's sex in the East was lovingly referred to as the "jade gate." Jade, and green stones in general, have always been associated with Venus.

It might be mentioned here that The Emerald City, which hails from Seattle, Washington, is only one of the many social organizations for the cross-dressing community of transvestites, transsexuals, transgenderists, Missy Cadets, Queen Dorenes, and other in-betweens—the behavior is irreversible by psychological methods—including the alphabet soup mix of CDs, DQs, FTMs, and MTFs. "Never, never throw out your Drag," advises Lois Commondenominator, editor in chief of Hollywood's *Dragazine,* addressing the ritual of Dress Hunt, the annual Halloween fete on Santa Monica Boulevard. "Even though your friends will hand you down their rejects, you'll always end up with a new Drag buddy who needs help at the last minute. . . . See you out on the Boulevard, Miss Thang!"

A "Gretna Green couple" is a phrase that indicates a pair who is married at Gretna Green, Scotland, without benefit of clergy—that is, simply by announcing their intention to marry before witnesses without license or fee or ceremony. It was tantamount to an elopement, in short, and a law was finally passed forbidding such unorthodox marriages.

Pale green is the color of male sexuality, according to a 1970 condom advertisement I once saw—they were being sold exclusively in that color—a fact that I could never understand or fully explain to myself, although that very color provides Solomon in his exquisite litany of love with a seductive if laconic detail: "Our couch is green" (Song of Sol. 1:16). The chile is synonymous in Mexico and South America with the penis, and the jokes are limitless. *"Soy como chile verde Llorona, picoso pero sabroso"* ("I'm like the green chile Weeper, hot but tasty"). There is no question that green eyeshadow looks wanton. Silent-film star and vamp Pola Negri's green-shadowed eyes, smoky and libidinous, were famous. ("But I am so boao-ti-ful!" she supposedly cooed, hugging herself as she watched the daily takes. "No one is more boao-ti-ful!") And what is it with sex and Jell-O— also called "shimmy," "shivering Liz," and "nervous pudding"? Jack Lemmon in the film *Some Like It Hot* describes Marilyn Monroe's walk as being "like Jell-O on springs." Women wrestling in Jell-O is popular in cowboy bars. Gonzo comedian (and near genius) Denis Leary, he of the machine-gun patter, in the movie *Demolition Man* mentions in one of his characteristically manic speeches about being covered in green Jell-O. Green Jell-O is also a sexual objective correlative in Amanda Filipacci's erotic novel *Nude Men* (1993). "I plunge my spoon into a cubical section of my green gelatin dessert and lift it to my mouth," says the male protagonist. " 'So, you paint nude men,' I say, squishing the sweet greenness between my tongue and palate." This bit of sensuosity leads him into an affair, not with the pretty artist, but rather with her thirteen-year-old daughter! (Could this be the reason why two million boxes of Jell-O are sold daily throughout the world?) A harlot in England was once referred to as a "green goose." William T. Vollmann's Poe-esque tale "The Green Dress" deals with a man's sexual obsession

("When my neighbor was wearing her green dress, the light beneath the door was green") with a woman whose body gives off "the fragrance of fresh green limes." To give a girl a "green gown" is a sixteenth-century descriptive phrase for romping with a girl in the fields and rolling her on the grass so that her dress is stained green. Robert Herrick writes in "Corinna's Going a-Maying,"

> *Many a green-gown has been given,*
> *Many a kiss, both odd and even*

It is a color associated, probably by way of country freshness and freedom, with amorous activity, as in the ballad of "Greensleeves" (Lady Greensleeves) and in such references as Ben Jonson's *Bartholomew Fair* (1614) when two loose women are busily being readied for a career of strumpetry: "Ursula, take them in, open thy wardrobe, and fit them to their calling in green gowns, crimson petticoats; green women, my Lord Mayor's green women! Guests o' the game, true bred." Is it for nothing in *Oliver Twist* that Bethnal Green is where poor Nancy, the unwilling prostitute, lived?

The "jade stalk," only one of several Chinese synonyms for the penis—some others are red bird, coral stem, swelling mushroom, and so forth—refers not to green jade but to the more precious, creamy-colored "white" jade, which describes how, engaged in the sexual act, the man, "about to ejaculate . . . can quickly and firmly, by using the fore and middle fingers of his left hand"—according to one Asian handbook I read— "put pressure on the spot between scrotum and anus, simultaneously inhaling deeply and gnashing his teeth scores of times . . . then the semen will be activated, but not yet omitted; it returns from the Jade Stalk and enters the brain." What takes place, apparently, is the diversion of seminal fluid from the penis into the bladder, from which it would later be flushed away with urine. It was a kind of coitus interruptus and had the same contraceptive effect. Speaking of China, woodwork was lacquered green in great mansions of the wealthy years ago, and privately operated "green bowers," sanctuaries, run by prostitutes, that offered relaxation and peace, food and drink, music and dancing, and hospitality for a night, flourished for men who wanted to find, in a rather paradoxical cross between a neo-Donatistic monastery and the Abbey of Thélème, not sexual intercourse, but rather the *escape* from it. Until the nineteenth century, the sex-only brothel was a rarity, except in districts where poverty and a concomitant monogamy prevailed. What would this be called, *coitus obstructus?*

Green is decadent color. Oscar Wilde in his essay *Pen, Pencil, and Poison* (1889) writes of that "curious love of green, which in individuals is always the sign of a subtle, artistic temperament, and in nations is said to denote a laxity, if not a decadence of morals." He often proudly wore—and popularized ("invented," as he said)—the green carnation as a badge of the aesthetic movement, "the unnatural flower of Decadance," Karl Beckson called it, symbolizing the superiority of artifice over nature, and he and his friends all wore such a flower on the opening nights in London of *Lady Windermere's Fan* (1892) and *The Importance of Being Earnest* (1895).

Aubrey Beardsley, Lord Alfred Douglas, Robert Ross, and other of Wilde's friends sported the flower. It was a loose group known as "the Green Carnation set," a small, artificial cult, unwholesome, precious, overexaggerated, and fey, whose badge was, in Wilde's own words, "the arsenic flower of an exquisite life." And hadn't he already referred in *Salomé* to dancers' penchant for "little green flowers of perverse forbidden desire"? Robert Hichens's *The Green Carnation* (1894), originally published anonymously by Heinemann—"The flower is a work of art," said Wilde. "The book is not"—is a broad satire on this very same aesthetic movement, as illustrated in the lives of various pale, callow, over-advantaged youths with gilt hair, Burne-Jones features, and eyes of blue. (Hichens was himself gay.) Lord Reginald Hastings, "impure and subtle," "too modern to be reticent," blasé at twenty-five, is the central subject of the novel, he and his exotic friend Esmé Amarinth, a dear thing who is brilliantly epigrammatic when intoxicated. It was the sly and pathomimetic symbol, indicative of homosexuality in Paris at the time, to which Noël Coward campily alludes in a song of the same name in *Bitter Sweet*:

Faded boys, jaded boys, each one craves
  Some sort of soul salvation,
But when we rise reluctantly, but gracefully from our graves
  We'll all wear a green carnation

"She was wearing a gown in three shades of green, with profusions of falling crystals," writes Ronald

Firbank in his story *A Tragedy in Green,* "her dull red hair shrouded in a silver net. As she moved, a diamond crucifix swung lightly from an almost imperceptible chain. 'I am a work of art,' she sighed, 'and this evening I feel nearly as wicked as Herodias.' " Later on we read: " 'Green!' she cried lyrically, 'colour-mine! I do not care about you in trees, nor do I like you in vineyards, or meadows, and least of all at sea! But in *rooms,* in *carpets,* in *brocades,* and oh! in *gowns,* you are the only colour that brings to me content.' " Was this mad lyrical apostrophe the reason that eccentric novelist Stephen Tennant, presiding over a sumptuous dinner in honor of Ronald Firbank, refused to eat anything except a single pea?

"My judges will regard all this as a piece of mummery on the part of a madman with a gross liking for the *fruit vert,*" says Humbert in Nabokov's *Lolita,* which author goes on to explain in notes of the annotated edition that the word is dated French slang for " 'unripe' females attractive to ripe gentlemen." And Baudelaire refers to *"Le succube verdâtre"* in "La Muse Malade" in *Les Fleurs du Mal* and to the French artist Gavarni (1804–1866) as *"poète des chloroses."*

A friend of Wilde's, the great actress Sarah Bernhardt played the part of Salomé—"Its one defect for Sarah," writes Oscar Wilde biographer Richard Ellmann, "was that Herod, not Salomé, was the central figure"—whose costume Wilde wanted to be "green like a curious and poisonous lizard." (She also wanted blue hair, but when Wilde objected—he badly wanted that color for the character of Herodias—Bernhardt furiously snapped at him, shitfitfully insisting, "I *will* have blue hair.")

Whenever Bernhardt got hungry, she would habitually stop work for what she called her *"déjeuner sur l'herbe,"* the *déjeuner* being her favorite lunch of cold cuts, cheese, and wine (or, for dinner, oysters, truffled pâté, a fruit omelet, and a Bordeaux of select vintage), and the *herbe* being the large green carpet on the floor of her dressing room, already vernal with laurel wreaths and bouquets, where she and whoever was with her, which might have included any one of a number of "protégés" or the thousand lovers she reputedly had, sprawled. Hadn't she once mused aloud that, no, she was not certain who the father of her child was, Victor Hugo or General Boulanger or Prime Minister Gambetta? She was so idolized that, according to legend, when she was to be notified later in the evening of the first-act curtain, the call boy would knock very quietly and respectfully on the door of her dressing room only to say in a near whisper, "Madame, it will be eight o'clock when it suits you."

That devotee's remark evokes in matters of perception and perspective what Benedetto Croce called "the probable as the object of art" and calls to mind a wonderful anecdote from Philip Bashe's *Teenage Idol* of Ricky Nelson's onetime drummer, the eccentric Richie Frost. "One summer, frustrated by the California sun constantly scorching his lawn brown, he painted it green."

It goes without saying that green is to nature what nature essentially is to food, for what in growing grains is not chlorophyllic? Green vegetables, a phrase that is clearly almost a tautology—there are more greens in produce than changes in the chins of the chopfallen—include almost every tint and hue of the color as there are kinds of produce, from spinach to okra, lima beans to arum leaf, celery to broccoli, cucumbers to beans, scallions to olives, watercress to swiss chard, collards to peas, zucchini to lettuce (an Egyptian symbol of fertility, which is also sacred to Adoni of the Phoenicians as representing ephemeral existence), endive to okra (called *Nkruma* in Africa, it was brought to this country by slaves), peppers to parsley, that relentless garnish of virtually every hotel entrée. (One should never cut parsley if one is in love, according to legend, and transplanting parsley is considered inauspicious.) Chayote, or green squash, can be smooth-skinned or spiny. Spinach, in my opinion, has the very *taste* of green and embodies that color—would it be from the iron in it?—matchlessly to that sense, except perhaps for the grassy taste of parsley or the slightly fur-green garden crunch of fresh string beans. And maybe watercress, which grows next to a clear natural spring in West Barnstable on the street where I live and can be greenfully munched by the fistful all summer and spring. There exist varieties of green tomatoes, of course: Evergreen, Green Grape, and Green Zebra. The perfect salad dressing to use with these is "Green Goddess"—a creation of the Palace Hotel in San Francisco (now the Sheraton Palace) during the thirties at the request of actor George Arliss, who was at that time appearing in William Archer's play *The Green Goddess*—a dressing made not only of anchovies, mayonnaise and tarragon vinegar, but also with green onions, chives, romaine, escarole, and chicory.

Gertrude Stein, on celery: "Celery tastes tastes where in curled lashes and little bits and mostly in remains."

And she helpfully notes for added lucidity, "A green acre is so selfish and so pure and so enlivened." And pickles of course show a spectrum of greens. "Pickles! Oh Sandra!" disdainfully cries wealthy Maggie (Bette Davis) in the movie *The Great Lie* to her concert pianist rival (Mary Astor) who, pregnant with her ex-husband Peter's (George Brent's) child and convinced he was killed in a plane crash, agrees to let scheming Maggie nurse her to term and even take the child, a great switcheroo that leads to Maggie nervously monitoring her diet, potential tragedy, and one of the strangest but sweetest endings in film.

Artichokes—were you aware that fresh ones *squeak* when rubbed together?—are a sort of purplish green, not unlike asparagus, which, according to Alexandre Dumas in his *Dictionary of Cuisine,* comes in three varieties: white, violet, and green. He observes of the *asperge:* "The white is the earliest. Its flavor is mild and pleasant, but it has little substance. The violet is the thickest and most substantial. The green is thinner, but more of it is edible. The Romans had a saying," he adds, "when they wanted something done quickly. 'Do it,' they said, 'in less time than it takes to cook asparagus.'" There is even the patina of green tannin on potatoes, making the peelings, I believe, the one natural item useless in compost piles. It is my amateur opinion in the matter of green vegetables that the taste of cooked fresh peas, just shucked, buttered and slightly salted, is the single greatest taste of all foods on earth—I mean *all,* with maybe the possible exception of lobster, and perhaps fresh blackberries in milk. I am still trying to figure out how, by the way—and why—John Ashbery could write a poem called "The Vegetarians" without making a single reference in one stanza to a vegetable, any growth, or the word *green!*

And how wide the variety of green fruits: pears, grapes, pineapples, apples. (The famous apple of Dionysus, incidentally, was supposedly a quince, which is green.) Cherimoya is a tasty greenish fruit that appears to be covered with large scales: the inner pulp is white with many black seeds. And in Oaxaca I once bought from a street vendor sliced sweet green melon on a stick, sprinkled with chili powder and salt, and it was delicious. Greengage is a dessert plum esteemed in Great Britain, a yellow-green fruit with juicy amber flesh. And kiwifruit—it is always to be written as one word—or "Chinese gooseberry" is green, as are limes. Have you heard the story that piercing a lime with pins causes love pangs in one's beloved? Glynda in Ronald Firbank's novel *The Princess Zoubaroff* says, "I'm fond of grapes, and apricots if they're green." Richard Crashaw's "Upon Two Green Apricockes Sent to Cowley by Sir Crashaw" goes, in part,

> *No fruit should have the face to smile on thee*
> *(Young master of the worlds maturitie)*
> *But such whose sun-borne beauties what they borrow*
> *Of beames today, pay back againe to morrow*

A green blackberry is white, as oranges are often— and quite naturally—green. Isn't it consoling to know that a flower named for its color stubbornly keeps its name if the color varies? White rose, blue violet, white violet, and so forth. Wittgenstein pronounced that "reddish green" is inconceivable, although every autumn we can see it in changing leaves. A close friend of mine from New Mexico who had recently been on a visit to Vermont complained to me that it is *too* green.

Civil War soldiers ate "green" beef, unappetizing unfresh cuts sent to the front. ("Green meat" is a rancher's term for meat that has not been aged. Their term for the meat of an unweaned calf is "blue meat" or "boarding-house meat.") No edible meat is green and, I am quite certain, no grain is green. Although there are green peppercorns, immature and wild peppercorns with a distinctive taste, harvested early, and often packed in liquid, usually wine vinegar or brine, and cherished by nouvelle cuisinistes. Who, by the way, was the author of the ill-tempered calumny, indicting Spain, that goes,

> *Carne es verdura;*
> *Verdura es aqua;*
> *Hombres son mugeres*
> *Y mugeres nada*

> (The meat is greens,
> The greens are water,
> The men are women,
> And the women nothing)
>   (my translation)

There is green cheese. "What's in the green sandwich?" asks one of the erstwhile poker players in Neil

Simon's play *The Odd Couple* of sloppy, unfastidious Oscar, who examines it and replies, "It's either very new cheese or very old meat." And Robert Graves writes in *I, Claudius:* " 'Men such as Antony, real men, prefer the strange to the wholesome,' Livia finished sententiously. 'They find maggoty green cheese more tasty than freshly pressed curds.' " True seafood diners, as opposed, say, to landsmen invincibly ignorant of gastronomic niceties, covet the green "tomalley" or liver found in female lobsters. What about green eggs? They actually exist, as Dr. Seuss well knew. Araucanas, a breed of chicken from Chile, lay beautiful colored eggs of a blue-green shade, natural Easter eggs, that run from turquoise to deep olive, hazel to a kind of copper green. An urban legend has it—or is it moronic rock stars alone who insist on believing this?—that green M&Ms are an aphrodisiac. Wintergreen Life Savers sparkle in the dark when you bite into them. Curad bandage wrappers, curiously enough, apparently cause the same phenomenon. (The adhesive used to seal them contains an ultraviolet dye, and the act of opening the wrapper causes a glow visible only in the dark.) And did you remember that Popeye the Sailor Man in the hold of his boat *Olive* keeps— *blecch!*—spinach bubble gum?

A ritual in the family of A. A. Milne, author of *Winnie-the-Pooh*, according to his son, Christopher Robin, in his memoir *The Enchanted Places*, was for family members after both lunch and dinner to have, as he says, their "Green Sweets." It was a candy called "Starboard Lights," which came in amber jars, "a sort of crème de menthe Turkish delight, round and flat, like a peppermint cream." It was a candy soon no longer made. After both of his parents had died, their houses sold, and all the family treasures dispersed, Milne writes, "one thing only I kept as a reminder: the pair of jars that had housed the Green Sweets since before I was born. Somewhere inside them was locked away the secret of the happiness they gave. I shall never discover it. I don't want to learn it. It is enough to look at them from time to time and know that it is there."

There is *potage vert,* a great bistro dish. Pea soup, of course. And turtle soup, Winston Churchill's favorite, brings to mind the Mock Turtle's song, which he sings, sobbing with good reason, in *Alice in Wonderland,*

> *Beautiful Soup, so rich and green*
> *Waiting in a hot tureen!*

Turtle soup made from scratch, *astonishingly* made from scratch, by what I can only think of as earnest gourmands, is organized after deshelling it—did you know that the upper shell of a turtle, or plastron, is commonly called the "callipash," the undershell the "callipee"?—by cutting the flesh into pieces six inches square, boiling all in a stockpot until tender, and adding a pint of Madeira, shallots, lemons, basil, butter, onions, bay leaves, and simmering until done. The green fat of a turtle, incidentally, has long been held in high esteem by gourmands.

Green sauces are not particularly common. There are various *sauces vertes*—technically a mayonnaise—made with, among other things, combinations of sorrel, parsley, and chives. Watercress cream sauce goes well with poached salmon. Green chile sauce *(salsa verde)* is a classic. Pipián, a spicy green (or red) sauce thickened with ground pumpkin seeds and flavored with chile peppers, is popular in Mexico. Mint sauce, which the French, having found no great poetry in it, refuse to consider a sauce. And of course pesto is green. Mulukhiyah or "Jew's mallow" *(Corchorus olitorius),* an Egyptian plant whose pounded leaves produce a soupy, dark green sauce and generally served with chicken over rice, is given mention by my Arabic-speaking brother Peter in his English translation of Abd al-Hakin Qasim's *Rites of Assent.* There is, finally, a green butter, used exclusively for fish.

For green drinks, there is limeade, grasshoppers (one-third each crème de menthe, crème de cacao, and light cream), and Green Chartreuse, which at 55 percent alcohol is one of the strongest liqueurs. The recipe, no longer made at la Grande Chartreuse but at Voiron, fifteen miles away, is as secret as Coca-Cola's 7X formula and is supposedly known only to three monks. The Chinese adore green tea. Pulque, a maguey-cactus distilled, is a green mash of high alcoholic potency. (I remember having it in Mexico with green waxy banana leaves, stuffed with tender iguana meat.) And we read in Malcolm Lowry's *Under the Volcano:* "Mr. Laruelle sipped his water-clouded anis which was first greenly chilling then rather nauseating." Isn't ginger beer green? And ouzo, doesn't its milky whiteness have a greenish tinge? Midori (Japanese for green) is a comparatively new liqueur that is made from the flesh of melons. There is the mint julep, of course, properly to be served in a chilled pewter Jefferson Cup. (A new University of Virginia graduate—the custom began with Mr. Jefferson, who so honored his friends—is traditionally presented a Jefferson Cup with his or her initials on graduation day by a friend, as I was in 1968.) And green Verveine Du Velay is an Auvergnat liqueur from France whose main flavoring ingredient is verbena, along with thirty-two other herbs. Going from herbs to health, a plethora of green drinks can be found in raw-food cookbooks. In Marcia Acciardo's *Light Eating for Survival,* where she asserts that "chlorophyll cells are very similar to the hemoglobin blood cells of our bodies" and that greens "are very effective blood cleansers and blood builders," she lists several, among them: "Rejuvenata" (two ounces wheatgrass, two ounces rejuvelac); "Green Glow" (four ounces each of comfrey leaves, parsley, spinach, celery, along with six ounces of apple, with mint for taste); and "Green Leaf" (a mixture of celery greens, watercress, and the garden tops of beet and turnip greens). And let it be noted that in the 1540s, explorer Jacques Cartier's men were taught by the Canadian Indians to check scurvy by drinking an infusion of evergreen needles.

What about a green beer? Try this. "The New York Metropolitan Museum of Art has in its possession a Babylonian clay tablet from about 1500 B.C. indicating that a form of beer was consumed in Mesopotamia long before the time of the ancient Celts, let alone the Germans," observes Mario Pei in *The Story of Language.* "The beverage, made with an ingredient called *bappir* and a mash named *patuti,* was manufactured in breweries called *sabitum*. *Sirde* and *sikarn-kas* were apparently names of ancient brands, and the month in the Babylonian calendar named *iti-manu-ku,* 'month for the eating of green malt,' appears to indicate some link with our bock beer."

Absinthe is strange. In 1792 Dr. Pierre Ordinaire actually created this elixir for its medicinal value—for its color he called it "The Green Fairy" (it was also later called "The Green Goddess," and even the hour of drinking it had a name, *l'heure verte*)—out of the clear extract of wormwood, although it was fully concocted, according to Stan Jones in his *Barguide,* from "a formula of fifteen plants, including Spanish anise, hyssop, Melissa, badian, coriander, veronica, camomile, persil, and even spinach, along with absinthium." It turned a milky greenish yellow when water was added to it and, steeped in high alcohol, was 136 proof! The concoction was drunk by slowly dripping it through a perforated spoon that contained a lump or two of sugar. It was arbitrarily banned on March 16, 1915, as a dangerous and mind-altering drink, after a farmhand named Jean Lanfray, after drinking six quarts of wine but only a few absinthes, shot his wife and children. The suspicious green drink was singled out as the cause. When the ban on anise drinks was later lifted in 1922, they were restricted to 40 percent alcohol, then later, in 1930, to 45 percent. The closest we have to absinthe today is the greenish drink Pernod. Finally, as to green drinks, in Rieti, Italy, I once drank an especially rare grappa that was as flaming bright as the "green fire" of King Solomon's emeralds. And did you ever hear of Cynar? It is an Italian liqueur made from—*grolch*—artichoke hearts!

A transition beckons. Indigestion in Ireland is relieved by measuring the waist with green thread in the name of the Trinity, then eating three dandelion leaves on a piece of bread and butter for three consecutive mornings. Try it after a wild night of quaffing Cynar!

Green is an official liturgical color in Roman Catholicism—oddly, the color blue is not—used on days (except saints' days) from Trinity Sunday until Advent and from the Octave of the Epiphany to Septuagesima Sunday, exclusively. Whatever is hopeful is green. It represents Pentecost, the Resurrection, the triumph of life over death, just as spring triumphs over winter, and is the color worn at Easter. It symbolizes charity, initiation, the Holy Spirit, the Trinity, St. John the Evangelist, and the final regeneration of the soul through good works. Van Eyck gave John the Baptist a jewel green cloak in *The Ghent Altarpiece,* the greatest monument of early Flemish painting. Spengler said that bluish green, a tone he especially admired in the paintings of Matthias Grunewald—"the color in which the interior of a great cathedral is so often clothed"—was *specifically* a Catholic color. Pale green is the color of Baptism. The crusaders wore green crosses on their shoulders. It is the color of victory in the Kabbalah; of Osiris, god of vegetation and death in ancient Egypt, the material aspect of solar divinity; and in Hinduism it is the color of the supernatural horse with seven heads that drew Om, the sun, across the daytime sky.

The Sangreal, or Holy Grail, was the drinking vessel said to have been carved from a single brilliant emerald, as a symbol perhaps of his coming resurrection into eternal life, and to have been used by Jesus Christ at the Last Supper. At the Crucifixion, according to legend, the blood that flowed from the wounds of his hands, feet, and side trickled into the jewel green cup, which was then carried to England by Joseph of Arimathea, where it remained for many years as an object of devotion and pilgrimage. At length, mysteriously it disappeared, whereupon many knights-errant, especially those of the Round Table, spent their lives searching for it, notably Sir Galahad, it was said, who was eventually successful in finding it. Various miraculous properties were attributed to the cup, such as the power of prolonging life, preserving chastity, and the like. In some versions of the tale, it was said to have been brought down from heaven by a group of angels and entrusted to the charge of an order of knights who guarded it in a templelike castle atop the inaccessible mountain Montsalvat, whence it would vanish from their sight if approached by any but a perfectly pure and holy person. At the death of Parsifal, the chaste knight reared in a forest, the Sangreal was carried up to heaven and has not been seen on earth again.

"All the verdant and life-affirming qualities of this color [green] have been earmarked as the color of healing throughout history," we read in *The Rainbow Book*. "An ancient Egyptian papyrus in calling for a remedy and healing, exclaims, 'Come Verdigris ointment! Come, thou verdant one!' . . . Stones and gems became known as cures throughout the world . . . green beryl were taken as a remedy for diseases of the eye, while jade assisted in childbirth, cured dropsy, quenched thirst, and was said to relieve palpitations of the heart."

Doesn't the color green, with its reparative, regenerative, and restorative powers, say, along with poet James Wright,

> *Be glad of the green wall*
> *You climbed across one day*
> *When winter stung with ice*
> *That vacant paradise.*

"Green Tara meditation," a form of *ch'i* cultivation, is one method of solving mental and physical health problems. The name comes from a bodhisattva, Tara, known for her compassion, usually represented as wearing lovely green robes and resplendent green jewelry and headdress. Green Tara, who is best known for helping Sakyamuni reach Buddhahood, is known for curing sickness. The Chinese call her Lu Du Fwo Mu, the Green-Colored Mother of the Buddha. We should not fail to mention here the Emerald Buddha *(Wat Phra Keo)* in the Royal Chapel next to the Grand Palace, in Bangkok, a figure of uncertain origin, high above the main altar in the temple, carved from a single piece of jade, thirty-one inches high, over which long wars were fought—the Laotians once stole it—and which in Thailand is greatly revered.

Islam holds green *(akhdar)* as a sacred color. The turret roofs of the Sacred Mosque at Mecca are green, as are the veils of the Holy Kaaba on which the Koran, in its entirety, was embroidered in silver letters by the hands of angels. Then there is the green dome rising over Mohammed's tomb at Medina, erected in 1860 under the patronage of Caliph Abd al-Mejid. The interior panels of the tomb are also green, containing verses from the Koran, which can be seen beautifully done in the dome of Al Aqsa Mosque, for example. It is the color of the banner of Mohammed, the color borne by his descendants, and the green-and-white flags of the Muslim Brotherhood, of whatever persuasion, whether it be the members of al-Jihad, Hizbollah, Gama's al-Islamiya, or Hamas, the Palestinian militant group. Almost every Arabic dictionary is green. Colors like red, bright orange, and ostentatious gold are avoided by pious Moslems, for, in the words of the Holy Koran, they are "for others." The Green Mosque, a beautiful example of the highly developed Brussa period of Turkish architecture, can be seen in Brussa itself. It is a brilliant green. And even in Persian rugs, this particular color, not rare but neither commonly seen—Bachtiari rugs tend to have many shades of green, whereas the Qashgais use a special shade, "cucumber green"—is considered spiritual and to be of especially sacred import.

King Farouk's mania for Egyptian royal green, for example, was aligned to his faith and patriotism, and his unending compulsion for that color was found in his coats, dressing gowns, neckties, slippers, rooms, and cars, even gifts of jewels.

Are you pondering symbolics? The most democratic countries, or so Guy Davenport once mentioned to me in passing, seem to use red and white on their flags

(Helvetia, Canada, Denmark, and so forth), next red and white and blue (England, the United States, Norway, and so forth), while fanatical or totalitarian or ireful people, or so it could be argued, tend to go in for green (Ireland, Mexico, South American dictatorships, and so forth). Curiously, the only fully green state flag in the United States is that of Washington State.

Redolent of vigor and energy, it is a color worn by everyone from Robin Hood to Peter Pan, including the Green Knight, Leslie Caron in the musical *Fanny,* wearing her "gray green clothes," beautiful Audrey Hepburn in *Funny Face* who sings, "How Long Has This Been Going On?"—her prop is a hat with a huge lime green scarf-tie, her first winning engagement with the superficial world of fashion—Mr. Greenjeans of Captain Kangaroo fame, and no end of superheroes and crime fighters, most of whom appeared in early-1940s comic books, like the Green Archer (Robin Hood outfit), the Green Arrow (green tights), the Green Lama (a ventriloquist whose scarf was his weapon), and the Green Mask (green domino). There is also Spider Man's archenemy, the Green Goblin, who hurls orange jack-o'-lantern gas bombs at people. Two infinitely greater green heroes have had wider appeal, however. The Green Hornet, Britt Reid—he is actually the son of Dan Reid, nephew of the Lone Ranger—habitually wears a green trench coat, snap-brim hat, and mask (a full-face one in the movies, covering only his eyes on TV), uses a gas pistol that induces sleep, and drives a souped-up car called "Black Beauty." His faithful Japanese companion Kato (who was, not coincidentally, transmogrified into a Filipino after the attack on Pearl Harbor!) wears a black mask. And the Green Lantern of *All-American Comics* wears green pants and a green-lined black cape with a high collar, and his preternatural "power ring"—its only weakness is wood—allows him to fly but has to be recharged once every twenty-four hours at the powerful green lantern, which is made of extraterrestrial material. And let us not forget Super Pickle, the dauntless green pickle of Hallmark pop-up book fame, who wears a red cape, white boots, and gloves!

Many characters in Dickens's work wear this lively color with preoccupation and almost crotchety monomania. Venerable Mr. Christopher, the patriarch of Bleeding Heart Yard in Dickens's *Little Dorrit,* wears a long, wide-skirted bottle green coat, bottle green trousers, and a bottle green waistcoat. Barnaby Rudge, the shrewd, kind, but half-witted youth, wears green clothes that are worn and soiled. So does Alfred Jingle in *The Pickwick Papers,* with his green coat faded and scarcely reaching to his wrists. " 'The bottle-green,' " says spindle-shanked old Arthur Gride in *Nicholas Nickleby,* " 'the bottle-green was a famous suit to wear, and I bought it very cheap at a pawnbroker's and there was—he, he, he!—a tarnished shilling in the waistcoat pocket. . . . I'll be married in the bottle-green Peg. Peg Sliderskew—I'll wear the bottle green.' "

Scarlett O'Hara loved green. (Nobody looked better in green than Vivien Leigh, with her scented décolletages and foxlike eyes.) She wore to the barbecue at Twelve Oaks the whitish green dress with green ribbons her sisters had coveted—India and Melanie and others attend, wearing subdued orange—reminding me not only of the gorgeous white-green gown worn by Spring in Botticelli's *La Primavera* (no dress was ever worn more beautifully) but of the lines in Wallace Stevens's "The Apostrophe to Vincentine": "Your dress was green/Was whited green/Green Vincentine." Later Rhett gives Scarlett the green bonnet from Paris and promises green silk for a dress to match. The deep red dress Rhett makes her wear to Melanie's birthday party in the film version of *Gone With the Wind,* by the way, in Mitchell's novel is actually jade green. Elizabeth Taylor's famous green gown—strapless with tulle, which she wore in the movie *A Place in the Sun* (1951)—virtually every teenage girl in America tried to duplicate, wearing it not only to her prom but to every high school social event she could think of. Scarlett and Liz at their best were, in my opinion, mere scullery maids next to Botticelli's Simonetta Vespucci, who put God's own beauty into his brush. Let me add, parenthetically, that the painting *La Primavera* reveals something like five hundred or more different species of grass, almost uncountable, which I think is also the case with Albrecht Dürer's print "Grasses," an astonishingly compact work. (A friend of mine from Texas insists that at least 350 kinds of grasses can be found in the Lone Star state.) As to that, count the greens sometime in Picasso's *Woman by a Window* (1956), a virtual *study* in that color, where a large-eyed woman sits in a rocking chair before a French window, revealing a verdant landscape.

Count Robert de Montesquiou, the dandy, had an extraordinary almond green outfit with a white velvet waistcoat. The walls of his effete and stately bathroom were painted with vague, dreamlike fish, and in his bathroom, "painted, molded, carved, cast in green bronze hortensias," according to writer Cornelia Otis Skinner, "bloomed, climbed, writhed, and swooned in fashionable convulsions." He also wore on his forefinger a large seal ring, set with a crystal that had been hollowed out to contain one human tear, though exactly whose it was he never revealed. Dr. John Thorndyke, the doctor, lawyer, and detective—he interrogates *things* rather than persons—who appears in R. Austin Freemen's *Blue Scarab* (1923), *Mystery of Angelina Frood* (1924), and so forth, always carries his research kit, the invaluable green case "with its collection of miniature instruments and array of chemicals." And speaking of chemicals, when Marlene Dietrich was starring in *Kismet,* she had to have her legs painted yellow at points, but when the paint came off, she found that her legs had turned green.

Green cloche hats, tight-fitting and bell-like, became a fashion craze in 1924 with the publication of Michael Arlen's best-seller *The Green Hat.* Katharine Cornell played its heroine, Iris Fenwick, on the Broadway stage, as did Tallulah Bankhead later, but it was Garbo who stunningly modeled *the* green hat for a *Vogue* layout in 1925 and later acted the role in the film version of the play, *A Woman of Affairs* (1929). A modern girl, the character of Iris, said to be based on Nancy Cunard, was so chic, so lacking in what was once thought of as femininity, that she became a model for the young "sophisticates" of the time, as a result. As regards Broadway, memorable as well was the huge billboard raised over the Great White Way advertising the 1954 movie *Green Fire,* starring Grace Kelly and Stewart Granger, with Kelly's face superimposed on a huge, busty, oversize body (not hers) wearing temptation green.

The world of fantasy, from Shakespeare's Arden to Avalon to Albion, is often green. In James Stephens's *The Crock of Gold* (1912), leprechauns in Gort Na Cloca Mora (as in "How Are Things in Glocca Morra?" from Burton Lane and E. Y. Harburg's 1946 hit show *Finian's Rainbow)* wear bright green clothes with leather aprons and tall green hats. In order to summon them, you knock three times, twice, and then once again, on the trunk of their tree, which, according to Kim Philby, was also, far less innocently, the secret knock of the Soviet KGB. There is no grass on the island of Balnibarbi in Swift's *Gulliver's Travels* (1726), but the soil is fertile, cucumbers grow well, and a major "project" there is extracting sunshine from them, which is then sealed in vials and released in inclement weather. In the Oz books, in L. Frank Baum's Emerald City, the capital built by the Wizard, a single gate is studded with emeralds, as are the interiors of the houses, and the lawns are smoothly smaragdine. The lovely Mangaboos, who cannot smile or frown (so their expressions are always calm and peaceful), in Baum's *Dorothy and the Wizard of Oz* (1908) always dress in green. (Is their color explained by the fact that they are not born, but rather grow on bushes in beautiful gardens?) Marie-Catherine d'Aulnoy's *La Serpentine Verte* is a beauty-and-beast fable where the Green Serpent, horrifying with his long, bristling mane, terrifies poor Hidessa, who is cursed at birth with "perfect ugliness" but eventually proves to be a handsome prince. Green is always associated of course with the fourteenth-century fable *Sir Gawain and the Green Knight,* in which story, on New Year's Day, to the astonishment of the court at Camelot, the Green Knight, dressed completely in green and riding a green horse, challenges any knight present to strike him with an axe, with the condition that he himself would agree to receiving a return blow a year later. When Sir Gawain decapitates him, the Green Knight, who had been enchanted by Morgan Le Fay, we find out later, blithely proceeds to pick up his own severed head and rides away with it under his arm.

Myths carry over to life. They are elemental, and usually sacrificial. Every year in Normandy on the twenty-third of June, the Eve of St. John, the Brotherhood of the Green Wolf chooses a new master, who always has to be chosen from the hamlet of Conihout. He wears a long green mantle and conical tall green hat (no brim), and, chanting the hymn of St. John, processes with a crucifix and holy banner to a place called Chouquet, where, after a mass is said, ritual dances follow. C. G. Jung mentions in his *Archetypes and Collective Unconscious* a vegetation or tree numen of Russian fairy tales who reigns in the woods, Och, King of the Forest, who has a green beard and a wife and children who are green, as are the little water-women who wait on him, even bringing him green food. "Green George," a ritual character in a kind of spring festival in Romania, Transylvania, Russia, and various Slavic countries, is clad from head to foot on St. George's Day (April 23) in green birch branches. An effigy of him—at one point he steps out of his leafy envelope, adroitly, so no one can perceive the change—is then as a propitiation dunked into a river or pond, to the chant:

> *Green George we bring,*
> *Green George we accompany,*
> *May we feed our herds well.*
> *If not, to the water with him.*

Star Trek characters are often chlorodermic. In Herbert Read's *The Green Child* (1935), the flesh of the people is a semitranslucent green, like the flesh of a cactus plant. (They also wear diaphanous robes.) Green Land, their underwater country, also has a language, which has no Aryan roots, however, and bears no relation to any other known language. It is only spoken, for they have never conceived the idea of writing, of an alphabet, letters, or books. It is useful to know that in Green language, *Si* means "I am." Rikki Durcornet, by the way, also refers to a "green alphabet" in the odd story "The Jade Planet." To the French, "green language" is slang or argot. And in her essay "The Green Talk," the late M.F.K. Fisher defines this chlorolinguistic gift ("in the same class with ESP") as "the ability to speak without sound—a kind of transference of speech from one spirit to another," *talk,* she stresses, not wordless understanding, "inaudible, invisible conversation between intimates" (long married people, kindred spirits, and so forth), involving gentle patience. Are language and the color green somehow mythologically linked? Man, the god of literature, holding a writing brush, is dressed in green (Mo, the god of war, is red) in Hong Kong's Man Mo Temple on Hollywood Road, the oldest and most famous temple in that colony. For that matter, the Boy Scout merit badge for reading is green! John Updike in *Buchanan Dying* mentions his Uncle Spotts, who "spoke with an antique voice, an old-fashioned super-palatal wheeze that merged with the dark, somehow tropical greenery outside his house." In Clark Ashton Smith's story *A Voyage to Sfanamoe*, travelers go to Venus and become transmogrified into plants, which would have won the approval of, among others, television's bratboy Bart Simpson. ("Tolstoy, Schmolstoy! *Space Mutants II* is what I call a work of genius!") And in *The Day of the Triffids* walking plants, like insect-eating sundews and pitcher plants, begin attacking people. But plants *are* a kind of people anyway, aren't they? Most Martians are green, of course, along with the Jolly Green Giant, Oscar the Grouch, and Mr. Oogie Boogie in Tim Burton's *The Nightmare Before Christmas,* who is spookily and incandescently verdant. As Francis Bacon says, "There is no excellent beauty that hath not some strangeness in the proportion."

I have always felt green to be a perfectly natural skin color for earthlings—didn't T. H. Huxley tell us that science commits suicide when it adopts a creed?—even the strangest, including people like Wolfman Jack. I recall reading an article about a black girl who once called him when he was a disc jockey at XERB-AM in Rosarito Beach and asked, "Wolfman, is you a spade?" And Wolfman shot back with, "No, darling, I is green, the international color." Who on earth is ever solidly or definitively one color? Nobody is black. Nor is anybody white. "And moreover we, whites, are not white at all," says the poet John Shade in Nabokov's *Pale Fire,* "we are mauve at birth, then tea-rose, and later all kinds of repulsive colors." Agreement is fairly universal. "Yellow isn't a skin color any more than white or black or red," observes Jeff Yang in the *Village Voice.* "Asians fall into a chalk-to-sienna spectrum, like most ethnic groups, and that radioactive lemon color—Pantone 130CV?—is an artifact of *The Simpsons.* (Then again, the art for *The Simpsons* is produced in Korea.)"

The raths of famous Jabberwocky Wood in Lewis Carroll's *Through the Looking-Glass, and What Alice Found There* (1871) are green pigs, who bellow and whistle when they lose their way and assemble on the *wabe.* In H. P. Lovecraft's "The Dream-Quest of Unknown Kadath," the old towers of Hlanith have casements of greenish bull's-eye panes. (The city is not visited, except to barter.) In Edgar Allan Poe's weird *The Island of the Fay,* the tombs of the Fays are green. The inhabitants of the Isle of Nothing in William Morris's *The Water of the Wondrous Isles* (1897) wear garlands of green leaves. And the Green Chapel, a weird standing oratory of unknown origin, is a rough cave completely overgrown with grass. In Italo Calvino's enigmatic city Anastasia in *Le città invisibili* (1972), if for eight hours a day any visitor works as a cutter of apple green chrysoprase, his labor, which gives form to desire, takes from desire its form, and he will believe he is enjoying Anastasia wholly when he is only its slave. It is a green trap.

Green has many negative connotations. It is the color of death, lividness, purulent sputum, mold, pus, bad baloney, unclean teeth, the spoor of cheap rings and jewelry, sickly gills—from smoking—and inexperience (as with youth), hence folly and naïveté. Chthonians, blob-monsters, and various oddball feature creatures invariably have green repulsive skin in most horror stories and books, just as Martians, according to general sci-fi ethnobotany, are always small, hydrocephalic, intelligent, and seem a sort of porraceous green. Spooky aliens emerging from spacecraft are inevitably green. Greenbluff, Illinois, is in fact the hometown of Capt. Arthur Black (Nicholas Hammond) in *The Martian Chronicles,* a 1980 film based on several Ray Bradbury stories, where a certain town and all of its inhabitants are duplicated on Mars by Martians! A green flag signifies a wreck at sea, a greenstick fracture a bone partly broken and partly bent. Death often wears the face of chlor. While vernal green in Buddhism means life, pale green depicts the kingdom of death and things pertaining to the realm of the dead. And John Ashbery in "School of Velocity" writes of "the green heartbreak/Of the eternally hysterical sun." Pale green often connotes Satan and negativism, evil and nihilism. M.F.K. Fisher in her vivid essay "Vomiting," graphically describes the "utter submission to an enveloping whirl of green brown urging, then helpless retching." Green apples are a traditional source of stomach upset. It is rarely a healthy color when applied to human behavior or the exercise of human appetites. The garb of the corrupt prelate in Hieronymus Bosch's *Death and the Miser* is arsenic green. Curiously, the feared "Boston Strangler," Albert De Salvo, the thirty-four-year-old schizophrenic who throttled thirteen women in the Boston area between 1962 and 1964—he crazily made bows with the nylon stockings after garroting his victims—was known as the "Green Man" to the police because so many women, the few who had managed to survive his attacks, had described their assailant as wearing green slacks. Bankrupts in England at one time had to wear, mortifyingly, a green cloth cap in public. Avarice is an aspect of envy as well, is it not? And not also intemperance? Overindulgence? Laziness? Accidia (sloth) and Gula (gluttony) are symbolically green in Bosch's strephosymboliac painting *Seven Deadly Sins*. Greenland *(Grönland)*, never green, was given that name by tenth-century Norsemen with the sly idea that if only they gave that distant, boulder-bestrewn, desolate country a good name, it would induce settlers to go there. And how sad and unpromising are the haunting and prescient echolike lines from Idris Davies's children's song *"Gwalia Deserta,"*

> *All would be well if-if-if*
> *Say the green bells of Cardiff*

"Where an English speaker is 'in the red,' his Italian counterpart is 'in the green,'" observes Mario Pei in *The Story of Language*, where he also notes that a "green reply" in France is a tart one. Pei also points out that "green words" in Sardinia mean spells and incantations used to inveigle and to seduce and to entice a person. A rude slang term for money is "dead presidents" and seems a perfect phrase for verdiphobes. Didn't Cecil B. DeMille, who refused to touch used currency and was always sending out to banks by messenger to get crisp new bills, hate smudged green as much as filthy lucre? Edward "Duke" Ellington, who incidentally greatly feared drowning all his life, also hated the common color of the sea. "Green he loathed and would never wear," writes Derek Jewell in *Duke: A Portrait of Duke Ellington.* "Once I asked why. He shrugged off the question. He was a city boy: green was like grass, and grass reminded him of graves." *Roheline,* for example, the Estonian word for green, comes—as is often the case in languages—from *rohi,* meaning grass.

Grass does recall graves, graves green, and green, at least mythopoetically—especially in the ancient art of alchemy—often poison itself.

> *O, what is greener than grass?*
> *And what is worse than woman was*

riddles the Devil of a woman in the ancient ballad "The Elfin Knight," and she correctly answers,

> *O, poison's greener than grass*
> *And the devil's worse than e'er woman was*

The first gas effectively used as chemical warfare, employed by the Germans against the French at Ypres on April 22, 1915, was chlorine gas, a greenish yellow cloud that smelled like bleach. Amelia Earhart's last message, "broken and choked," on her 1937 flight suggests that she was possibly gagging on chlorine gas, which may have formed as seawater corroded the radio batteries in the plane. Another "choking" gas, phosgene, was later fired in shells, and mustard gas followed in 1917, the breathing of which caused bronchitis after twenty-four hours. Wilfred Owen, who was himself killed in action in 1918, in his poem "Dulce Et Decorum Est" witnessed, through his gas mask, a soldier being gassed, "flound'ring like a man in fire or lime":

> *Dim through the misty panes*
>   *a thick green light*
> *As under a green sea, I saw him drowning*
> *In all my dreams before my helpless sight*
> *He plunges at me, guttering,*
>   *choking, drowning.*

On Omaha Beach during the Normandy invasion on June 6, 1944, Dog Green, Easy Green, and Fox Green were the names of several memorable beachheads, those grim tidal flats where losses were among the heaviest of the war, filling a good part of the 9,386 American graves there. As many as 1,557 bodies were never recovered. And the day after the plutonium bomb was exploded at Alamogordo, New Mexico, the Trinity site, seen from the air, revealed a radioactive crater of green, glassy, fused desert sand, an awful, blasphemous parody of growth and vegetation.

Kryptonite has various forms, and green is the most deadly (and the most common) to Superman. Dr. Seuss's Grinch is green. The Green Knight of mythic literature (unlike the *jolly* Green Giant) denotes death as impartiality and represents treason as slaying youth and beauty. I can never forget that Sharon Tate was sitting on lime-green-and-orange sheets, pulled down, the night she was murdered. " 'At the fatal stroke of 11 P.M., Rocky [Sullivan] was led through the little green door of death,' " reads Billy Halop in the newspaper account of James Cagney's cowardly and unheroic death, as he goes to the chair, clawing and screaming, in Michael Curtiz's film *Angels with Dirty Faces*. And of course at the U.S. penitentiary at Alcatraz, from 1934 to 1963, the lockup for incorrigible federal convicts, the prison cells—measuring five feet by nine feet, less room than many animal shelters allow a dog—were painted a putrid green. While it is a color that has always stood by way of colloquial metaphor as an adjective—a synonym—for innocence, stupidity can also apply. Greenhorns are novices at any trade or profession, gullible and immature. ("My salad days/When I was green in judgement," we read in Shakespeare's *Antony and Cleopatra* [I,v].) An unsophisticated youth at Oxford, the victim of endless practical jokes in the Rev. Edward Bradley's novel *Cuthbert Bede* (1860), is actually named Verdant Green. "Wearing a green hat" in China means to be cuckolded. According to Sarah Rossbach in *Living Color*, "An Irish beer producer discovered [this] when it sought to increase consumption of its ale in Hong Kong. Sales badly dropped off significantly after the airing of a television advertisement that featured the tossing of a green hat." "Pulling the heather green" is slang in England for seeking abortifacient herbs. Even bus glass green in windows is ruinously distortive. "It is a pity that now they color bus windows, where one sees only a sad permanent twilight," observed cartoonist Saul Steinberg, an ardent rider of buses, the height from which, he happily feels, gives a person the view of a horseman, as opposed to the false view from cars, where, seated too low, he complains, a horrible feeling takes over, "like watching TV in the middle of a highway." There is often with green an inexactitude of unevenness even in color reproduction. I am thinking of those early carbo color photographs found in magazines during the Depression—especially in food spreads—opaquish, off center, jittery-edged, unreal looking, and gelatinous.

Speaking of green distortion, a huge curtain was once deceitfully raised and lowered in the center field of Yankee Stadium. As Dan Schlossberg observes in his book *The Baseball Catalog,* "If a power pitcher worked for New York, the curtain was up, so that every batter had trouble picking up the ball against a sea of white shirts. If an ordinary pitcher was on the mound, the curtain was down to help Yankee batters." No wonder the Yankees have won so many World Series and the Boston Red Sox—well, they won their last one in 1918! Chalk it up to what magicians call "indirection"! Or *is* there a curse?

Green is the color of mucous, slime, poison sumac, cancerous tumors, the faces of evil witches—the lead-green dead complexion of the Wicked Witch of the West in the film *The Wizard of Oz* is horrifying—as well as deadly snakes. The "Mojave green" is a fiercely aggressive rattlesnake, but whereas the venom of most snakes is either a hemotoxin or a neurotoxin, the venom of this serpent is *both*. Who can forget the green pods containing half-formed bodies growing in a greenhouse in *Invasion of the Body Snatchers?* Without freedom of thought, people *are* vegetables, are they not? "People allow their humanity to drain away," cries Miles Pennell (Kevin McCarthy) in the film, "and don't realize how precious it is until it is directly threatened." *"Il mio male ha nuovo verde"* (My grief bears new green), writes poet Salvatore Quasimodo, making even sadness green. I have seen greenish *mano de léon* flowers (cockscomb, or *Celosia argentea),* along with limes, decorating the *ofrendas* or altar offerings on the Day of the Dead in Veracruz. And as Philip Larkin observes in his poem "The Trees,"

> *The trees are coming into leaf*
> *Like something almost being said;*
> *The recent buds relax and spread.*
> *Their greenness is a kind of grief*

Remember how beleaguered Sybil with her multiple personalities greatly fears the "green kitchen" of her childhood, as it was that location where her mother restrained and abused her? Ironically, the nineteenth-century Irish statesman Charles Stewart Parnell had a superstitious *aversion* to the color green, which predictably caused him in that country, of all places on earth, many unpleasant and embarrassing moments. And in Virginia Woolf's *To the Lighthouse,* Mrs. Ramsay, who appears as a sort of nature mystic, presciently winds her green shawl around and around and around the "horrid [boar's] skull" with its great horns which, throwing its shadows every which way across the room, stands in the novel, portentiously, for death.

"Greens" was also the pejorative name applied to independent looters during the Russian Revolution who savaged areas in which no Red or White Russian would dare enter. "A comet with a filthy tail of robbery and rape," Tolstoy called them with great disdain. Green is also the color of disloyalty in Chaucer's "The Squire's Tale." It is a curious phenomenon how the secondary colors can often seem artificial, repulsive, sharp, untrue, even neonesque, simply because they are mixtures, alloys, adulterated, manufactured, two degrees removed, so to speak, from the prime Platonic form. I have tasteless neighbors who leave out on their property, all year round, a plastic Wal-Mart jungle gym of poisonous green, orange, and purple, which shouts through the chopped-down woods like an obscenity. It can be an ugly and relentless color. "Love those greenwalls," says peckerwood Eddie (Randy Quaid) to Clark Griswald (Chevy Chase)—"We had a little trouble in St. Louis"—looking at his car tires in the movie *National Lampoon's Vacation,* during the Griswalds' stopover in Coolidge, Kansas, on their way to Wally World. And Flaubert, in his *Dictionnaire des Idées Reçues,* with a caustic eye sardonically defines "Landscapes (By Painters)"—was he thinking specifically of Cézanne?—as "Always platters of spinach."

Contagion is green. In the tobacco industry, "green spot" on leaves is caused by the death of the leaf tissue before the green pigments have been eliminated in the curing process. "Green scum," a minute algae that spreads, is a plant-bed disease characterized by moist green growth. Green rot in plant pathology is the decay on fallen oak, beech, birch, and other deciduous trees in which the wood is colored a malachite green by the cup fungus. Green rose is a monstrous variety of the China rose *(Rosa chinensis viridiflora)* in which the petals are replaced by green leaves. Verdigris is a gruesome patina that forms on metal by overexposure to sea air. Saliva leaves a green mold on brass instruments. "Eyewitnesses to the bread riots," writes Carolly Erickson in *To the Scaffold, The Life of Marie Antoinette,* "reported that the protesters [during the French Revolution] did not scruple to cut open loaves and dye them green and black to make them look moldy, then wave them in the faces of the police and other officials." And Soylent Green is a grim wafer food made from human corpses in the film of that name. Speaking of human corpses, the "thread" virus named Marburg, the deadliest ever known, almost instantly fatal—your liver liquifies, your skin melts, and you actually weep blood—was traced to cells from African green monkeys. The "greenhouse effect" is the result of the ozone affected by chlorofluorocarbons (CFCs) in gases widely used in refrigeration equipment and aerosol spray propellants. The "green sickness," an old or rustic name for chlorosis, was a form of anemia characterized by a green pallor—old physicians and quacks concluded that it was from sexual abstinence—now fairly rare, but once common among young girls. It was an idea that was widely spread by popular handbooks of female disorders, such as the *De Mulierum Affectibus,* reinforcing the old notion that the illness of hysteria was caused by an absence of healthy coitus. *Suffocatio matriciis* is in fact mentioned as a unique indisposition by the perhaps overingenious Constantine the African in his eleventh-century *Viaticum:* "When the woman has no commerce with a man, the sperm *{sic}* accumulate and there is born from it a smoke which rises to the diaphragm, for the diaphragm and the womb are linked. . . ."

A curious parallel to this idea can be found in art theory, where, it is suggested, a full imagination, like passion, if unexpressed, can lead to costiveness. "The painter," Picasso points out, "goes through states of full-ness and evaluation. That is the whole secret of art. I go for a walk to the forest of Fontainebleau. I get 'green' indigestion. I must get rid of this sensation into a pic-ture. Green rules it. A painter paints to unload himself of feelings and visions." And as Gertrude Stein said of Picasso, "He was a man who always has need of empty-ing himself, of completely emptying himself."

As we have mentioned, not only even in but often because of its unhealthy, eerie-looking, neo-chloasmatic, neon-chlorotic brightness, green is often linked, for its Technicolor incandescence, to poison. An old English proverb goes, "If you wear green, your relatives will soon wear black." We know the insecticide Paris Green kills malarial mosquitoes. A further example may be found in Peter Lories's book *Superstitions,* where he says, "In Vic-torian times many of the colors dyed into cloth and even wallpapers contained a coloration made with arsenic, particularly the color green, so green wallpaper was con-sidered highly suspect, as during the night it might somehow leak the arsenic and poison the sleeper."

The round unornamented stones in Boston's old King's Chapel Burial Ground—the oldest is 1658, William Paddy's—are green with age, mold, growth. "Mold is something the buyer of a name-brand packaged item no longer fears," says Thomas Hine in *The Total Package*, a shift, he points out, in the business of food packaging of the perception of green, for previously there was a "long-held wisdom that green is associated with moldiness and decay and thus very tricky to use with food products that are not themselves predominantly green in color." Fear is a hideous contagion and can turn one green. Hector in the *Iliad*, about to face, and be slain by, the wrathful, indomitable Achilles outside the walls of Troy, is actually described as turning "pale green" (χλώρος δέος) with fear. The Homeric verb for complexion changes is τρέπεται. Chaucer, incidentally, also uses green as meaning "pallid."

Interestingly enough, chloros (χλωρός) or pale green is translated "pale" (of a horse) in Revelation 6:8, symbolizing death. Pale green is a word used in relation to grass, as we have seen in Sappho, but it is also the color word for young grass in Mark 6:39, as well as in Revelation 8:7 and 9:4, and in this usage is akin to *chloe,* tender foliage, with the name Chloe (cf. 1 Cor. 1:11) being cognate to the English word *chlorine.*

It is the complexion of motion sickness, general illness, and nausea, when a person is "green around the gills." (Curiously, in the nineteenth century, *white* and *yellow* about the gills meant looking ill, while Sir Francis Bacon used *red* about the gills to signify anger.) On April 10, 1888, Friedrich Nietzsche wrote to Georges Brandes from Turin, saying, "I had two hundred days of torment in the year. . . . My specialty was to endure extreme pain, *cru, vert* [raw, green], with perfect clarity, for two or three consecutive days, accompanied by constant vomiting." Kermit the Frog, when he says, "It's not easy being green," is often correct. "Two members of the cast, years later, said they had never forgotten the expression on James' face," writes Leon Edel in *Henry James,* on the opening night performance of his play (and failure) *Guy Domville,* "as he came into the wings. To Franklyn Dyall, who had a small part, and was just beginning his career, James seemed 'green with dismay.' " And green is of course with almost malign exactness the chloral tint of envy, the blind fury of being traduced by another, "the green-eyed monster" Iago describes in *Othello* (III.iii). A green complexion indicates that unappeasable vice, that self-devouring misery, for, just as cats, lions, tigers, and all the green-eyed tribe "mock the meat they feed on," so jealousy murderously mocks its victim by the pain of loving and loathing someone at the very same time. There is even a calliste green, or yellowish green, taken from *kalliste* (Greek for "fairest") in reference to the notorious Apple of Discord, inscribed *"Detur Pulchriori"* (For the fairest) and jealously thrown by Eris, goddess of discord, into the nuptials of Peleus and Thetis, from which she had been excluded. All of the goddesses claimed the apple as their own, especially Juno, Venus, and Minerva, and in the subsequent contention the Trojan War began.

There is more than one word for jealousy in Greek. The word *zelos* incorporates righteous and sinful jealousy, both. *Phthonos* (φθώνος) has a purely negative meaning.

The phthoneric man differs from the competitive man in that his neurotic aim is not so much to win as to keep others from winning—to deprive. "Cain grew hot with anger" (Gen. 4:5); "Saul was continually looking suspiciously at David from that day forward" (1 Sam. 18:9); Jacob's sons were jealous of the favor shown Joseph, their younger brother. Rachel was jealous of her sister's fruitfulness in childbearing. Miriam was jealous of her non-Israelite sister-in-law. Korah, Dathan, and Abiram enviously formed a conspiracy against Moses and Aaron. Envy is on the Marcan list of what defiles (Mark 7:22). And Matthew, along with Mark, specifically uses the word *phthonos* to describe the motive of the Jewish authorities, driven by envy, who were responsible for the execution of Jesus (Matt. 27:18; Mark 15:10). Even Jesus's disciples got involved in repeated arguments as to who was the greatest among them. Is all jealousy improper? We read in Scripture that God "is a jealous God" (Exod. 34:14). "When applied to God," explains G. H. Livingston in *The Pentateuch in Its Cultural Environment,* "the concept of jealousy does not carry the connotation of a warped emotion"—Milton in *Paradise Lost* is, in spite of himself, less certain—"but, rather, of insistence on the singleness of worship of Jehovah." And so the password is? Pity, I suppose. For the meretricious victim of this vice in the process of hoping to eat his victim is instead himself devoured by what he feels. Joan Didion in her novel *Democracy* (1984) writes, " 'You see how the green comes out?' was something Carol Christian said often . . . she seemed to believe herself the object of considerable 'envy.' . . ." And banter follows: "I detect

just the slightest tinge of lime." "Positively chartreuse."
Leonard Cohen's "One of Us Cannot Be Wrong" begins,

> *I lit a thin green candle*
> *to make you jealous of me*

Which came first, I wonder, envious green or the
grass that grows on the other side?

I believe I actually *saw* jealousy once, in the sick face
of a newspaper reporter, an old fart and failed writer,
who had once been assigned to do a "profile" on me and
who in asking me several louche questions established
almost instantaneously a gnawing envy of all he sur-
veyed, my house, my novels, my land, my library, in
short, my way of life—why can't an interviewer see he is
also interviewed?—and it came out vividly not only in
his crapulous article but in the venomous way he later
attacked me, without a full investigation, of a particular
accusation he so badly wanted to believe (a rumor will
always travel fastest to the place it will cause the great-
est harm) that it infected both his fuddled profile and
the very prose style he pixilatedly tried to use in imita-
tion of me, for envy is at bottom, in its blundering and
misbegotten notions, almost always flattery.

Is that so strange? Life is an incavation, and paradox
the lantern we raise by which to hobble along. Shame is
often a weapon to purify the self, and so a dilecta. "I
ache in all the places where others get pleasure,"
Antonin Artaud once remarked. Half the time we don't
know one from the other, which as a consolation in our
blindsight at least allows for both Galen and homeopa-

thy, if it doesn't for happiness. "Green is both envy *and* hope," novelist James McCourt once brilliantly remarked to me. "And who can tell them apart?" I certainly cannot for they coalesce in a whirl of wishes and misses. My only reverie takes place in the validating dream of having the swanky and resplendent Louise Brooks—with her shiny black helmet of hair, playing Lucienne, mean me as she sings in the rapturous final scene of Augusto Genina's film *Prix de Beauté* (1930),

> *Ne sois pas jaloux, tais-toi—*
> *je n'ai qu'un amour, c'est toi*

> (Quiet, don't be jealous—
> I've only one love, it is you)

Sir Richard Burton loathed the imposing green of the jungle, so alien to an explorer who preferred the softer yellows and creams of the vast wastelands of the Arabian desert. The naturalist Henry Walter Bates expressed a "feeling of inhospitable wildness" in the rain forests of the Amazon basin, as did Charles Darwin elsewhere in South America. H. M. Tomlinson found the jungle "securely aloof and indifferent to the point of impartial hostility." William Beebe in *High Jungle* concluded that "it is a silent, terrible warfare of the plant world which is most impressive. A great tree at the trailside," he writes, "perhaps two centuries from saplinghood, is being strangled by the snakelike coils of a huge liana or climbing vine, and not only by constriction but by smothering." Amelia Earhart spoke repeatedly of her fear of green jungles, and the thought of going down into one in a plane horrified her beyond words, far more than plummeting into the sea. We may recall as well how vegetation repels the urbane, cosmopolitan, and overfussy Svidrigailov in Dostoyevsky's *Crime and Punishment.* In the filthy hotel on the night of his suicide, when he hears the leaves in the garden under his window, he thinks, "How I hate the noise of trees at night in a storm and in darkness." Nor can he abide the sight of water, even in landscape paintings. A far deeper and more spiritual person, Raskolnikov, on the other hand, at one point badly yearning to be saved from his criminal plan, dreams of water in an oasis and of green vegetation, finding something salvific, at least by projection, in soft and supervirent nature. Before committing the murders, in fact, he purposefully takes himself over to the verdant St. Petersburg islands, where "the greenness and freshness pleased his tired eyes, used to the dust of the city," and he lies down on the grass—a Watteau painting *manqué*—and falls asleep.

So what of Svidrigailov? What of those who despise nature—the abhorrence of what Picasso felt intimidated by *("Je déteste la Nature")* or what Theodore Roethke calls "this urge, wrestle, resurrection of dry sticks/Cut stems struggling to put down feet"? What is it that terrifies them so or that they fear losing or feel threatened by, unlike their opposites, such as, for instance, Charles A. Lindbergh, who once said, "Real freedom is in wildness, not civilization. I'd rather have birds than airplanes." Was the rite of Stravinsky's spring, as we have mentioned, correctly if portentously conveyed, in intending to show spurts of growth, vegetable birth pangs, and explosions of sap by a musical din of portentous arpeggios, horripilant squawks, rubbery shrieks, and terrifying glissandos? What ultimately is declared in the tidy person's horror of nature? What is found to so hate in the face of unrelenting *verdezza?* ("All plants must be potted!") A tropism for order? A fear of sex? Strangulation? Vivisepulture? Being enveloped? Loss of dominion? Terror of where the wild things are? Are such zones, unruly, possessed, and secret, always so haunted and primitive for them, like the work of Henri Rousseau or Haitian voodoo artists like Philome Obin? What animates the verdicide? What does his soul disinter that he so abhors? On what sharp psychometric spindle is he so badly impaled?

The implications are much deeper and far more ominously theo-eschatological than François Boucher's objections that the natural world is "too green and badly lit"—doubtless a response to Diderot's grumpy complaint against him that he "never saw nature for an instant" ("This man takes the brush only to show me buttocks and breasts. He knows not what grace is")—for if it is true that Adam in Milton's *Paradise Lost* (IV.624–29) tames nature almost as a moral act

> . . . *we must be ris'n,*
> *And at our pleasant labor, to reform*
> *Yon flow'ry Arbors, yonder Alleys green,*
> *Our walk at noon, with branches overgrown,*
> *That mock our scant manuring, and require*
> *More hands than ours to lop thir wanton growth.* . . .

what is involved in the very cosmos we find underfoot of what should be, not so much avoided, as tamed? ("Nature is hard to be overcome," notes Thoreau in *Walden,* "but she must be overcome.") Isn't it the reverse of Italo Calvino's theory which he advances as the reason Federico Fellini's films disturb us so, because we are forced to admit that what is most intrinsically *close* to us we most need to distance ourselves from? Symmetry to the ancient Greeks, it may profitably be mentioned here, was an aspect of reason. They hated shapelessness and, preferring formalism, generally sought to impose patterns where they were otherwise not to be found. "In the works of Man," observes H.D.F. Kitto in *The Greeks,* "Reason and Perfection assume a symmetrical form; Man is part of nature; therefore Nature too, being *ex hypothesi* based on Reason, will be symmetrical." As to natural symmetry, remember, Herodotus was even comforted ("Reason supports this") that the Nile bisected Africa and the Danube Europe!

But isn't feral nature—abnormal plants, the menace of vegetation, fly traps, meat-eating flowers, and so forth—almost a topos in our deep-down dreams? A fear, under the ramparts of the natural and the vital, of the irrational? Doesn't the jungle-like garden in Tennessee Williams's *Suddenly Last Summer* ("There are massive tree-flowers that suggest organs of the body, torn out, still glistening with undried blood") speak to us of nature's savagery and menace and quite obviously prefigure not only the theme of madness ("Such a nice name. Sounds like a disease. Night-blooming *dementia praecox*") but also the graphic scenes of cannibalism later in the play? Isn't choking and overgrowing jungledom a threat, in the very same way, for instance, that creeping and relentless and implacable grass devoured everything of the Mayans, who every fifty years or so abandoned whole cities? (Dr. David Livingstone on his Zambesi Expedition [1858–1863] found grass that was eight feet high!) "The grass is so durable," writes Charles Olson in "Human Universe," "neither forest nor corn can come again." As Ezra Pound notes,

> *Jungle:*
> *Glaze green and red feathers, jungle*
> *Basis of renewal, renewals;*
> *Rising over the soul, green virid, of the jungle,*
> *Lozenge of the pavement, clear shapes,*
> *Broken, disrupted, body eternal,*
> *Wilderness of renewals, confusion*

(Cantos, XX)

Isn't the revelation of a terrifying universe, like trolls, lava, gruff billygoats, and things like quicksand, implicit in what by personification or anthropomorphism we project of fear from the wild, over-ravenous clutching grove of apple trees in the film *The Wizard of Oz*? From the crossbred plant in *The Little Shop of Horrors* ("Feed me! Feed me!")? From the ten-foot people-eating Triffids? Edith Sitwell's fear of the male—she apparently never felt the yearning for an erotic relationship until very late in life—was aligned, she felt, to the rankness of a nature she realized she herself sadly embodied when seen by men, people like her father or men in general. Her body, its incessant calls, its urges, its needs, were, by all accounts, dead to her, and for the longest time she would not even leave the house or even deign to stir. Who but men or a man, in her poem "Green Song," asks one critic, is boring into her with such accusatory looks when in response she fearfully prays, "No more the accusing light revealing the rankness of nature"?

In Samoa, Robert Louis Stevenson often spoke of waging a long, unavailing struggle against green nature and the relentlessness of its force. He confessed in various letters of his "horror of creeping things, a superstitious horror of the void and the powers about me." In *Songs of Travel* he writes of nature, "There the green murderer throve and spread/Upon his smothering victims fed," a strange and continuing preoccupation that finds echoes in his poem "The Woodman," where he speaks of being "at the beast's work," thrashing vegetation, where he adds, as if to recall the essential task of Adam in plucky *Paradise Lost,* taming the wilderness, "thick round me in the teeming mud/Briar and fern strove to the blood." Stevenson goes on to describe in martial metaphors how

> *Green conquerors from overhead*
> *Bestrode the bodies of the dead;*
> *The Caesars of the silvan field,*
> *Unused to fail, foredoomed to yield:*
> *For in the groins of branches, lo!*
> *The cancers of the orchid grow. . . .*

It is ironic, given the theme of the corruption of native life by civilization in much of his Pacific writings, the idea of taming verdure should have irked—or surprised—him so, but perhaps Stevenson could not, as Byron said of Coleridge, explain his explanation. A jungle is sucked dry of all green in Steve Erickson's cyberpunk novel *Arc d'X,* which would have pleased Stevenson. Curiously, Stevenson's gardening wife Fannie's nervous breakdown was partly traceable, as she later told Edmund Gosse, to being driven mad "by the monstrous rapidity of the growth of vegetation in Samoa"—shades of Joel 1:4!—and her attitude influenced him in his *Pulvis et Umbra,* an essay that shows man stripped to an abhorrent nakedness, echoing not only a superstitious view of nature but a refusal to believe that the elements are neutral. Wilderness to Stevenson, the untamed jungle, he somehow took as a personal insult, forkshoveling away in the vegetation, as he did, with almost Gnostic fanaticism or madness, the way Roethke in his poem "Cuttings" also did:

> *When sprouts break out*
> *Slippery as fish*
> *I quail, lean to beginnings, sheath-wet*

or in "Root Cellar":

> *And what a compass of stinks!—*
> *Roots ripe as old bait*
> *Pulpy stems, rank, silo-rich*
> *leaf-mold, manure, lime, piled against slippery planks.*

Nothing would give up life:
Even the dirt kept breathing a small breath

Strangely enough, the Greek word for punishment is *kolasis*—it often emerges in various theological discussions of hell—but it is not really an ethical word at all. It is a farm word. Significantly, it originally meant the pruning of trees or the lopping off of limbs. The linking of savagery with nature is also reflected in our word *culture,* which is the direct root of *colere,* to till soil, its opposite, synonym for barbarity, being nature without the order of humanity. One thinks of relentless grasses, like rye grass and centipede grass, running and clumping grasses, kudzu vines, and "evasive" trees that escape from ornamental situations and take over native species, not unlike viruses.

Oddly, Stevenson was especially bedeviled by the color brown. He loathed it. It terrified him in his childhood nightmares. It was the color of diabolical fog in his fears, in his dreams, and in his stories, particularly in *Dr. Jekyll and Mr. Hyde.* Stevenson called the springs of his unconscious imagination "the Brownies," which he imagined as being underground creatures, and, not without some ambivalence, he always said he owed his creativity, his fantasy, to them, although he seems to link them in their chthonic and tentacular ominousness to the same green, enveloping possessiveness he associates with gross succulent grasses and incessant growth and rank *ginestrella,* creeping and coiling around one's whole being.

Color, felt Delacroix, has a more mysterious and

more powerful influence on us than anything else, an insight or epiphany on the irrational mysticism of color that came to him at one point while he was traveling in Morocco—"It acts, we might say," he writes, "without our knowledge."

Green in its virtuosity is like an aria, the basic and essential cantata, its elemental color, providing a melodic skeleton or frame, as it were, completed by the song of nature in spectral and splendiferous *bel canto* from her vast repertoire of ornaments, graces, roulades, trills, embellishments, portamenti, arpeggios, octave skips, slurs, and rapid scale passages. Green in its jubilance is lyrical, though variations can be dark and deficient, its cadences iridescent and born of the ideal. Its personality, its powers, defining our world, announcing itself in every lake and leaf, midge and mountain, blossom and bugwing, is so beguiling, it softens our hearts with its soothing chroma and lets us sleep—or flares and cries, "Be bright, be bright!" I have always felt, even at the worst of times, that if only the largeness of life could ever be overpoweringly felt, how green, how deeply green, how very deeply green it would be. And what a sign of grace.